T0246343

SEARCHING FOR FRANKLIN

Other Books by Ken McGoogan

ARCTIC EXPLORATION:

Dead Reckoning: The Untold Story of the Northwest Passage

Race to the Polar Sea: The Heroic Adventures and Romantic Obsessions of Elisha Kent Kane ‡

*Lady Franklin's Revenge: A True Story of Ambition, Obsession
and the Remaking of Arctic History* *

*Ancient Mariner: The Amazing Adventures of Samuel Hearne,
the Sailor Who Walked to the Arctic Ocean* *†

*Fatal Passage: The Untold Story of John Rae, the Arctic
Adventurer Who Discovered the Fate of Franklin* *†

THE VIEW FROM CANADA:

Flight of the Highlanders: The Making of Canada

Celtic Lightning: How the Scots and the Irish Created a Canadian Nation

50 Canadians Who Changed The World

How The Scots Invented Canada

Canada's Undeclared War: Fighting Words from the Literary Trenches (Detselig Enterprises)

FICTION & MEMOIR:

Visions Of Kerouac / Kerouac's Ghost / Le Fantôme de Kerouac
(Pottersfield, Robert Davies, Balzac-Le-Griot)

Chasing Safiya (Bayeux Arts)

Calypso Warrior (Robert Davies)

Going For Gold, co-author, Catriona Le May Doan (McClelland & Stewart)

All HarperCollins Canada unless otherwise indicated

UK: Bantam/Transworld * · USA: Carroll & Graf † · Counterpoint Press ‡

SEARCHING FOR
FRANKLIN

NEW ANSWERS *to the* GREAT ARCTIC MYSTERY

KEN McGOOGAN

Douglas & McIntyre

DOUGLAS AND McINTYRE (2013) LTD.
P.O. Box 219, Madeira Park, BC, V0N 2H0
www.douglas-mcintyre.com

EDITED by Derek Fairbridge
INDEXED by Colleen Bidner
DUST JACKET DESIGN by Dwayne Dobson
TEXT DESIGN by Libris Simas Ferraz / Onça Publishing
MAPS DESIGNED by Stuart Daniel / Starshell Maps
PRINTED AND BOUND in Canada
PRINTED on 100% recycled paper

DOUGLAS & McINTYRE acknowledges the support of the Canada Council for the Arts,
the Government of Canada, and the Province of British Columbia through the BC
Arts Council.

LIBRARY AND ARCHIVES CANADA CATALOGUING IN PUBLICATION
Title: Searching for Franklin : new answers to the great Arctic mystery / Ken McGoogan.
Names: McGoogan, Ken, author.
Description: Includes bibliographical references and index.
Identifiers: Canadiana (print) 20230237487 | Canadiana (ebook) 2023023755X |
   ISBN 9781771623681 (hardcover) | ISBN 9781771623698 (EPUB)
Subjects: LCSH: Franklin, John, 1786-1847. | LCSH: Great Britain. Royal Navy. |
   LCSH: John Franklin Arctic Expedition (1845-1851) | LCSH: Explorers—Great
   Britain—Biography. | LCSH: Canada, Northern—Discovery and exploration—
   British. | LCSH: Northwest Passage—Discovery and exploration—British. |
   LCSH: Arctic regions—Discovery and exploration—British.
Classification: LCC G660 .M34 2023 | DDC 917.1904/1—dc23

This book is dedicated to
Louie Kamookak (1959–2018)

And to
Sheena Fraser McGoogan
(Long May We Run)

Contents

~

Maps   viii

Author's Note   xiii

PROLOGUE – The Myth of the Explorer   1

PART ONE – SEARCHING FOR FRANKLIN

Chapter 1 – A Vault on This Island   11

Chapter 2 – John Franklin Goes Missing   19

Chapter 3 – Beechey Island Graves   30

Chapter 4 – A Hint of Catastrophe   38

Chapter 5 – Lady Franklin Responds   52

Chapter 6 – The Victory Point Record   59

PART TWO – THE ROYAL NAVY MAN

Chapter 7 – Who Was This John Franklin?   71

Chapter 8 – Voyage to York Factory   82

Chapter 9 – Upriver to Cumberland House   91

Chapter 10 – Once a Prisoner of War   101

Chapter 11 – Second-in-Command   107

Chapter 12 – Journey to Fort Chipewyan   113

Chapter 13 – The Great Mustering   125

Chapter 14 – Akaitcho Leads the Way   133

Chapter 15 – The Indispensable St. Germain   144

Chapter 16 – The Dene Leader's Question   150

PART THREE – HAUNTING THE LAND

Chapter 17 – The Gjoa Haven Mystery Box   161

Chapter 18 – Hunters, Interpreters, Eyewitnesses   168

Chapter 19 – The Peter Bayne Complication   181

Chapter 20 – What Do We Know for Sure?   189

Chapter 21 – The Second-Worst Disaster   197

PART FOUR – THE TRUE BELIEVER

Chapter 22 – The Resolute Back   205

Chapter 23 – The Immovable Simpson   212

Chapter 24 – Akaitcho's Warning   219

Chapter 25 – Crisis at Bloody Falls   228

Chapter 26 – Franklin Reaches the Coast   236

Chapter 27 – East of the Coppermine   242

Chapter 28 – Obstruction Rapids   251

Chapter 29 – St. Germain Finds a Way   258

Chapter 30 – Shock at Fort Enterprise   268

Chapter 31 – Cannibalism, Murder, Starvation   275

PART FIVE – INTERWEAVING EXPEDITIONS

Chapter 32 – Rescue from Enterprise   287

Chapter 33 – The Trouble with Polar Bears   294

Chapter 34 – The Man Who Could Do No Wrong   305

EPILOGUE – On Top of the World   311

A Note on Sources   318

Endnotes   320

Acknowledgements   325

Selected References   328

Image Credits   335

Index   337

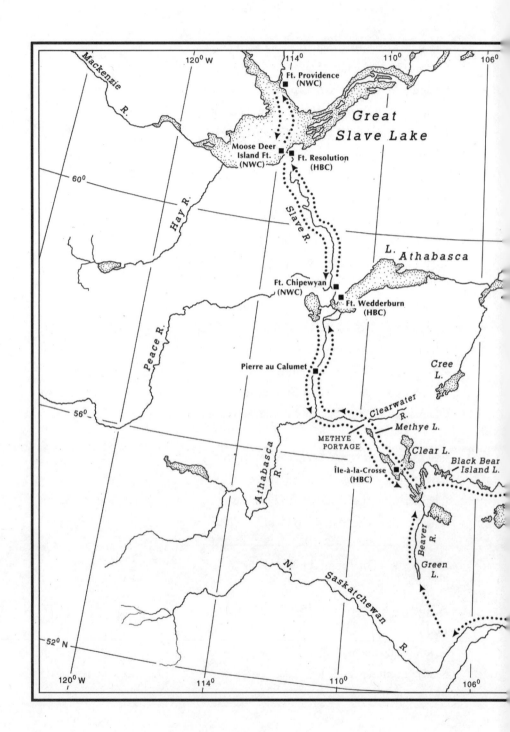

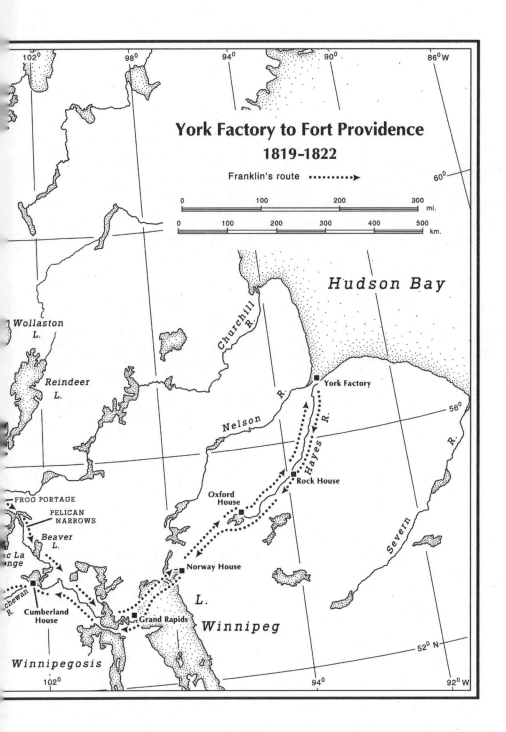

York Factory to Fort Providence
1819–1822

Franklin's route ●●●●●●●●●●➤

0	100	200	300
			mi.

0	100	200	300	400	500
					km.

102° 98° 94° 90° 86°W

60°

Hudson Bay

Churchill R.

York Factory

Wollaston L.

Reindeer L.

Nelson R.

Hayes R.

56°

Rock House

FROG PORTAGE

PELICAN NARROWS

Oxford House

Severn R.

Beaver L.

c La nge

Norway House

chewan R.

Cumberland House

Grand Rapids

L. Winnipeg

52° N

Winnipegosis

102° 94° 92°W

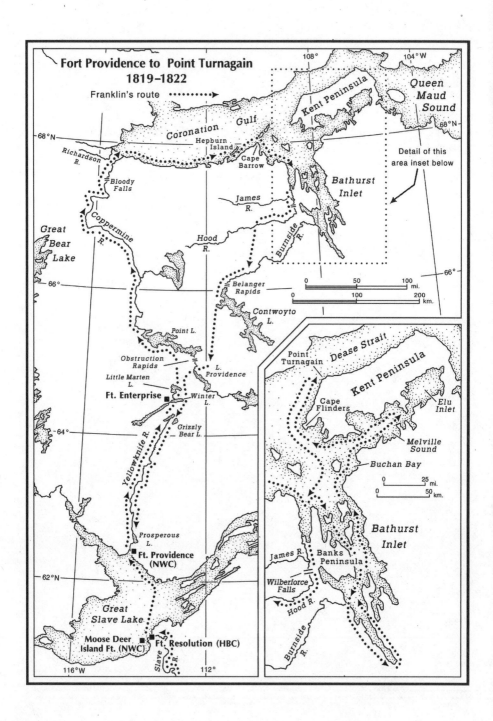

Fort Providence to Point Turnagain
1819–1822

Franklin's route ●●●●●●●●➤

Queen Maud Sound

Kent Peninsula

108°
104° W

68° N

Coronation Gulf

Hepburn Island

Cape Barrow

Richardson R.

Bloody Falls

Coppermine R.

James R.

Bathurst Inlet

Detail of this area inset below

66°

Great Bear Lake

Hood R.

Belanger Rapids

Burnside R.

Contwoyto L.

Point L.

Obstruction Rapids

L. Providence

Little Marten L.

Ft. Enterprise

Winter L.

Grizzly Bear L.

Yellowknife R.

64°

Prosperous L.

Ft. Providence (NWC)

62° N

Great Slave Lake

Moose Deer Island Ft. (NWC)

Ft. Resolution (HBC)

Slave R.

116° W

112°

0   50   100 mi.
0   100   200 km.

Point Turnagain

Dease Strait

Kent Peninsula

Cape Flinders

Elu Inlet

Melville Sound

Buchan Bay

0   25 mi.
0   50 km.

Bathurst Inlet

James R.

Banks Peninsula

Wilberforce Falls

Hood R.

Burnside R.

x

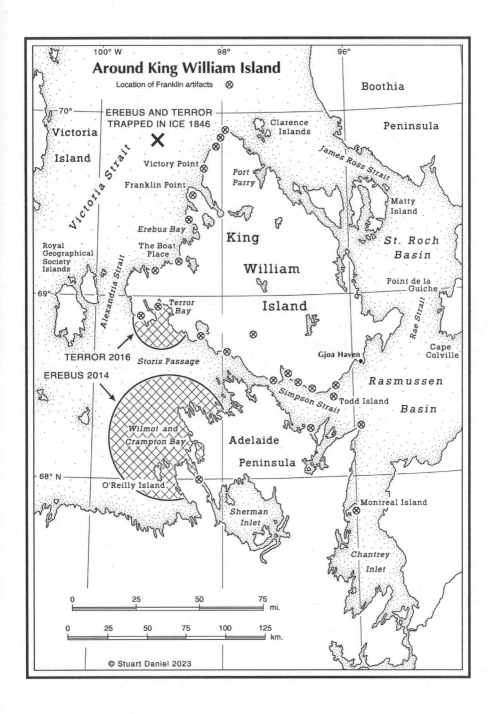

Around King William Island

Location of Franklin artifacts ⊗

100° W   98°   96°

Boothia

70°

EREBUS AND TERROR
TRAPPED IN ICE 1846

Peninsula

Victoria

✕

Clarence
Islands

Island

Victory Point

Victoria Strait

Franklin Point

Port
Parry

James Ross Strait

Matty
Island

Erebus Bay

King

The Boat
Place

William

*St. Roch
Basin*

Royal
Geographical
Society
Islands

Alexandria Strait

Island

69°

*Terror
Bay*

Point de la
Guiche

Rae Strait

TERROR 2016

Storis Passage

Gjoa Haven

Rasmussen

EREBUS 2014

Cape
Colville

Simpson Strait

Basin

*Wilmot and
Crampton Bay*

Adelaide

Todd Island

O'Reilly Island

68° N

Peninsula

Montreal Island

*Sherman
Inlet*

*Chantrey
Inlet*

0   25   50   75
mi.

0   25 50 75 100 125
km.

© Stuart Daniel 2023

Author's Note

~

Contemporary writers face special challenges when working with journals two centuries old. I have let stand idiosyncrasies of grammar and spelling while modernizing some usages, preferring "Inuit" to "Eskimo," for example, and "Dene" to "Northern Indians." Where an individual name gets two or three spellings (Samandrie, Semandré, Semandrie), I have settled on the most likely. After identifying William Ouligbuck Jr., I refer to him as Ouligbuck. Where John Franklin and his men spoke of Augustus and Junius, I prefer Tattannoeuck and Hoeootoerock. And while Charles Francis Hall spoke of Hannah and Joe, and wrote of them as Tookoolito and Ebierbing, I follow the modern phonetic consensus: Taqulittuq and Ipiirvik. I keep trying to write an impeccable book. But if this one is flawless, devoid of inconsistencies, omissions, and gaffes, it will be the first. Fingers crossed.

The Myth *of* *the* Explorer

~

On day two of our Arctic voyage we sail into a blizzard. It's three-thirty in the afternoon, and underwater archaeologist Marc-André Bernier is halfway through a presentation in the Nautilus Lounge on "The Search and Discovery of Sir John Franklin's Lost Ships." Bernier is the expert running the investigation for Parks Canada. During the next couple of days, he proposes to lead a visit to the site of the *Erebus*, where many of us—as many as wish to—will go snorkelling over the site. Now, while outside the wind gusts above fifty knots (gale force), he talks about Parks Canada search operations over the past eight years.

The hunt for the ships dates back almost to 1845, when Franklin disappeared into the Arctic with the *Erebus*, the *Terror*, and 128 men. Now, Bernier reviews the unprecedented search, driven at first by the Royal Navy and the widowed Lady Franklin. He highlights the contributions of Inuit testimony as relayed through such explorers as Dr. John Rae, Charles Francis Hall, and Frederick Schwatka, who relied on interpreters William Ouligbuck, Taqulittuq (Tookoolito), and Ipiirvik (Ebierbing). Bernier explains that these accounts "gave us an area but did not establish a location." That is why the Canadian search, which located *Erebus* in 2014 and the *Terror* two years later, required so much time and energy.

Adventure Canada uses the *Ocean Endeavour* for several Arctic voyages each year. The ship can accommodate 360 people, including passengers, crew, and professional staff.

Now, in September 2017, the storm rages unabated into late afternoon. And when Bernier finishes presenting, he hurries up onto the bridge to confer with the captain and Adventure Canada expedition leader Matthew James (M.J.) Swan. None of them like it, but Geography is having its way with History. Geography is manifesting as ice, heavy seas, and gale-force winds, while History is bidding to extend the narrative of the lost Franklin expedition by bringing adventure tourism to the wreck of the *Erebus*.

To that end, we are sailing with a full complement: 197 passengers, 124 ship's crew, and 37 professional staff. These include Inuit culturalists, medical doctors, a marine biologist, an archaeologist, two professional photographers, an activist filmmaker, a seabird biologist, a botanist, a singer-songwriter, a team of videographers, two expert divers, and an author-historian (yours truly).

At this point I have been voyaging with Adventure Canada for ten years, leading excursions and giving talks about exploration history. This time around, sailing *Out of the Northwest Passage*, we expected to board the *Ocean Endeavour* on Canada's Arctic coast at the northwestern edge of Nunavut—more specifically, in Kugluktuk, at the mouth of the Coppermine River. Heavy ice cut short the preceding voyage, however, and so, with about 200 others, I flew 270 miles to Cambridge Bay and embarked there.

The plan now is to sail through a narrow channel to anchor in Wilmot and Crampton Bay off the Adelaide Peninsula—roughly three hundred miles away. In groups of thirty, passengers will take a forty-minute Zodiac ride to an island near the *Erebus* site. There, in a collection of heated tents, we will meet underwater archaeologists and Inuit guardians and Elders flown in from Gjoa Haven on King William Island, the township nearest the site. I am especially excited to see Louie Kamookak, my old friend and fellow traveller.

From the designated island, having relinquished any instruments that can record geographical co-ordinates, we will ride to the *Erebus* site in Zodiacs. There, while some people go snorkelling above the wreck, others will view the site from Zodiacs using viewing buckets, and still others will watch onscreen as an ROV (remotely operated vehicle) visits the wreck. Maybe we will be present when divers surface with documents relating to Franklin's final expedition. Who can say?

That's the plan. Geography insists on a different scenario. As the ship sails toward the channel (as narrow as half a kilometre), the wind blows thirty to thirty-five knots, gusting to forty, and the swell reaches 1.5 metres. Swan says later that if the wind had dropped to fifteen or twenty knots, he stood "ready to make an attempt." Instead, fog engulfs the entire region. At evening briefing, Bernier says he arranged for a Twin Otter to fly people in from Gjoa Haven—among them Louie Kamookak. But the pilot would need at least one thousand feet of visibility, and that does not exist. At the Inuit guardians' campsite, which comprises five tents, "three of those tents have been blown off."

Somebody asks—it might be me—what about lingering in the vicinity for a couple of days to wait out the storm? Speaking from experience, Bernier responds that these wind and wave conditions will have stirred up sediment so badly that at best the wreck will become visible in three days. And if the storm continues, we might have to wait a week. Bottom line: on this voyage, none of us will be snorkelling over the *Erebus*. I go out onto the top deck and stand in the wind as the *Ocean Endeavour* sails east along the southwest coast of King William Island toward Gjoa Haven. I can't help thinking about John Franklin's men, many of whom starved to death in the late 1840s as they struggled along this coastline.

Late that evening, we anchor off Gjoa Haven, so named by Norwegian explorer Roald Amundsen, who wintered here in the early 1900s while completing the Passage in his tiny ship the *Gjøa*. Come morning, there lies the town, population 1,350, snow-dusted and shining in the sun. By 8:30 a.m., passengers are piling into Zodiacs. Onshore, having accomplished a "wet landing" in rubber boots, we split into half a dozen groups, say hello to local guides, and head out to explore the town. I go looking for Louie but he is nowhere to be found. I do spot the *Martin Bergmann* tied up to a dock. The previous year, guided by local Inuk Sammy Kogvik, searchers on that vessel had located Franklin's second ship, HMS *Terror*.

Early afternoon, everyone gravitates to Qiqirtaq High School, a big modern building, for a cultural presentation. As I take a seat on one of the tiered benches overlooking the gym, finally I spot Louie in a crowd of standees. He catches my eye and gestures toward the main entrance and we make our way into the hallway. After greeting each other, we fall to our usual kibbitzing. By now, age fifty-nine, Louie is widely recognized as the leading Inuit historian of his generation. We commiserate about not getting to meet at the *Erebus* site. He mentions speaking recently with an Elder, interviewing him, and I say, "Wait, aren't you an Elder yet? When are you going to become an Elder?"

"I'm still too young," he says, grinning. "Way too young."

Then he comes back at me: "When are you going to write your big Franklin book?"

"My big Franklin book?"

"You've written about everybody else. Don't you think it's time?"

"No way." I shake my head. "I'm still too young."

Together we laugh. Six months later, Louie is dead.

∼

Research-based non-fiction is the most conservative of literary genres. If a particular work is also historical in nature, the conventions are especially tight and restrictive. In recent years, history-based narrative has relaxed enough to allow for a strong voice and personal presence. I have sought to establish both in writing five books about northern exploration. All five have highlighted the importance of the Indigenous contribution to the Arctic enterprise.

This sixth work does the same. But it differs from those previous books in structure and, in a small way, point of view. Over the past decade, while teaching in the MFA program in Creative Nonfiction at University of King's College, I have deliberated on how to structure a story. One presentation, which I have given to sundry writing groups, I call *Adventures in Nonlinear Narrative*. Harold Pinter, Doris Lessing, Quentin Tarantino, Martin Amis, Toni Morrison, Mordecai Richler, Günter Grass, Thomas King, Christopher Nolan, Linden MacIntyre—all provide grist for the mill.

Where my previous Arctic books tell a single, roughly chronological story, *Searching for Franklin* interweaves two main storylines. In novels, plays, movies, biographies, or memoirs, such a structure raises no eyebrows, causes no alarm. In historical non-fiction, it flashes red: *Whoa! What is going on here?* Nor is that the only way this book challenges convention. I mentioned point of view. In the beginning (chapter 1) and at the end (Epilogue), I directly address one of the figures in the book—my late friend Louie Kamookak. In addition, when writing from personal experience, to

Louie Kamookak (left) kibbitzing in Gjoa Haven in 2017, asking the author, "So when are you going to write your big Franklin book?"

channel immediacy I use not the past but the present tense. Can historical narrative accommodate all this exuberance? I like to think so.

Louie Kamookak asked after my "big Franklin book." In belated response, although it's just average in size, I offer *Searching for Franklin: New Answers to the Great Arctic Mystery*. To be clear: this is not a work about the countless expeditions that went hunting for the Franklin ships after they disappeared into the Arctic in 1845—a quest that, during the past quarter-century, has inspired sundry novels, documentaries, and poems. Rather, here we go searching for the man behind the myth. To that end, this book takes what it needs from both the physical search and the life.

My first encounter with the myth of Franklin came in 1998, when I spent three months on a fellowship at the University of Cambridge. One rainy night, with a floor lamp at my elbow and a mug of coffee in my hand, I sat reading a particularly cogent description of how Sir John Franklin had earned the right to be recognized as the discoverer of the Northwest Passage. The book was *Frozen in Time*. Co-authors John Geiger and Owen Beattie observed that the last survivors of the Franklin expedition had completed the passage only after a final doomed march from their ice-locked ships. They quoted the eminent naturalist Sir John Richardson, who had twice travelled with Franklin: "They forged the last link with their lives."

Even as I admired that line, I thought, *Well, so you're suggesting that while metaphorically they succeeded, in reality those men discovered nothing.* They marched south along an ice-choked channel that would remain impassible for decades. And then they died, reporting nothing. Franklin himself had perished on June 11, 1847, months before a large party of men abandoned the ships. More to the point, the remnants of his ill-starred crew had struggled along a permanently frozen strait and died in a region where no passage existed.

That night in Cambridge, I set aside the book, rose to my feet, and began pacing the floor. My newly acquired grasp of Arctic geography had enabled me to see what Richardson was hiding with his eloquence. John Franklin discovered nothing. This realization left me shaking my head. I had come face to face with the myth of Franklin as Arctic hero. Soon enough, I found clarification in *The Myth of the Explorer*. Author Beau Riffenburgh argues that the creation of a powerful hero myth requires an exotic setting, a single-minded hero, the death of that figure, and mediators to celebrate him. Creating such a hero requires public relations experts and already, at Cambridge, I was beginning to see that, in his formidable widow, the dead Franklin had one of the best.

∾

Flash forward two decades. Soon after I began writing this investigation, I realized that I would have to write a dual narrative—to interweave two stories. The first, which begins with "Part One: Searching for Franklin," is a framing tale that revolves around my two-decades-long engagement with Arctic exploration. To create a complete experience, I have reworked a few incidents about which I have previously written, either in one of my books or in one of the thirty or forty pieces I have published in newspapers, magazines, logbooks, and academic journals.

While tracking my journey, complete with red herrings, wrong turns, and dead ends, this story encompasses key aspects of the physical hunt—the finding of graves on Beechey Island, the discovery of a written document at Victory Point, and the first reports of cannibalism. And it comprises several searches: Lady Franklin's for the two lost ships, Louie Kamookak's for the Franklin vault or burial site, and my own for the man behind the myth. Finally, it offers a new answer to the most famous of exploration mysteries: What happened to the 1845 expedition? In 1833, Captain John Ross and his men had emerged alive after surviving four winters trapped in the Arctic ice. What caused this later expedition to go so strangely and tragically wrong?

The second narrative here, which opens with "Part Two: The Royal Navy Man," treats Britain's first overland expedition (1819–22) in search of the Northwest Passage—a neglected story that excited me to write this book. It finds a young Lieutenant Franklin rejecting the advice and pleadings of an outstanding Dene leader, Akaitcho, and a peerless voyageur, the Dene–French Canadian Pierre St. Germain. An evangelical Christian who believed in miracles, John Franklin prays to the Lord while losing eleven of his twenty men to starvation, cannibalism, and murder.

Yet in 1823, when he published his official narrative of this nightmare expedition, he became a celebrity. He became The Man Who Ate His Boots—a reference to how, in extremis, he and his men were driven to consuming their leather moccasins. Today, Franklin stands revealed as a classic exemplar of an age and its admonitions, both naval and religious, and might best be described as The Royal Navy Man Who Couldn't Listen.

PART ONE

Searching *for* Franklin

~

CHAPTER I

A Vault *on* This Island

~

I see it all again, Louie. It's 2017 and as we stand laughing and joking in the front hall of Qiqirtaq High School, an announcer tells everyone to please take their seats: the show is about to begin. We agree to reconnect afterward, you and I, and rush back to our seats. We don't get to meet, though, because over the next half-hour, the wind grows fierce. We visitors have to cut short our stay and rush out into the howling afternoon. The Zodiac ride back to the ship, hanging onto a cord while pounding through two-metre waves, shows doubters like me why we didn't get to the wreck of the *Erebus*.

Because of the sudden rush, we never get to talk about polar bears. That's one of my big regrets, Louie, one among many. But forgive me! I neglected to say, *Ublaakut!* Good morning! That's how you greeted us each day when you came online. *Ublaakut*, Louie, from a future you will never know. In September 2017, I never get the chance to talk with you about my polar bear theory. That too-short visit at the high school is the last time we meet face to face. Now I count on my fingers and see you had six months to live.

During your final months, we do chat occasionally on the phone. I am helping polar adventurer David Reid organize an "Arctic Return

Expedition" to the memorial plaque we erected to honour nineteenth-century explorer John Rae and his two travel companions. David is bent on replicating Rae's 1854 journey to the site from Repulse Bay (Naujaat). Yes, I was present at the conception, which happened on the *Ocean Endeavour* as we sailed into Rae Strait. When I tell you about this, later, you make no secret of the fact that you are travelling regularly from Gjoa Haven to Yellowknife and Edmonton, that you are in and out of hospital and receiving chemotherapy. But I happen to know you are not yet sixty years old. For some reason I think you will be with us for many years yet. How stupid is that?

In my defence, Louie, I have to say you did encourage me to believe that you would survive indefinitely. At one point you raised a subject we had discussed as early as 2013—the idea of me helping you write an autobiography. I said I'd be delighted—that, in fact, we *must* do it. Not only that, but in January 2018, you agree to become the Gjoa Haven consultant to the Arctic Return Expedition, which is slated to set out in the spring of 2019. I am going to fly to Gjoa Haven. Together, you and I and a few young hunters will travel by snowmobile to greet David Reid's overland expedition at its culminating point—the memorial plaque we installed in August 1999. We would celebrate our twentieth anniversary at the site.

Two months later, Louie, you went and died. For me, that drains the Arctic Return project of energy. I no longer want to go and meet the overlanders. I let slide that part of the plan. In spring 2019, David Reid does lead a three-person excursion, retracing the original route. So that ends well. But now, as I write, I find myself spinning off into our own expedition.

From Calgary, via Edmonton and Yellowknife, I fly north to Gjoa Haven. I travel with your old friend Cameron Treleaven, that adventurous antiquarian book dealer with whom you have already done some Arctic rambling.

You meet us at the airstrip—thirty-nine years old, full of laughter and energy. But now I think of those reading over my shoulder—people who never met you. Shall I catch them up, tell them that you emerged into the world on August 26, 1959, Louie Iriniq Kamookak, at a seal-hunting camp on Boothia Peninsula near Taloyoak (formerly Spence Bay)? You were the second oldest child born to Mary Kamookak and her hunter husband, George. Now, in 1999, you head a family of six, supervise the maintenance of community housing, and find yourself immersed in two historical projects—one involving Inuit place names, the other, traditional oral stories. Above all, as emerges quickly enough, you are obsessed with finding the Franklin vault—the grave in which, you believe, the celebrated explorer lies buried.

In 1999, most strangers to Gjoa Haven stay at the barn-like Amundsen Hotel, where a shared room costs more than $200 per person per night—the equivalent today of roughly $330. Thanks to you, Cameron and I will spend four nights in Gjoa Haven in a one-room cabin you built three or four miles out of town. One evening, you take us by motorboat to the Todd Islets, fifteen miles west of Gjoa. You show us the Franklin site your grandfather, William "Paddy" Gibson, discovered in the 1930s—a scattering of white bones on the ground, with a few larger ones protruding from beneath the earth. These remains lay along a known route of the Franklin retreat. I find them interesting, but I am no forensic archaeologist, and to me they can reveal nothing new.

You note proudly that Gibson, your Irish grandfather on your mother's side, was a district inspector for the Hudson's Bay Company. At this site in 1945, still searching, he found and reburied a complete human skeleton, plus skulls and bones belonging to Franklin's men. He published his findings in the *Geographical Journal* and *The Beaver* magazine. Two generations later, as his grandson, already you are more involved in the Franklin search than any other living Inuk.

You tell me, "I believe Franklin is lying in a vault on this island." For years you have been hunting that burial site. Your obsessive search is rooted in a yarn you heard from Hummahuk, your great-grandmother, as a boy. When she was very young, six or seven, she was travelling with her family along the northwestern coast of King William Island, looking for driftwood. The party spotted a ridge, went to investigate, and came across artifacts they hadn't seen before—spoons and forks and other utensils, even musket balls.

Hummahuk said she also saw a long rope or chain trailing into the water, and nearby, a strange stone slab. "Her stories always stayed in my head," you told me. You used to say, "One of these days, I'm going to find that spot." When you were twelve or thirteen, one of your teachers talked about Franklin's men dying as they walked along the west coast of King William Island. That's when you put the two together—the history of the lost expedition and the story your great-grandmother told. To you, Hummahuk's description of a stone slab suggested the cover of a burial vault. As an adult, you are bent on finding that site and returning Franklin's body to England to rest beside that of his wife. And the vault? "The vault will be a tourist benefit for the community and for students to go see."

~

You never did find the Franklin vault, Louie. But you did become an honorary vice-president of the Royal Canadian Geographical Society. You received the Erebus Medal, the Lawrence J. Burpee Medal, the Canadian governor general's Polar Medal, the Order of Canada, the Order of Nunavut. So—no small recognition, all thanks to your successes in interpreting between cultures and arriving at a comprehensive understanding by comparing Inuit stories and the narratives of the *qallunaat*, or white men. Down through the years, encouraged by your wife, Josephine, you interviewed (informally) dozens of local people and sifted through their stories. "The oral tradition tells a lot of history," you told me once, "but it isn't always easy to interpret."

Somehow you managed. Even so, the Louie Kamookak I most like to remember is the one who in 1999 introduced me to the High Arctic. I see you now, Louie. Two nights after visiting the Todd Islets, and immediately after supper, we all three climb into your twenty-foot boat and roar north up the east coast of King William Island. We make a brief stop below a high plateau that your people, the Netsilingmiut, or Netsilik Inuit, call Avak. We hike to the top of this ridge and take in the spectacular view over Rae Strait—nothing but water as far as the eye can see. Around 9:45 p.m., we regain the boat and, while a stiff north wind surrounds us with white caps and spray billows over the canopy of the boat, thump fourteen miles across Rae Strait. In the pounding, exhilarating ride, much rougher than along the coast, I realize, "Whoa, Louie! Shouldn't we be wearing life jackets?"

How you laugh, Louie! You jerk your thumb at three orange lifejackets jammed behind my seat. "Put one on if you like," you say. "Out here, you go into the water, a lifejacket will only make things worse. Too cold. You won't survive ten minutes."

I don't doubt it, but I do don one of those life jackets. And that is the kind of memory I've been reliving, Louie, ever since, at your behest, I turned my attention to John Franklin himself. You were the one, Louie, who brought me to him. The Inuk brings the *qallunat* to the English naval officer—surely one of life's little ironies. When we met, as you know, I was obsessed not with Franklin but with Dr. John Rae, an explorer who listened to the Indigenous Peoples. About the Royal Navy officer I cared not a whit, except as he impacted the story of John Rae, who trained in Edinburgh as a medical doctor before entering the fur trade with the Hudson's Bay Company.

But in 1999, as we ramble around the Arctic tundra, you keep bringing me back to the good Sir John. You insist that searchers "will find his body in a vault on King William Island." One group of Inuit, you tell me, witnessed "the burial of a great chief under the ground—under a flat stone." Traditionally, the Inuit wrap their dead in caribou skins, place them on the surface of the ground, and build cairns over them. In this case, the hunters investigated the site, but "all they found was a flat stone. They said the dead man was a great shaman who turned to stone."

Another group of hunters chanced upon a large wooden structure. "They took a piece to use as a crosspiece for a sled. The man who told the

Louie Kamookak in 1999, examining the ruins of the John Rae cairn.

story said there was a large, flat stone, and he could tell the stone was hol-low." You never did stop searching for Franklin's vault. As late as the spring of 2016, you mounted an all-terrain-vehicle expedition and led two young hunters in setting out across the island toward its northwest coast. Heavy rain and mud caused you to run low on gas. Progress impossible, you had to turn back.

Never mind. Now, in what for me is that magical, ever-present August, we reach the west coast of Boothia Peninsula at twenty minutes past midnight. With daylight dwindling to dusk, we guide the motor-boat carefully through the shallows into a nondescript bay. To me, it looks indistinguishable from every other indentation. But you say you know it and that is good enough for me. Fifty yards from shore, your twenty-foot boat runs aground in the shallow water and we three adventurers pull on rubber boots, clamber over the side, and drag the craft farther onto the reef before burying two anchors in the sand.

Around half past one, as dusk yields to twilight, we finish lugging our equipment and supplies onshore and, on the rocky, treeless ground, pitch a floorless, handmade canvas tent, securing it with stones. Knowing the sun will rise above the horizon in just two hours, we unroll our sleeping bags and crawl into them, hoping to fall asleep quickly. At my urging, we have come to this desolate spot to honour Rae and the only two men who could keep up with him—the Ojibwe (Anishinaabe) Thomas Mistegan and the Inuk William Ouligbuck. From Calgary, Cameron and I have brought a plaque of weather-resistant anodized aluminum screwed to a slab of Honduran mahogany. In Gjoa Haven, you took us to a workshop and welded the plaque to a heavy metal stand. We are good to go.

Our late-twentieth-century campsite sits by the strait through which Roald Amundsen sailed in 1903–06 as the first explorer to navigate the Northwest Passage. And half a century before that, when John Rae realized that this strait was almost certainly the missing link in the Passage between north and south channels, he built a stone cairn. Our objective was to find this cairn and, during this last summer of the twentieth century—and indeed the millennium—erect the plaque where he and his two fellow travellers fit the final piece into a centuries-old geographical puzzle.

Fortunately, Rae not only described the place where he created the marker but also noted its geographic co-ordinates. After breakfast, we set out. Remember, Louie? After rambling around inland for a few hours, and finding nothing at Rae's specified longitude, we cross a waterway and follow the coast north. Finally, at around 4:30 p.m., we again approach Rae's latitude, only now we are hiking along the coast, the three of us strung out seventy or eighty yards apart. Of course, you are leading the way, walking along the top of a ridge. As we approach the tip of the peninsula that Rae named Point de la Guiche, suddenly you stop. You bend down to examine the remains of a cairn. Instead of hollering, you simply place your GPS receiver on the capstone, kneel over the cairn, and wait for Cameron and me to catch up.

The cairn has been dismantled but is still clearly recognizable as a human creation, even with its stones covered in yellow and black lichen. Nor is it the kind of cairn, you explain, that Inuit hunters build to cache game. The builder of this cairn placed big rocks in the centre on top of smaller ones, a practice that would crush fresh meat. This is the only human-made structure for miles. And the GPS tells us that although the longitude of this spot differs from Rae's by three minutes and thirty-six seconds, a considerable distance, the latitude agrees within a few yards. This is it—John Rae's cairn.

Standing in the wind, with open water visible to the west, the northwest, and the northeast, I try to see the scene as it unfolded in the blowing snowscape of early May 1854. A resolute man of forty-one, Rae had led his small party across ice and rough country for over 320 miles, man-hauling sledges through blizzards, gale-force winds, and temperatures as low as sixty-two degrees below zero Fahrenheit. Only he and his two hardiest men—Ouligbuck and Mistegan—reached this location on the west coast of Boothia Peninsula. And here, John Rae built this cairn. I kneel across from you and place my hand on the capstone.

CHAPTER 2

John Franklin Goes Missing

~

In June of 1844, ten years before John Rae built that cairn, Sir John and Lady Franklin arrived back in England from Van Diemen's Land. Having lived away for six years, with Sir John serving as lieutenant-governor of the Australian penal colony, they were thrilled to learn that the British Admiralty was showing renewed interest in solving the riddle of the Northwest Passage. Five years before, in 1839, two Hudson's Bay Company explorers had sailed east along the Arctic coast of North America in two small boats, travelling from the mouth of the Coppermine River to Boothia Peninsula.

Thomas Simpson and Peter Warren Dease had determined that, by using this newly charted waterway, a ship could sail from Boothia to the Pacific Ocean. All that remained to solve the whole riddle was to discover a north–south channel linking Barrow Strait, already proven to be accessible from the Atlantic, and the newly discovered coastal channel. How hard could it be?

The Admiralty had decided to dispatch an expedition to accomplish this task.

Whoever led the expedition, which was expected easily to "achieve the Passage" by sailing from the Atlantic to the Pacific, would receive ten thousand pounds (in contemporary terms, something like US$1.3 million)

to share as he chose among officers and crew members. Equally important to some, that individual would be immortalized as Discoverer of the
Northwest Passage. And so there ensued a fierce behind-the-scenes com-
petition—precisely the kind, involving family connections and powerful
allies, at which Jane Franklin excelled.

Early on, like Edward Parry, who was four years younger than him,
the fifty-eight-year-old John Franklin had been disqualified from consideration for the leadership role as too old for the rigours of the Arctic. Under
normal circumstances, Franklin himself would probably have accepted this
assessment. But events in Van Diemen's Land (an island penal colony soon
to be renamed Tasmania) had inspired a destructive smear campaign that
virtually destroyed his reputation. First, Lady Franklin—a far better writer
than Sir John—had got caught up in making key decisions on government
policy. This had led to the public allegation that she was secretly leading
a "petticoat government"—an accusation that, in the fiercely patriarchal
society of the times, did serious damage. *What? Was Franklin a weak-
ling dominated by his wife?* Franklin suspended Colonial Secretary John
Montagu, the senior civil servant in the colony, after the latter published a
series of scurrilous articles. The well-connected Montagu, a cold-blooded,
Machiavellian liar, returned to England and orchestrated the ignominious
recall of Franklin.

Now both Franklins felt driven to see Sir John appointed leader of
this looming Arctic expedition as a signal of exoneration. *Look! His reputation remains untarnished.* Later, when published reports insinuated this
motivation, Lady Franklin would fiercely deny it, insisting "nothing can
be more false and more absurd than the idea that he went on his Arctic
expedition from any other motive than the pure love of Arctic discovery
and enterprise."

James Clark Ross, now Sir James, topped the Admiralty list of leadership candidates. He had accepted a knighthood after returning from his
last Antarctic expedition. Ross had taken part in more polar voyages than
any of his contemporaries. But at forty-four and recently married, he

wished to live as a country gentleman on his estate southeast of London. And so he demurred, declaring that before marrying, he had promised his father-in-law to undertake no more polar voyages. Ross also had an alcohol problem. Yet, as the first choice of many, he wielded a great deal of influence . . . and he had become friends with both Franklins—especially Jane—during a visit to Van Diemen's Land.

Left to his own devices, Sir John Franklin would never have gained the leadership. But behind him, driven by the same desperate need for vindication, the formidable Jane went to work. To James Clark Ross, who had presented her with a beautiful gold bracelet on her arrival in Portsmouth (an inscribed gift from the Tasmanian Philosophical Society), Jane wrote with her usual astute mix of flattery and forthrightness. If Ross, who was clearly "the right person," chose not to lead the expedition, then she hoped Sir John would not be overlooked because of his age. She dreaded "exceedingly the effect on his mind of being without honourable and immediate employment, and it is this which enables me to support the idea of parting with him on a service of difficulty and danger better than I otherwise should."

Soon after receiving this communication, Ross went public: the only possible leader for the definitive expedition of 1845 was Arctic veteran Sir John Franklin. At the Admiralty, second secretary John Barrow—the civil servant who controlled naval appointments—could only shake his head in dismay. Barrow had failed in his campaign to give command to thirty-three-year-old Captain James Fitzjames, a family friend known for his wit and good humour. Long ambivalent about Franklin, Barrow then tried to tempt J.C. Ross into taking on the task, offering him a baronetcy and a pension. As delicately as he could, he offered to postpone the mission for a year so the explorer could resolve his drinking problem. Ross stood firm.

Two experienced, highly competent officers in their forties remained in contention: Sir George Back, who two decades before had distinguished himself as an overland Arctic traveller, and Francis Crozier, who had sailed on significant polar voyages and would go, ultimately, as second-in-command of the expedition and captain of the *Terror*. George Back asked Ross to support his candidacy. Having twice journeyed with Franklin in the Arctic, Back insisted that the older man did not tolerate cold well and argued that he was not physically fit to undertake such an adventure. The influential Ross remained adamant, though even his friends—among them Edward Sabine, astronomer, and Francis Beaufort, Admiralty mapmaker—also urged him to rethink his support for Franklin.

Ross was no doubt feeling the heat when Lady Franklin brought up reinforcements. Remarkably, using family connections and moral suasion, she had got through not only to the Royal Geographical Society, which sent a ringing endorsement of Franklin's candidacy, but to the redoubtable Sir Edward Parry, who told Thomas Lord Haddington, the First Lord of the Admiralty, that Sir John was a better man than any other he knew: "If you don't let him go, he will die of disappointment."

Lord Haddington buckled. He overruled Barrow. And on February 7, 1845, he announced that the leader of this epochal Northwest Passage expedition would be that Arctic veteran Sir John Franklin. Under Franklin, James Fitzjames would sail as captain of the *Erebus*.

~

By early spring, the Royal Navy had two state-of-the-art ships sparkling like success in the sun: the *Erebus* and the *Terror*, freshly painted black and yellow with a wide stripe running the length of each vessel. Had not James Clark Ross sailed these ships to the Antarctic? Jane Franklin herself had boarded them, and more than once, when Ross sojourned in Van Diemen's Land. Since then, they had been refitted for Arctic service, supplied with adapted railway engines and retractable screw propellers and also a heating system that drove hot air through twelve-inch pipes.

John Franklin was well satisfied with his eager officers—"a fine set of young men, active, zealous, and devoted to the Service"—and likewise the crew: "Many say that no ships could go to sea better appointed than

In 1845, the Royal Navy fitted out two state-of-the-art vessels, HMS *Erebus* and HMS *Terror*, to undertake an epochal voyage in search of the Northwest Passage.

we are." Above all, as Jane understood, Sir John felt vindicated—that his appointment to the leadership of this high-profile expedition signalled his exoneration.

From her London home, Jane Franklin travelled twenty-five miles southeast to the village of Greenhithe, four miles above the main docks at Gravesend. On Sunday, May 18, 1845, less than one year after arriving back in England, she boarded the *Erebus* to hear Sir John read his first divine service on that vessel. Next morning, the steamboat *Rattler* towed the *Erebus* and the *Terror* into open water. And away they sailed.

About the first two stages of the voyage—to Orkney and then onward to Greenland—Jane received several letters, the last of which her husband dispatched from Disko Island via whaling ship. The men remained in high spirits: "I think perhaps that I have the tact of keeping officers and men happily together in a greater degree than James Clark Ross, and for this reason: he is evidently ambitious and wishes to do everything himself."

As far as that island, Jane could reconstruct the expedition. Before quitting England, Franklin had read out an order stipulating that every officer and crewman would, on his return, immediately surrender journals, diaries, and other papers to himself as captain. Jane had long since determined that, in creating his first Arctic narrative, which made him famous as The Man Who Ate His Boots, Franklin had drawn extensively on the journals of John Richardson, his more literary second-in-command. But that was in keeping with naval tradition.

This time out, to all those on board, Franklin opened the ship's library, whose 1,700 volumes included Arctic reference books and a huge selection of works on the Christian faith, but also novels by Charles Dickens and William Makepeace Thackeray, collections of plays by William Shakespeare, and bound volumes of the magazine *Punch*. Jane could easily imagine Franklin conducting religious services and providing slates to illiterate crewmen who attended evening classes.

From Greenland, in the last letters he would write home, Sir John Franklin emerges as popular and admired by his men. He also shows himself to be deeply concerned, if not obsessed, with the pamphlet he had recently written in rebuttal to his ignominious recall from Van Diemen's Land, where from 1837 to 1843 he had served as lieutenant-governor. As noted, Franklin had got into a simmering power struggle with Montagu, the nasty but well-connected colonial secretary. Things went from bad to worse when Franklin, at the urging of his wife, overturned a decision to fire a hard-working country doctor without cause. An enraged Montagu returned to England and spread vicious, barefaced lies to destroy Franklin's reputation among government decision makers. Hence the pamphlet.

Above all, in his final letters, Franklin reveals himself to be an evangelical Christian—a man much given to prayer and Christian exhortation. Examples abound in *May We Be Spared to Meet on Earth: Letters of the Lost Franklin Arctic Expedition*. Franklin's contributions are notable for their religiosity. To the young man who would later wed his only daughter, Franklin praised the way his loved ones bore his leave-taking with "a very proper spirit" and "who in fervent prayer committed me & my companions & our cause to the infinite Mercy of God who alone can order the issues of the voyage, and trusted that the Lord would graciously receive their petitions."

In a later letter to that young man's father, a Protestant minister, Franklin wrote that he believed sincerely that this expedition would eventually, "though in ways perhaps undiscernible by us, promote the cause of true religion." He would delight in introducing the blessings it imparts "to all who humbly seek to embrace & follow its holy precepts through faith in the Crucified Redeemer." One more example? To a favourite sister, Franklin insisted that the officers and crew of every ship sailing to strange lands should go forth with "a Missionary Spirit and may God grant such a spirit on board this ship!"

$\sim$

Those who received such letters were initially optimistic. In the spring of 1846, after wintering in Madeira, Jane Franklin took passage on a ship that sailed through the West Indies to the United States. She hoped to be in that country when Sir John emerged into the Pacific Ocean, and to greet him and share in his moment of glory on the west coast of the continent. But Franklin failed to emerge. And that December, back in London, she began to worry. To James Clark Ross, she wrote that she "dare[d] not be sanguine" as to the success of the absent voyagers. "And should it please Providence that we should not see them return when we are led to expect them, will you be the man to go in search of them as you did so nobly for the missing whalers?"

Ross assured her that all would be well. But the following month, his maverick uncle, Sir John Ross, began clamouring for a search expedition. That veteran explorer, now nearing seventy, proclaimed the obvious:

that as Franklin's ships had not arrived in the Pacific Ocean, they had got locked in the ice. Even before Franklin sailed, this same Arctic veteran had warned that the *Erebus* and the *Terror*—refurbished bomb ketches weighing 370 and 326 tons, respectively—were too big and heavy to accomplish their objective. He himself had got trapped in vessels with a nine-foot draught, and these, weighed down with coal, extended nineteen feet below the surface.

The elder Ross revealed that he had promised Franklin that if England received no news of the voyage by 1847, he would mount a relief expedition. Some experts doubted this, but perhaps he spoke the truth. Either way, the Lords of the Admiralty dismissed his concerns: they had offered a reward for news of Franklin and remained confident that whalers and fur traders would deliver it to them. Jane Franklin's Royal Navy friends—among them Beaufort, Parry, and James Clark Ross—became an informal Arctic Council. They stressed that Franklin had been gone less than two years and carried provisions for three. He would acquire additional food by trading and hunting. They saw no reason to worry. Lady Franklin followed their lead. She dismissed John Ross's proposed expedition as "an absurdity."

Yet that old seadog did not stand alone in offering dark prognostications. Before Franklin even left England, Dr. Richard King had predicted that the polar expedition would become "a lasting blot in the annals of our voyages of discovery." A surgeon and naturalist who had travelled overland to the Arctic coast in the early 1830s, King claimed the good Sir John was being dispatched "to form the nucleus of an iceberg." Having descended the Great Fish River (now called the Back River) with George Back, King had been clamouring to lead another expedition down that same river, travelling light with a small party. He insisted that this was the only way to solve the riddle of the Northwest Passage. He was not far wrong because the Back River reaches the Arctic coast at Chantrey Inlet, south of King William Island, and does offer direct access to Rae Strait. In any event, King's relentless carping had earned him a reputation as a self-interested crank.

Now, insisting that Franklin would be trapped not far from the Arctic coast, King sought support to lead a rescue party by his old favourite route. Of recognized Arctic experts, only naval officer Frederick Beechey said publicly that King might be onto something. Nobody else would listen. In March 1847, James Clark Ross declared, "I do not think there is the smallest reason of apprehension or anxiety for the safety and success of the expedition under the command of Sir John Franklin."

That summer, while sojourning in Italy, Jane Franklin told her diary that "as the autumn advances we must be at home again, as we shall then be tremblingly looking for the return of the Arctic Ships. Sir John Richardson tells me that if they do not return by December there will be reason to fear some disaster." In August, when she arrived home at 21 Bedford Place, overlooking Russell Square, she learned that Richard King had resurfaced. In June, he had written the colonial secretary arguing that Franklin and his men had by now probably been forced to abandon their ships. King offered yet once more to take a relief expedition down the Great Fish River. Again, the Admiralty dismissed him. *He was not a Royal Navy man. What could he know?*

But Lady Franklin began to wonder whether King might have a point. Was the Admiralty doing everything that could be done? In September, from Bedford Place, she wrote to the First Lord requesting a copy of her husband's original orders. And she turned her attention to what might happen next. The Admiralty announced plans to dispatch a supply ship, the *Plover*, to the Pacific coast of North America to meet Franklin as he emerged into the Beaufort Sea. But what if he did not emerge?

The Admiralty also approved a proposal for an overland search party to be led by Sir John Richardson, second-in-command during Franklin's two overland expeditions. Richardson would lead two dozen men to the northern coast—not down the Great Fish River, which culminates 125 miles due south of Gjoa Haven, but much farther west, along the better-known Coppermine, down which he had ventured with Franklin in 1819–22.

Richardson was casting about for a competent second-in-command, sifting through scores of applications, when on November 1, 1847, he read a report in the London *Times* by a Hudson's Bay Company doctor, John Rae. It detailed how he had wintered over in the High Arctic, living off the land. Rae had spent more than a decade based at Moose Factory, learning from the Indigenous Peoples, mainly Cree and Inuit. On July 5, 1846, along with a dozen men, he had sailed north out of Fort Churchill in two small boats. He had reappeared just over one year later, on August 31, 1847, with eight bags of pemmican and four of flour—a pointed response to those doubters who had had predicted that any men who travelled with him would starve to death.

For Richardson—now fifty-nine years of age and serving as chief medical officer at Haslar naval base on the south coast of England—Rae's report arrived like manna from heaven. On reading it at his residence in Portsmouth, he jumped to his feet and cried out to his wife, "I have found my companion—if I can get him." By mid-November, Richardson had appointed as second-in-command the remarkable John Rae, "who had recently led a dozen men into the High Arctic and wintered over, relying on his own resources."

In London, meanwhile, Jane Franklin invited Arctic insiders to her home. There, with James Clark Ross and several other members of the Arctic Council—Edward Parry, Francis Beaufort, Frederick Beechey, Edward Sabine—Jane perused a map of the Arctic. Immediately after that meeting, J.C. Ross brought a proposal to the Admiralty.

On November 8, he wrote that he was "willing and desirous to take command" of a search expedition, one that would travel not by land but by sea. Five days later, his uncle, the irascible Sir John Ross, resubmitted his own plan to seek Franklin, using shallow-draft vessels. "Unknown to me," he wrote afterward, "a meeting was held at Lady Franklin's residence, at which all my proposals were sneered at and my opinions scouted, while I was represented to be too old and infirm to undertake such a service."

In December 1847, the Admiralty announced that James Clark Ross would lead a search by water. There was no talk now of any alcohol problem, no talk of promises to keep. With two ships, the *Enterprise* and the *Investigator*, Ross would sail the following May. Though pleased with this, Jane Franklin remained haunted by Richard King, and to Ross she wrote, "Of Dr. King himself, I wish to say nothing. I do not desire that he should be the person employed, but I cannot but wish that the Hudson's Bay Company might receive instructions or a request from Govt. to explore those parts which you & Sir John Richardson cannot immediately do, & which if done by you at all, can only be done when other explorations have been made in vain. And then, does he *not* say truly, it will be *too late*—?"

CHAPTER 3

Beechey Island Graves

~

I n August 2007, while sailing for the first time as a resource historian on an expeditionary cruise ship, I finally visit Beechey Island. It overlooks Lancaster Sound, the northern channel of the Northwest Passage, and is really a peninsula attached to massive Devon Island. At last I see the grave-sites of the first three men to die on the 1845 Franklin expedition. A fourth grave is that of a sailor who died nearby in 1854. With six or eight other voyagers in the late morning, I stand gazing at the wooden headboards (facsimiles, in fact) while a Scottish bagpiper plays "Amazing Grace" and a light snow falls and instantly melts. At this desolate spot, in 1846, still hoping to discover the Northwest Passage, Sir John Franklin would have conducted three sonorous burial services.

A mere four years later, in August 1850, American explorer Elisha Kent Kane was standing nearby on an ice-locked ship called the *Lady Franklin*. He was chatting with its captain, William Penny, and a couple of other naval officers when he heard a cry. Gazing out over the snow-covered shores of Beechey Island, he was startled to see a sailor charging over the rise. "Graves!" the man shouted. "Graves! Franklin's winter quarters!" Searchers for the lost expedition of Sir John Franklin had found what is now the most famous historic site in the Arctic.

Drawn by James Hamilton after a sketch by Elisha Kent Kane, and engraved by John Sartain, this is a romanticized view of the three graves found on Beechey Island.

Kane and his fellow officers "hurried on over the ice," as he wrote later, "and, scrambling along the loose and rugged slope that extends from Beechey to the shore, came, after a weary walk, to the crest of the isthmus. Here, amid the sterile uniformity of snow and slate, were the head-boards of three graves, made after the old orthodox fashion of gravestones at home."

Such was the first breakthrough in the Franklin search. Earlier that same month, Kane and his fellow Americans aboard the *Advance* had realized that they would have to winter, as Kane put it, "somewhere in the scene of Arctic search." Having lost three weeks to the ice off Greenland near the Devil's Thumb and two more to Melville Bay, they had sailed west, entered the open North Water, and begun finally to make good time.

Several weeks previously, at the Whalefish Islands, the Americans had learned that a couple of British search ships had already visited Disko

Island. Those vessels could draw on small steam engines for emergency use and would now be far, far ahead. Kane and his companions had dreamed of enjoying the fellowship of the British searchers, "dividing between us the hazards of the way, and perhaps in the long winter holding with them the cheery intercourse of kindred sympathies. We waked now to the probabilities of passing the dark days alone."

But on August 19, as the *Advance* neared the entrance to Lancaster Sound, its sailing master spotted two British vessels following in the ship's wake. Within four hours, the larger of the two drew alongside. It proved to be the *Lady Franklin*, engaged in the Franklin search under the redoubtable Penny. He, too, had encountered problems in Melville Bay. Before sailing on past the slower *Advance*, he reported that Commodore Austin's four-vessel expedition was in the area, and also the provision ship *North Star*.

A couple of nights later, while sailing through Lancaster Sound, driving before a strong wind and taking water at every roll, the Americans overtook yet another British vessel. This small schooner, towing a launch and "fluttering over the waves like a crippled bird," proved to be the *Felix*. Kane watched as "an old fellow, with a cloak tossed over his night gear, appeared in the lee gangway, and saluted with a voice that rose above the winds." Two decades before, Sir John Ross had been shipwrecked and survived four winters in the Arctic. Now he roared joyfully, "You and I are ahead of them all!"

Ross boarded the *Advance*, a vigorous, square-built man who looked younger than his seventy-three years. He reported that Austin's four-boat squadron had taken refuge in various bays, and that Penny was lost in the gale. At age thirty, Kane knew enough Arctic history to delight in meeting John Ross here, near Admiralty Inlet, where seventeen years before the old seadog had contrived to escape an icy incarceration. Kane marvelled that, despite opposition and even ridicule, Ross had sailed in search of his old friend in "a flimsy cockle-shell, after contributing his purse and his influence."

During the next couple of weeks, while the ships remained within hailing distance, Kane would seek out John Ross to solicit his opinions and hear his stories. Ross told Kane that he had talked with Franklin before the latter sailed. He had warned Sir John against "the caprice or even the routine of seasons," and urged him to ensure that he always had an escape route in case he got trapped in the ice. Easier said than done, obviously.

In August 1850, explorer Elisha Kent Kane was present at the finding of the graves.

Later, in the book that Kane would write and publish about this first Arctic expedition, he would indicate the significance he attached to his meeting with Ross by quoting the old sailor at length, explaining, "I have given this extract from my journal because the tone and language . . . may be regarded as characteristic of this manly old seaman."

On August 25, 1850, from the deck of the *Advance* as it neared Beechey Island, Kane spotted two cairns on Cape Riley, the larger marked with a flagstaff. A couple of hours later, near enough to land, Kane went ashore and found a tin canister in the larger cairn. It contained a note saying that two days before, the British captain Ommanney had called in here. Inspecting the area, notebook in hand, Kane identified five distinct "remnants of habitation"—four circular mounds of crumbled limestone, clearly designed as bases for tents, and a fifth such enclosure, larger and triangular, whose entrance faced south toward Lancaster Sound. He also found large square stones arranged to serve as a fireplace and, on the beach, several pieces of pinewood that had once formed part of a boat. In Kane's view, the evidence was meagre but conclusive: "All these speak of a land party from Franklin's squadron."

Next morning, the *Advance* sailed on toward Beechey Island, which "rode up in a lofty monumental block" of characteristic mountain limestone, and which Kane insisted on identifying more precisely as a promontory or peninsula because a low isthmus linked it to Devon Island. By August 27, five vessels under three commanders—William Penny, Sir John Ross, and the American Edwin De Haven—stood anchored within a quarter mile of each other.

Not far from Beechey, between Cape Spencer and Point Innes, Penny had discovered some additional traces of Franklin's expedition: tin canisters with the manufacturer's label, scraps of newspaper dated 1844, and two pieces of paper bearing the name of one of Franklin's officers. In his private, 161-page journal, Kane revealed his persistent belief that the lost expedition might yet be found: "Penny seemed to think that these [relics and their scattered situation] indicate a party in distress. Cast away and now perhaps on road to England via Cape Riley. Cannot agree with these [conclusions]. A migrating party they certainly are or were, but the ships may yet be in the land of the living."

After breakfast on August 27, Kane was talking with William Penny, who had recently speculated in print about the existence far to the north of an Open Polar Sea, when he heard that cry and looked up and saw the sailor hurrying across the ice, hollering against the noise of the wind and the waves. *Graves?* "Graves! Franklin's winter quarters!"

The officers hurried to meet the messenger. After catching his breath and responding to questions as best he could, the crewman—one of Penny's—led the way onto Beechey Island and then to the crest of a ridge. Now Kane saw what had so excited the sailor: against the snow, three wooden head-boards. They would not have been out of place at a cemetery in his hometown Philadelphia. Astonished, he stood marveling.

The three mounds adjoining them formed a line facing Cape Riley, visible across a cove.

The boards bore inscriptions declaring them sacred to the memories of three sailors: W. Braine of the *Erebus*, who died April 3, 1846, at age thirty-two; John Hartnell of the *Erebus*, no date specified, dead at age twenty-three; and John Torrington, "who departed this life January 1st, A.D. 1846, on board of H.M. Ship *Terror*, aged 20 years." In describing this scene, Kane drew attention to the words "on board"—and added, "Franklin's ships, then, had not been wrecked when he occupied the encampment at Beechy."

The excitement of this discovery of graves would be felt down through the decades, leading even to a 1980s exhumation as searchers sought to determine what happened to the Franklin expedition. Now, on August 27, 1850, Elisha Kent Kane copied the inscriptions from the headboards and sketched the three graves against the desolate landscape. He then scoured the area, which abounded in fragmentary remains—part of a stocking, a worn mitten, shavings of wood, the remnants of a rough garden. A quarter mile from the graves, he came upon a neat pile of more than six hundred preserved-meat cans. Emptied of food, these had been filled with limestone pebbles, "perhaps to serve as convenient ballast on a boating expedition."

Countless other indications, including bits and pieces of canvas, rope, sailcloth, and tarpaulins, as well as scrap paper, a small key, and odds and ends of brasswork, attested that this was a winter resting place. Nobody turned up any written documents, however, or even the vaguest hint about the intentions of the party. Kane judged this remarkable—"and for so able and practiced an Arctic commander as Sir John Franklin, an incomprehensible omission."

~

Other researchers, given the benefit of hindsight and the accretion of evidence, have questioned whether Franklin was as competent as some of his contemporaries believed. In 1850, Elisha Kane noted only that it was impossible to stand on Beechey without forming an opinion about what had happened to the British explorer. Before offering his own, he reviewed the incontestable facts. During the winter of 1845–46, the *Terror* had wintered here. She kept some of her crew on board. Some men from the *Erebus* were also here. An organized party had taken astronomical observations, made sledges, and prepared gardens to battle scurvy.

Beyond this lay speculation. Kane inferred the health of the expedition to be generally satisfactory, as only three men had died out of nearly 130. He puzzled over the abandoned tin cans, "not very valuable, yet not worthless," and speculated that they might have been left if Franklin departed Beechey in a hurry—as a result, for example, of the ice breaking up unexpectedly.

The main question, of course, was, where had Franklin gone? Kane judged that Franklin "had not, in the first instance, been able to prosecute his instructions for the Western search; and the examinations made so fully since by Captain Austin's officers have proved that he never reached Cape Walker, Banks' Land, Melville Island, Prince Regent's Inlet, or any point of the sound considerably to the west or southwest."

In fact, though all the Arctic experts present at Beechey shared this belief, Austin's officers had proven nothing. Kane and his fellow searchers, entranced by speculations of an Open Polar Sea, never considered that before he put in at Beechey, Franklin might have sailed north up Wellington Channel and then south again. Instead, Kane imagined that in spring 1846, Franklin had gazed out anxiously, waiting for the ice to open. The first lead to appear would almost certainly run northwest along the coast of Devon Island. Would Franklin wait until Lancaster Sound opened to the south, and then sail back to try the upper reaches of Baffin Bay? "Or would he press to the north through the open lead that lay before him?"

Anybody who knew Franklin's character, determination, and purpose, Kane insisted, would find the question easy to answer. "We, the searchers, were ourselves tempted, by the insidious openings to the north in Wellington Channel, to push on in the hope that some lucky chance might point us to an outlet beyond. Might not the same temptation have had its influence for Sir John Franklin? A careful and daring navigator, such as he was, would not wait for the lead to close."

CHAPTER 4

A Hint *of* Catastrophe

~

I n the autumn of 1852, two years after the discovery of graves on Beechey
Island, explorer John Rae travelled north from London to visit his
widowed mother in the northern reaches of Scotland. At her home in
Stromness, Orkney, Rae developed a plan to complete the mapping of
the Arctic coast of North America. This he outlined in a letter published
in the *Times* on November 26, 1852. Rae proposed to sail into Hudson
Bay aboard a Hudson's Bay Company vessel then make his way north to
Repulse Bay (Naujaat), where he had previously spent a winter. From there,
having put together a crew, he would set out west and north, sextant in
hand. In a postscript he added, "I do not mention the lost navigators as
there is not the slightest hope of finding any traces of them in the quarter
to which I am going."

Rae gained the backing of George Simpson, the so-called "little
emperor" who ran the inland operations of the HBC. He swung into
action, amending his plan as he went. In March 1853, he sailed on the
steamer *Europa* to New York City. He made his way to Montreal and visited Simpson to finalize arrangements. Travelling north and west by canoe,
Rae reached Norway House, just above Lake Winnipeg, on June 12. Here
he greeted the dozen men he had hired at a distance. They included the

Orcadian explorer Dr. John Rae happily learned travel and hunting techniques from Indigenous peoples. In this 1862 watercolour by Canadian artist William Armstrong, Rae wears Cree/Métis clothing of fur and leather, so signalling his allegiance.

Ojibwe Thomas Mistegan, a "splendid deer hunter" who had served with Rae and Richardson as a steersman or boat leader in 1848–49. Farther north, near Fort Churchill, Rae added the Inuk interpreter William Ouligbuck, son of Ouligbuck Sr., who had who served with both Rae and, in 1825–27, John Franklin.

At York Factory, Rae switched from canoes to two York boats. Early in August, well past Fort Churchill, he judged the existing party too large and sent back seven men and one boat. He proceeded north with seven men. Besides Mistegan and Ouligbuck, these included four Scottish Métis (John Beads, Jacob Beads, John McDonald, and James Johnston) and one Scottish Highlander (Murdoch McLennan). Finally, on August 15, 1853, in a cold, drizzling rain, Rae sailed into Repulse Bay. He found the place bleak, dreary, and far more forbidding than he remembered from his first overwintering. Thick ice clogged the shoreline, and immense snowdrifts filled every ravine and every steep bank with a southern exposure. A mass of ice and snow several feet deep covered his old landing place.

Now came a long, dark Arctic winter. Rae kept the men busy hunting and foraging. He calculated provisions for a sixty-day journey, among them 390 pounds of pemmican, 128 of flour, 70 of biscuit, 35 of preserved potatoes, 5 of tea, 40 of sugar, 5 of chocolate, 12 of condensed milk, and 135 of cooking alcohol and tallow, for a total of 820 pounds. The bedding, guns, and ammunition brought the total to 996 pounds. Rae would haul 70 pounds himself, leaving 926, or 232 per large sled—a total he later reduced. In mid-January, to cache food for the looming expedition, and to test his equipment and men, Rae practised man-hauling with three men at a time.

With the arrival of what might loosely be called spring, Rae hoped to buy sled dogs and sent three men to search one last time for any sign of Inuit. They found none and the explorer resigned himself to the famously brutal work of man-hauling. On March 31, 1854, the forty-year-old explorer left Repulse Bay, leading four men at least ten years younger than himself. The five began their journey in bright sunshine and, despite the heavy slog before them, in excellent health and spirits.

Two days out from Repulse, when he saw that one of the men could not keep up, Rae sent him back and brought forward Thomas Mistegan, previously left behind (bitterly disappointed) because of his ability to hunt and provide for the others. In addition to being the expedition's second-best hunter (after Rae himself), Mistegan was an admirable snowshoe walker and sledge-hauler who could tolerate cold. The Ojibwe hunter caught up with the party on April 4. The men made him a special supper, to which he did ample justice after his forced march of thirty-five miles.

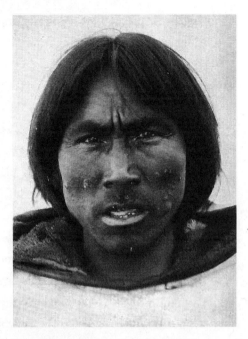

The Inuk hunter and interpreter William Ouligbuck played a crucial role in helping Dr. John Rae ascertain that the Franklin expedition of 1845 had ended in disaster.

Rae led the men northwest along the route he had taken in 1847. He proposed now to cross Boothia Peninsula and chart its western coast northward from the mouth of the Castor and Pollux River—which Peter Warren Dease and Thomas Simpson had reached from the west—to the western mouth of Bellot Strait, charted in 1852.

As always, Rae travelled Inuit-style, building snowhuts as he went. These small igloos remained impenetrable to stormy winds. They required, on average, one hour to build, but stood ready, with doors blocked up, for the return journey. A traveller would not have the trouble of using a cumbersome tent—pitching, taking down, packing on a sledge, and hauling.

Also, like bedding, it would keep gaining weight from moisture. Another advantage was that moisture from the men's breath adhered firmly to the igloo walls instead of condensing and dripping onto the bedding as in a tent.

Unlike naval explorers, who cooked twice a day and stopped for lunch, Rae travelled non-stop, usually breakfasting on dried fruit (from England), a piece of frozen pemmican, and half a biscuit: "We never stopped to eat or drink but put a small piece of our breakfast allowance of pemmican in our pockets, which we munched at our pleasure." Supper usually consisted of more pemmican, boiled with flour and preserved potato or other vegetable into a porridge called rubaboo, a dish that originated with the Plains Métis.

At night, all five men "lay under one covering," Rae wrote, "taking our coats off, so that our arms might be more closely in contact with our bodies. This and the changing of our moccasins was all the undressing we went through. I *always* occupied an outside place, and the cook for the next day the other. Those inside were warm enough, but when either of the outsiders felt chilly on the exposed side, all he had to do was turn round, give his neighbours a nudge and we'd all put about, and the chilly party was soon warmed. We got so speedily accustomed to this that I believe we used to turn over from one side to the other when required without waking."

Rae had started out as early as he dared in the travelling season, and now the weather turned wintry again. Gale-force winds and heavy, drifting snow confined the men to snowhuts or reduced them to travelling as little as six miles a day. The temperature fell to sixty-two degrees below zero Fahrenheit, and Jacob Beads, one of the Scottish Métis, froze two of his toes. By April 10, when the party reached the point on the coast of Committee Bay from which the explorer intended to travel due west across Boothia Peninsula, all the men, including Rae, had endured some degree of snow-blindness, their eyes stinging as if filled with sand.

Rae led the men forward through the zero visibility of a violent snowstorm, steering by compass. For a while the skies cleared, but at Pelly Bay (now Kugaaruk), a dense fog descended and again the compass became necessary. Confronted by impassable mountainous terrain, Rae veered southwest across Boothia Peninsula and came across the fresh footprints of an Inuk hauling a sledge. Rae sent Mistegan and Ouligbuck to find the traveller.

After eleven hours, they returned with seventeen Inuit, among them five women. Rae had met some of these people at Repulse Bay in 1847, but others among the Inuit had never seen Europeans before and proved truculent and even aggressive. "They would give us no information on which any reliance could be placed," Rae wrote in his official report to the HBC, "and none of them would consent to accompany us for a day or two, although I promised to reward them liberally." The hunters objected to the party's travelling farther west, insisting that a hostile band of Inuit lay in that direction.

Rae surmised that they had cached provisions in those parts and didn't want them stolen. To avoid that, they sought "to puzzle the interpreter and mislead us," he wrote. "I declined purchasing more than a piece of seal from them, and sent them away—not however, without some difficulty, as they lingered about with the hope of stealing something; and, notwithstanding our vigilance, succeeded in abstracting from one of the sledges a few pounds of biscuit and grease."

The falsity of the assertion about hostile Inuit living farther west would be demonstrated almost immediately, because two men from Pelly Bay joined the party in travelling that way, quite without fear. Rae encountered the first of these, See-u-ti-chu, driving a team of dogs with a sledge laden with muskox meat. Rae hired the man, who cached his booty on the spot and recommended heading west along the route he had just travelled. The party had no sooner loaded the dogsled and started out than a second Inuk, In-nook-poo-zhe-jook, arrived with more dogs and offered to join the party. He would emerge, over time, as a key player in ascertaining what happened to the Franklin expedition.

The observant Rae noticed immediately that In-nook-poo-zhe-jook wore a gold-braided capband—clearly Royal Navy—and asked him where he had got it. The Inuk replied that it came from the place where the dead white men were. He had traded for it. The dead white men? With the help of William Ouligbuck, Rae proceeded to interrogate the man. Later that day, he recorded field notes: "Met a very communicative and apparently intelligent [Inuk]; had never met whites before but said that a number of Kabloonas [white men], at least 35 or 40, had starved to death west of a large river a long distance off. Perhaps 10 or 12 days' journey. Could not tell the distance, never had been there, and could not accompany us so far. Dead bodies seen beyond two large rivers; did not know place. Could not or would not explain it on a chart."

In 1859 or 1860, after Leopold McClintock had come and gone, Inook-poo-zhe-jook would visit King William Island and investigate scenes of the Franklin tragedy. Just over half a mile from a boat McClintock had searched, he located a second boat, untouched. He told American explorer Charles Francis Hall, through the interpreter Taqulittuq, that he had discovered "one whole skeleton with clothes on . . . as well as a big pile of skeleton bones near the fireplace & skulls among them." He found bones broken up for their marrow and knee-high boots containing "cooked human flesh—that is human flesh that had been boiled."

These revelations lay in the future. Now, in 1854, In-nook-poo-zhe-jook could provide no detailed knowledge. Over the next few decades, searchers would find the remains of thirty-five or forty men on the west coast of King William Island. More remains would turn up on the North American coast near Starvation Cove. The discussion of what happened, where exactly, and when, would continue into the twenty-first century.

In 1854, John Rae bought the Inuk's capband on the spot. He wondered whether it might have come from the lost Franklin expedition but regarded that as unlikely. Half a dozen ships were searching the waters and islands far to the north, up Wellington Channel. That, the naval experts agreed, was where the Franklin expedition would be found. Besides, what did he have to act upon? Some white men had died ten or twelve days away in a spot that these Inuit hunters had never visited and that now lay under a thick blanket of snow. The information was too vague.

Both dog teams were tired, and the man-haulers made slow progress along a river to Simpson Lake. After a couple of days, the two Inuit who had joined the party wished to leave for home. See-u-ti-chu feared that wolverines might plunder his cache of muskox meat. Rae paid both men well. He told In-nook-poo-zhe-jook that if he or his companions had any other relics from white men, they should bring them to Rae's winter quarters at Repulse Bay, where he would pay handsomely for them. And on he travelled.

Two of his men, the Scottish Métis Jacob Beads and James Johnston, were suffering from frostbite. On April 25, after a hard days' hike of more than eighteen miles, they could hardly walk. After helping the two set up a camp near a big rock, Rae told them to await his return. Then, with Mistegan and Ouligbuck, he took four days worth of provisions and set out man-hauling. Two days later, he found a cairn built in 1839 by Thomas Simpson and Peter Warren Dease at the mouth of the Castor and Pollux River. Rae returned to the snowhut where he had left Beads and Johnston—a fifteen-hour march over thirty miles of rough terrain.

Jacob Beads could hardly move, and Rae insisted that the two men remain where they were and await his return. At two o'clock in the morning on April 30, 1854, Rae loaded provisions for twenty-two days onto three sledges and, with his two best men, set out to trace the last uncharted coastline of North America. The three beat their way west and north along the coast through fierce winds and blowing snow. To Rae's surprise, the coast showed no sign of turning west, as maps indicated it would, to encompass King William Land. Finally, on May 6, he arrived at a promontory and stood gazing out over the ice of a frozen channel where naval charts indicated he should be seeing land.

Slowly he realized that this frozen strait separated Boothia Peninsula from what in fact was a distant island—King William Island. More than that, he could not help wondering whether this channel, when the ice melted in the spring, would not become the missing north–south link in the Northwest Passage. At that point, the practical Rae put

Ouligbuck to work building a snowhut. Taking out his instruments and charts, he sent Mistegan north across the ice beyond the tip of Point de la Guiche, as he would name this peninsula. Mistegan hiked some distance north and climbed a hill of rough ice to gain a higher vantage. The land was still trending northward, while to the northwest, at a considerable distance across the ice—perhaps twelve or fourteen miles—more land appeared: "This land, if it was such," Rae wrote in his journal, "is probably part of Matty Island, or King William Land, which latter is also clearly an island."

Rae had reached a point where, except for the unknown strait before him, his survey matched that made by Sir James Clark Ross in 1830, providing "a very singular agreement . . . considering the circumstances under which our surveys have been taken." In snowy weather, Sir James had missed the strait and charted the area as an enclosed bay—albeit with a dotted line and a question mark. His uncle Sir John Ross had closed the line while preparing the final copy of the expedition map and called the strait Poctes Bay.

Rae contemplated the frozen passage before him. It contained what he called "young ice," radically unlike the much rougher ice he had encountered three years before while trying to sail a boat to the western side of King William Island. Clearly, the island protected this channel from the impenetrable pack ice that flowed from the north. He had ventured into Victoria Strait in small boats and, this being the Little Ice Age, found it impassible. But the passage before him would be navigable when that strait was not.

Now, although he could not prove it, John Rae realized that, with the help of Ouligbuck and Mistegan, he had solved the first great mystery of nineteenth-century Arctic exploration. Here, between Boothia Peninsula and King William Island, he had discovered the hidden gateway in the Northwest Passage. Half a century would elapse before Roald Amundsen would prove him right by becoming the first to navigate the Passage from the Atlantic to the Pacific. But now, Rae marked the location of his discovery by building a small cairn just south of the tip of Point de la Guiche—a cairn whose ruins three adventurers located 145 years later.

A satisfied Rae and his two hardiest men began the long journey back to Repulse Bay. On reaching the two men he had left waiting in a snowhut, Rae felt confirmed in his decision to turn back. Both were badly worn down and, while James Johnston could walk reasonably well, Jacob Beads was losing a big toe at the joint. On other occasions, farther south, Rae had treated frostbite with great success by applying a poultice made of the inner bark of the larch fir. Now, under more difficult conditions, he could do little. Beads insisted on hobbling along, stoutly refusing to be hauled. The weather had cleared, the snow was hard-packed, and the party of five made better time returning than coming out. The men reached their Pelly Bay snowhut on May 17, shortly after midnight, with the bright sun low on the horizon.

They were still almost two hundred miles from Repulse Bay. Rae allowed all the men to rest. Then, noticing tracks in the snow, he sent Mistegan and Ouligbuck to follow them. Eight hours later, the two returned with a dozen Inuit men, women, and children. One of the Inuit produced a silver fork and spoon, which Rae promptly bought: "The initials F. R. M. C., not engraved, but scratched with a sharp instrument, on the spoon, puzzled me much, as I knew not at the time the Christian names of the officers of Sir John Franklin's expedition." Still convinced that Franklin had become lost far to the north, Rae speculated about Captain Robert McClure, who had sailed with a search expedition in 1850, and wondered whether the initials might be his, with the small *c* omitted—perhaps F. Robert McClure?

Rae expressed keen interest in seeing any further relics and promised to pay handsomely for them, back at Repulse Bay. Nine days later, at five in the morning, Rae and his men arrived at that destination. They had covered in twenty days the distance (minus forty or fifty miles) that, going out in rougher weather, had taken thirty-six days. Rae found the three men he had left behind—John Beads, John McDonald, and Murdoch

McLennan—living on friendly terms with several newly arrived Inuit families who had pitched tents nearby. "The natives had behaved in the most exemplary manner," wrote Rae, "and many of them who were short of food, in compliance with my orders to that effect, had been supplied with venison from our stores."

More Inuit arrived from Pelly Bay with relics to trade and stories to tell. At last, Rae had an opportunity to glean answers about the white men who had apparently died of starvation. Only now did he begin to realize and understand, with growing horror, that the visitors were almost certainly talking about men from the lost Franklin expedition, which had sailed from England nine years before. While trading for relics, and then more thoroughly afterward, Rae asked questions through Ouligbuck. The Inuit visitors told him that all the kabloonas had died several years before. No survivors had ever reached any HBC trading post, where the Hudson's Bay Company had sent Yellowknife Dene to seek them with ammunition, clear instructions, and promises of reward.

The Inuit newcomers explained that four winters earlier, in 1850, some Inuit families killing seals near the northern shore of a large island (which Rae now understood to be King William Island) had encountered at least forty kabloonas dragging a boat and some sledges south. None of these white men could speak Inuktitut, but they communicated through gestures that their ships had been crushed by ice and that they were travelling to where they hoped to hunt deer.

The men looked thin and hungry, and all except the leader hauled on the drag ropes of sledges. The leader was a tall, stout, middle-aged man who wore a telescope strapped over his shoulder. The party, obviously short of provisions, bought seal meat from the Inuit, then pitched tents and rested. These kabloonas then headed east across the ice toward the mouth of a large river—a river that, Rae now recognized by its description, could only be Back's Great Fish River.

The following spring, when Inuit visited that river to fish, the newcomers continued to explain, they discovered about thirty corpses. They found graves on the main part of the continent and five dead bodies on an island a long day's journey northwest of the river. Rae surmised that these references were to Ogle Point and Montreal Island. The Inuit discovered some dead bodies in tents and others under a boat that had been overturned to provide shelter. A few other bodies lay scattered about.

None of the Inuit Rae questioned had themselves seen the kabloonas alive or dead, but Rae had worked long enough in the north to appreciate the reach and reliability of the Inuit grapevine. This was an oral culture. Sitting in his tent, he conducted repeated interviews through Ouligbuck, checking the veracity of his informants against information recorded in the narratives of John Ross and Edward Parry.

The Inuit had considered it odd that they found no sledges among the dead, although the boat remained. Rae pointed out that the kabloonas, if they reached the mouth of the Great Fish River, would need their boat to proceed farther but might have burned the sledges for fuel. "A look of intelligence immediately lit up their faces," he wrote, "and they said that may have been so, for there had been fires."

In his report to the HBC, Rae continued, "A few of the unfortunate men must have survived until the arrival of the wild fowl (say until the end of May) as shots were heard and fresh bones and feathers of geese were noticed near the scene of the sad event. There appears to have been an abundant store of ammunition, as the gunpowder was emptied by the natives in a heap on the ground out of the kegs or cases containing it, and a quantity of shot and ball was found below highwater mark, having probably been left on the ice close to the beach before the spring thaw commenced."

One night, having gleaned all the information he could, Rae sorted through the relics he had acquired. Among them were pieces of telescopes and guns, broken watches and compasses. Again he counted the identifiable items, those bearing the crests and initials of officers on Franklin's two ships. These totalled fifteen. They included a gold watch, a surgeon's knife, several silver spoons and forks bearing the Franklin crest, an order of merit in the form of a star, and a small silver plate engraved with the name of Sir John Franklin.

Rae studied the engraved plate by lantern light and marvelled: Franklin himself had eaten from it. The presence of this silver dish, together with the other relics, verified the Inuit story beyond doubt. He knew the answer, or at least the beginning of one, to the second great mystery of Arctic exploration. He knew that the Franklin expedition had suffered a fate as terrible as the imagination could conceive.

But now Rae faced a difficult decision—perhaps the most important of his life. He returned the silver plate to his leather bag, then stepped out the door of the tent. It was almost midnight, but here in the Arctic, the sky was merely grey and streaked with clouds. Beside the tent, Rae paced back and forth, as he was given to doing. Should he return immediately to England to report what he had learned? Or should he wait here until next spring and then travel overland to see whether he could find human remains?

With summer imminent, he could not hope to begin that prodigious trek for another eight or ten months. The ice would soon melt, rendering long-distance travel impossible. Nor did he have waiting on the Boothia coast at the far end of his trek a boat he could then use to reach King William Island or Back's Great Fish River. And he could hardly hope to haul the boat he did have several hundred miles.

On the other hand, he had enough pemmican to last three months. If he so decided, he could conceivably wait until next winter and make the journey overland. Should he do it? Staring up at the scudding clouds, John Rae decided not. At least half a dozen ships, and maybe more, were seeking John Franklin in all the wrong places. Their captains had orders to continue searching. Under the circumstances, Rae had a duty to communicate what he had learned as soon as possible, and so reduce the risk of more lives being needlessly lost.

After countless difficult hours of talking with visiting Inuit through Ouligbuck, John Rae accepted that the lost Franklin expedition had ended in catastrophe, with the final survivors driven to cannibalism—to boiling human flesh and eating it. How could he keep this secret? On August 4, 1854, when at last the pack ice cleared, Rae sailed south out of Repulse Bay to begin his journey back to England. The explorer could not know it, but having made a career of testing himself, he was about to face the most difficult ordeal of his life.

CHAPTER 5

Lady Franklin Responds

~

On October 23, 1854, on its front page, the *Times* of London published the detailed report John Rae had written for the Hudson's Bay Company. In that account, he laid out the facts—all of them. Rae related how, while crossing Boothia Peninsula with a few men, he had chanced to meet some Inuit hunters. From one of them, he learned that a party of white men had starved to death some distance to the west. Subsequently, he had gleaned details and purchased a variety of articles that placed "the fate of a portion, if not all, of the then survivors of Sir John Franklin's long-lost party beyond a doubt—a fate as terrible as the imagination can conceive."

To secure information, he had offered rewards. At his Repulse Bay campsite, with spring sunshine melting the Arctic ice, he had sat with interpreter William Ouligbuck and conducted interviews with visiting Inuit. He determined that a large party of Franklin's men had abandoned their ships off King William Island in Victoria Strait. Contrary to all expectations, they had trekked south toward mainland North America, many of them dying as they went.

The Inuit had discovered thirty-five or forty dead bodies. Some lay in tents or on the ground, others under an overturned boat. One man, apparently an officer, had died with a telescope strapped over his shoulder and a double-barrelled shotgun beneath him. Writing for the Hudson's Bay Company and the Admiralty, rather than a public readership, and accustomed to facing realities beyond the experience of most of the British newspaper audience, Rae reported the unvarnished truth in words that would resonate throughout the British Empire, then well on its way to encompassing almost one-quarter of the globe and more than 400 million people. "From the mutilated state of many of the corpses and

Painted in Van Diemen's Land (Tasmania) in 1838 by Thomas Bock, this portrait of Jane, Lady Franklin, is one of the few that survive.

the contents of the kettles," Rae wrote, "it is evident that our wretched countrymen had been driven to the last resource—cannibalism—as a means of prolonging existence."

Doctor Rae's report, as it came to be called, made European front pages in translation. Sir John Franklin and his noble crew had been reduced in the frozen north ... to cannibalism? *What?* Historian Hendrik van Loon, author of *The Story of Mankind*, would write that his father, who lived in Holland during this period, forever remembered "the shock of horror that ... swept across the civilized world."

Lady Franklin took to her bed. Friends had prepared her, relaying rumours of a preliminary account that had appeared in a Montreal newspaper. That John Franklin had been personally involved in cannibalism she rejected as inconceivable. Even the notion that some of his crew, the flower of the Royal Navy, could be reduced to measures so desperate—no, it exceeded credibility.

Yet when at the Admiralty offices she examined the relics Rae had brought back from the Arctic—the ribbons, the buttons, the gold braid, the broken watch—Jane Franklin found herself confronting an awful reality. For nearly ten years she had kept hope alive. Now, as she recognized an engraved spoon that had belonged to Sir John and felt its silver heft in her hand, she felt the dark truth crash over her like a wave. Never again would she see her husband alive.

~

Late in 1854, Lady Franklin rose from her bed determined to respond. John Rae's allegations of cannibalism threatened her husband's reputation, and so her own. They could not be allowed to stand. Rae's relics had convinced her that Franklin had died, but never would she accept the narrative that came with them. She thought of Charles Dickens, whom she had met socially and who at forty-two had already published such classic novels as *Oliver Twist*, *David Copperfield*, and *Bleak House*. Dickens also produced a twice-monthly newspaper called *Household Words*, as Lady Franklin well knew. Through a friend—Carolina C. Boyle, formerly lady-in-waiting to Queen Adelaide, wife of King William iv—she communicated her wish that Dickens might visit her as soon as possible.

The desperately busy author dropped everything and, on November 19, 1854, came calling at Lady Franklin's elaborate apartment in Spring Gardens, the most fashionable quarter in London. The lady did not mince words. She wanted John Rae repudiated—particularly his allegations of cannibalism. The foremost British writer of the age listened and undertook to accomplish that task. In *Household Words*, Dickens published a devastating two-part analysis entitled *The Lost Arctic Voyagers*—part one as the lead article on December 2, and part two the following week.

Acknowledging that Rae had a duty to report what he had heard, Dickens castigated the Admiralty for publishing his account. He then attacked Rae's conclusions, arguing that the explorer had shown no reason to believe "that our wretched countrymen had been driven to the last resource—cannibalism—as a means of prolonging existence." Lacking any new evidence, Dickens suggested that the remnants of "Franklin's gallant band" might well have been murdered by the Inuit: "We believe every savage to be in his heart covetous, treacherous, and cruel; and we have yet to learn what knowledge the white man—lost, houseless, shipless, apparently forgotten by his race; plainly famine-stricken, weak, frozen, helpless, and dying—has of the gentleness of Esquimaux nature."

Dickens offered more along these lines, lambasting Rae for having taken "the word of a savage." He presented an argument that, from the vantage point of the twenty-first century, can only be judged profoundly racist. Time has proven his two-part essay to be a tour de force of obfuscation, self-deception, and wilful blindness. But late in 1854, it engulfed John Rae like an avalanche. The explorer responded with dignity and truth, and Dickens had the decency to publish his rebuttal in *Household Words*. But Rae had only right on his side, and few writers in any time or place could have contended with Charles Dickens in full rhetorical flight. When Dickens was done, John Rae's reputation was deader than Jane Franklin's late husband.

Eventually, the explorer would be vindicated. Down through the decades, and even into the twenty-first century, researchers would contribute nuance and clarification. But the thrust of Rae's initial report—and the Inuit oral history on which he based it—would stand. Some of the final survivors had been driven to cannibalism. Such was the fate of the Franklin expedition.

Jane Franklin refused to accept this reality. Many questions did remain unanswered and she had no shortage of influential allies. Early in 1855, she began clamouring for more search expeditions. Sir Edward

Belcher, having sailed with five ships on what was supposed to "The Last of the Arctic Voyages," had arrived back in London. Despite the protests of his senior officers, he had abandoned four of his ships in the Arctic, revealing himself as both indecisive and cowardly. His outraged subordinate officers saw to it that he faced a court martial, but he escaped censure, narrowly, because he could point to equivocal orders from the British Admiralty, which controlled the Royal Navy. Belcher brought no news of the lost Franklin expedition.

Jane Franklin pressured the Hudson's Bay Company to complete the search John Rae had begun. Now that the correct search area had been identified—she accepted those parts of the Inuit testimony that suited her—surely, the Royal Navy had a moral obligation to seek more complete answers. Rae's evidence that Franklin had died in the Arctic only intensified Lady Franklin's sense of urgency.

By 1856, she had spent 35,000 pounds searching for her husband—the equivalent today, by conservative estimate, of US$3.7 million (almost $5 million Canadian). Some of that came from her own accounts, and some she had raised through public subscription. She had inspired Americans to contribute as well—more than $1.3 million in contemporary terms, two-fifths of which came from shipping magnate Henry Grinnell.

Of the three dozen expeditions that had sailed in search of Franklin by 1856, Lady Franklin had organized, inspired, and financed ten. As well, using both public opinion and influential friends, she had exerted relentless pressure on the Lords of the British Admiralty, compelling them to spend between 600,000 and 675,000 pounds.

At the same time, during the two years ending in March 1856, the British government had spent massively on the Crimean War, battling Russia—in alliance with France and the Ottoman Empire—to reduce that country's influence around the Black Sea. Faced with increasing pressure to reduce expenditures, and as one expedition after another returned from the Arctic with nothing to report, the Lords of the Admiralty yearned to dispense with the long-lost Sir John.

In 1857 Jane Franklin purchased this small 177-ton vessel, refitted it for use in the Arctic, and sent it in search of her lost husband under Captain Leopold McClintock.

Jane Franklin did not intend to let that happen. In spring 1856, she organized yet another petition. She solicited signatures from dozens of prominent figures, among them scientists, naval officers, and presidents and past presidents of the Royal Society and the Royal Geographical Society. The signatories appealed for yet another search expedition "to satisfy the honour of our country and clear up a mystery which has excited the sympathy of the civilized world."

In June, Lady Franklin sought and received support from the House of Commons. The president of the Royal Society informed her that she would receive assistance if she provided a ship and a commanding officer. She still owned the schooner *Isabel* and thought she might return that ship to Arctic service. Needing a captain, she looked first to that heroic American Elisha Kent Kane. He had just finished writing what would become a two-volume classic about narrowly surviving two winters trapped off the coast of Greenland: *Arctic Explorations: The Second Grinnell Expedition in Search of Sir John Franklin.*

Jane Franklin wrote requesting his services. But in October 1856, when he arrived in London, anybody could see that his chronic heart condition was taking a toll: weight loss, emaciation, physical weakness, lack of energy. Doctors advised a change of climate. Kane sailed for Cuba but, on February 16, 1857, he died in Havana. Lady Franklin would have to look elsewhere for her ship's captain.

Not only that, but experts had pronounced her schooner unfit for service. She had to find another ship. Jane Franklin lobbied to acquire a British vessel called the *Resolute*, which Americans had recently retrieved from the Arctic ice. The British Admiralty refused to lend her the ship. Within a week, Jane Franklin had arranged to purchase a newly available vessel of 177 tons. The ship had belonged to a wealthy man who had died after using it for a single cruise. Considerably smaller than the *Resolute*, the ship was 124 feet long, 24 feet wide, and 13 feet deep. Refitted for Arctic service, it would suit admirably. Lady Franklin renamed it *Fox*. Now only two questions remained. How would she acquire the funds to pay for provisions and men? And, equally crucial, whom would she appoint to command the expedition?

CHAPTER 6

The Victory
Point Record

~

A fter consulting friends and naval officers, Jane Franklin solicited
Captain Francis Leopold McClintock to captain the *Fox*. Born in
Dundalk, Ireland, in 1818, McClintock had joined the Royal Navy as a
gentleman volunteer at the ripe old age of seventeen. Once before, in 1848,
as a second lieutenant, he had sailed in search of Franklin, with James
Clark Ross. That two-ship expedition had got locked in the ice off Port
Leopold, at the northeast corner of Somerset Island. After eleven months,
the ships had sailed back to England.

Five years later, serving with Captain Henry Kellett, McClintock
conducted a notable sledging journey, travelling 1,400 miles in 105 days
and charting 768 miles of previously unmapped coast. He was a capable,
careful officer who, on receiving Lady Franklin's offer, wrote to James Clark
Ross wondering "how far the Admiralty sanction ought to be obtained, as
I do not wish to be so impolitic as to act counter to their wishes."

In April 1857, from Dublin, McClintock sent Lady Franklin a con-
ditional acceptance. He enclosed, for forwarding, his application for a
leave of absence from the Royal Navy. Jane wrote to Prince Albert through
his private secretary, asking that the prince consort—husband of Queen
Victoria—intercede on McClintock's behalf so that he would not have to

resign his commission—so making the result a foregone conclusion. On April 23 she wired McClintock, "Your leave is granted; the 'Fox' is mine; the refit will commence immediately."

Six days later, under the heading "Lady Franklin's Final Search," the *Times* carried an advertisement for subscribers to finance the expedition. Private companies contributed boats, food, stoves, and tents, and the Admiralty came through with arms, ammunition, and three tons of pemmican. Later, a newspaper report published by "friends of Lady Franklin" would indicate that the expedition cost 10,434 pounds—the equivalent today of US$1,763,700 (over $2.4 million Canadian). More than 250 donors contributed, among them numerous well-known Victorians: inventor Charles Babbage, novelist William Makepeace Thackeray, art patron Lady Trevelyan, the diplomat Lord Dufferin (later governor general of Canada), and, most surprisingly, G. Julian Harney, a militant Chartist who fought for universal suffrage and associated with Karl Marx and Friedrich Engels.

As money poured in, Leopold McClintock travelled to Aberdeen to oversee the refitting of the *Fox*. This involved replacing velvet furnishings, stowing provisions, and transforming the vessel from a pleasure craft into an ice-worthy vessel. He was there when Lady Franklin, mindful always of social niceties, summoned him to London to meet Queen Victoria at a public ceremony. With that accomplished, McClintock returned to Aberdeen.

Lady Franklin followed a few days later, travelling by train. On the last day of June 1857, she and her niece, Sophia Cracroft, went aboard the *Fox* for a farewell luncheon. Later McClintock would write of Lady Franklin, "Seeing how deeply agitated she was on leaving the ship, I endeavored to repress the enthusiasm of my crew, but without avail; it found vent in three prolonged, hearty cheers. The strong feeling which prompted them was truly sincere: and this unbidden exhibition of it can hardly have gratified her for whom it was intended more than it did myself."

On July 2, 1857, with a complement of twenty-five men, including seventeen Arctic veterans, Captain Leopold McClintock sailed out of Aberdeen. He went to gather evidence of what had happened to the Franklin expedition. But in the weeks before sailing, he found time to consult with John Rae in London, to discuss his findings and whether he might sail the *Fox* through Rae Strait, which separated Boothia Peninsula and King William Island. If he could make his way through there, he could almost certainly carry on to the Pacific Ocean, and so become the first explorer to navigate the Northwest Passage.

In the mid-Atlantic, as ordered, McClintock opened a letter of instructions from Jane Franklin. In it, she laid out three priorities: he should rescue any survivors, recover any written records, and seek confirmation that Franklin's men had travelled over water to the northern coast of the North American continent. This last affirmation would enable Jane to argue that her husband had preceded Captain Robert McClure as first discoverer of a Northwest Passage even though he had got nowhere near the Pacific Ocean and this alleged Passage, the ice-choked Victoria Strait, was just as fictional as the one McClure "discovered" by viewing distant islands and sledging across frozen straits. No ship would sail through Victoria Strait until 1967, when a powerful icebreaker, the *John A. Macdonald*, pounded through the ice.

Confident that McClintock would strive to attain her stated objectives, and mindful always of posterity, Jane Franklin had added, "My only fear is that you may spend yourselves too much in the effort; and you must, therefore, let me tell you how much dearer to me even than any of them is the preservation of the valuable lives of the little band of heroes who are your companions and followers." In western Greenland, McClintock bought two dozen sled dogs and added an Inuk interpreter called "Christian" to assist official interpreter Carl Petersen, who had sailed with William Penny and Elisha Kent Kane.

McClintock proceeded north along the west coast of Greenland to Melville Bay, a crescent-shaped indentation extending, south to north, for 150 miles. Like Kane before him, the captain then headed directly west into Baffin Bay and the Middle Ice—that floating mass of icefields dotted with giant icebergs, scores of them larger than the *Fox*. The Middle Ice was almost always impenetrable, although a few ships had managed to traverse it. Six years previously, Kane had managed it by hitching his ship to a massive iceberg, which extended so far beneath the surface that it reached into a deeper current and dragged the ship against the wind.

McClintock proved less lucky. In September, he and his twenty-five-man crew got trapped in the Middle Ice of Davis Strait, which runs between Greenland and North America. Later, Sophia Cracroft would observe that the cool-headed captain "never lost the equanimity which is his most remarkable characteristic." He organized a school, unpacked an organ to allow for music, and had the two Inuit hunters on board teach the other men how to build snowhuts. As the ice-locked ship moved south, those hunters contributed seals and the occasional polar bear to the larder.

On April 25, 1858, after having been trapped for 250 days, the *Fox* began grinding and heaving. The pack ice broke up with surprising violence. The shuddering knocked crewmen off their feet and caused the ship's bells to ring. In his journal, McClintock would write of one eighteen-hour stretch, "Such a battering . . . I hope not to see again."

Then, suddenly, the ship floated free. At this point, McClintock could have retreated south to Newfoundland, but no. He sailed north up the coast of Greenland and resupplied the ship at Disko Island. In mid-June, he again tackled the Middle Ice. This time, he entered Lancaster Sound and, without mishap, sailed west to Beechey Island. There, just above Northumberland House, he erected a splendid memorial tablet entrusted to him by Lady Franklin.

From Beechey, McClintock started due south down Peel Strait. But on August 16, having travelled twenty-five miles, he found his way blocked by pack ice. He retreated north and east and then swung south down Prince Regent Inlet. He hoped now to sail west through Bellot Strait to King William Island. When he reached the western end of the strait, he found a wall of ice blocking Victoria Strait. He withdrew and, late in 1858, established winter quarters at the eastern end of Bellot Strait, within easy viewing distance of a ridge overlooking present-day Fort Ross.

Today, at the highest point on that ridge, visitors can stand beside "McClintock's Cairn" while gazing out over Bellot Strait, Prince Regent Inlet, and the Fox Islands. In the winter of 1858–59, anyone scrambling to that spot would have been able to see the *Fox* locked in the ice and battened down for the winter—and also a magnetic observatory 210 yards from the ship, "built of ice sawed into blocks," as McClintock wrote, "there not being any suitable snow."

Prevented by pack ice from sailing, McClintock turned to the dogs he had brought aboard in Greenland, now twenty-two in number. In Petersen and the two Inuit crewmen, he had three dog drivers. Starting with scouting sorties, he contrived to mix and match sledge teams—four men hauling an eight-hundred-pound sledge, for example, with seven dogs hauling one of seven hundred pounds. Like Rae before him, he took to building snowhuts to save the extra weight of tents. In mid-February, taking Petersen and one other man, he went scouting through Bellot Strait and down the west coast of Boothia Peninsula. He met some Inuit hunters and then a village of forty-five people, who were happy to trade. McClintock procured silver cutlery, a medal, part of a gold chain, and several buttons and knives, all of it pointing to a wrecked ship. None of the Inuit had seen any white men, but one older man, Oo-na-lee, said the relics came from a place where some white men had starved on an island in a river containing salmon. Others spoke of a ship, McClintock wrote, that had been "crushed by ice out in the sea to the west of King William's Island."

Bad weather prevented further excursions until April. But then, after returning to Cape Victoria, McClintock met another group of Inuit, including a young man who sold him a knife. "After much anxious inquiry," McClintock wrote, "we learned that two ships had been seen by the natives of King William's Island; one of them was seen to sink in deep water, and nothing was obtained from her, a circumstance at which they expressed much regret; but the other was forced on shore by the ice, where they suppose she still remains, but is much broken. From this ship they have obtained most of their wood; and Oot-loo-lik is the name of the place where she grounded."

Most of this McClintock learned from the young man who sold him the knife. "Old Oo-na-lee, who drew the rough chart for me in March, to show where the ship sank, now answered our questions respecting the one forced on shore: not a syllable about her did he mention on the former occasion, although we asked whether they knew of only one ship? I think he would willingly have kept us in ignorance of the wreck being upon their coasts, and that the young man unwittingly made it known to us." The savvy Oo-na-lee was probably thinking of somehow acquiring more valuable trade goods from off the ship.

Here the story grows more dramatic. The young man "also told us that the body of a man was found on board the ship," McClintock wrote, "that he must have been a very large man, and had long teeth; this is all he recollected having been told, for he was quite a child at the time." Both men said that the ships were destroyed in August or September: "that all the white people went away to the 'large river,' taking a boat or boats with them, and that in the following winter their bones were found there."

⁓

On April 28, 1859, at Cape Victoria on Boothia Peninsula, McClintock split his expeditionary team in two. He sent William Hobson, his second-in-command, to trace the northern and western coasts of King William Island. Then, with Carl Petersen driving the dogs, he himself made his way south through Rae Strait. He crossed Simpson Strait to Montreal Island and the estuary of the Great Fish River (now called the Back River). Finding nothing but a few relics in an Inuit cairn, he recrossed Simpson Strait and followed the south coast of King William Island west. He came across an unburied skeleton—a few rags clinging to the bones—and a number of Franklin expedition relics. At Cape Herschel, he dismantled the cairn Thomas Simpson had built twenty years before . . . and found it empty.

Twelve miles on, McClintock spotted a new cairn containing a note from his second-in-command. William Hobson had found two notes scrawled on a single page of a Royal Navy form and deposited in a metal cylinder near Victory Point. The first note, written on May 28, 1847, indicated that the *Erebus* and the *Terror* had spent the previous winter in the ice just northwest of King William Island off Cape Felix. It said Franklin had spent the winter before that (1845–46) at Beechey Island after ascending Wellington Channel to latitude 77 degrees. All was well.

The second message, which was added to the original page eleven months later, on April 25, 1848, said that the *Erebus* and the *Terror*, trapped twelve to fifteen miles northwest of Victory Point since September 1846, had been "deserted" three days before: "The officers and crews, consisting of 105 souls, under the command of Captain F. R. M. Crozier, landed here [it gave geographical co-ordinates]. Sir John Franklin died on the 11th of June 1847; and the total loss by deaths in the Expedition has been to this date 9 officers and 15 men." This was signed by captains James Fitzjames and Francis Crozier, with the latter adding a final few words: "And start (on) tomorrow 26th, for Back's Fish River."

What had happened to reduce the expedition's numbers so dramatically, from 129 to 105? Why had such a high percentage of officers died? The Victory Point Record raised more questions than it answered. Halfway down the west coast of King William Island, near a large bay, Hobson had found a twenty-four-foot boat sledge and a boat containing two dead bodies and a curious array of goods. These included eight pairs of boots, four neckerchiefs, some scented soap, two pocket chronometers, a piece of sealing wax, a pair of slippers, two pairs of goggles, a beaded purse, tinted spectacles in a case, and the gold band of an officer's cap.

McClintock, arriving after Hobson, also puzzled over the boat, which was facing north. Were the men trying to haul the boat back to the ship off Victory Point? Surely, that would be madness. Having charted the

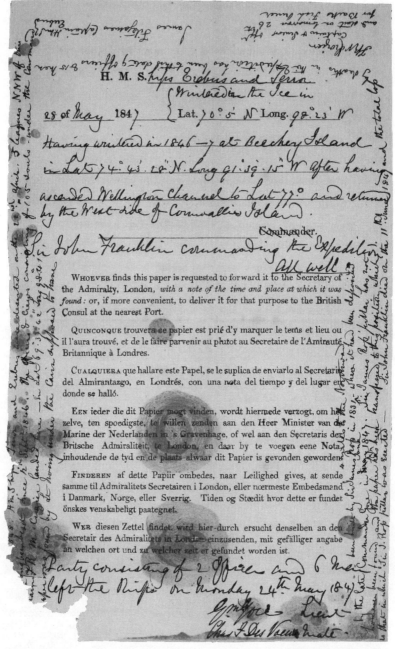

H. M. S. *ships* Erebus and Terror

Wintered in the Ice in

28 of May 1847 Lat. 70° 5' N Long. 98° 23' W

Having wintered in 1846-7 at Beechey Island
in Lat 74° 43' 28" N. Long 91° 39' 15" W after having
ascended Wellington Channel to Lat 77° and returned
by the West side of Cornwallis Island.

Sir John Franklin commanding the Expedition.

all well

Commander.

WHOEVER finds this paper is requested to forward it to the Secretary of
the Admiralty, London, *with a note of the time and place at which it was
found*: or, if more convenient, to deliver it for that purpose to the British
Consul at the nearest Port.

QUINCONQUE trouvera ce papier est prié d'y marquer le tems et lieu ou
il l'aura trouvé, et de le faire parvenir au plutot au Secretaire de l'Amirauté
Britannique à Londres.

CUALQUIERA que hallare este Papel, se le suplica de enviarlo al Secretario
del Almirantazgo, en Londrés, con una nota del tiempo y del lugar en
donde se halló.

EEN ieder die dit Papier mogt vinden, wordt hiermede verzogt, om het-
zelve, ten spoedigste, te willen zenden aan den Heer Minister van de
Marine der Nederlanden in 's Gravenhage, of wel aan den Secretaris der
Britsche Admiraliteit, te London, en daar by te voegen eene Nota,
inhoudende de tyd en de plaats alwaar dit Papier is gevonden geworden.

FINDEREN af dette Papiir ombedes, naar Leilighed gives, at sende
samme til Admiralitets Secretairen i London, eller nœrmeste Embedsmand
i Danmark, Norge, eller Sverrig. Tiden og Stœdit hvor dette er fundet
önskes venskabeligt paategnet.

WER diesen Zettel findet, wird hier-durch ersucht denselben an den
Secretair des Admiralitets in London einzusenden, mit gefälliger angabe
an welchen ort und zu welcher zeit er gefunden worden ist.

Party consisting of 2 Officers and 6 Men
left the Ships on Monday 24th May 1847

Gore Lieut
Chas F Des Voeux Mate

The handwritten Victory Point Record or Note, discovered on King William Island
in 1859, indicates that in May 1847 all was well with the expedition. An addition to
the note, written in April 1848, states that twenty-four men were dead, including
John Franklin, and that those remaining had left the ships and were making for the
Back River on the coast of the continent.

coastline, McClintock decided to name "the two principal bays after [Franklin's] two ships & all the minor bays,—points, islands, etc. after officers of these ships; those of the Erebus being grouped about 'Erebus Bay', similarly those of the Terror about 'Terror Bay.'" In an 1880 letter to American explorer Frederick Schwatka, McClintock explained that he regarded the western coastline of King William Island as sacred to the memories of those officers, and so used no other names.

McClintock's findings, notably the Victory Point Record and the so-called Boat Place, would focus subsequent searches and speculations. Through the nineteenth century and most of the twentieth, amateur historians set aside Inuit testimony. Nobody gave much credence to the notion that all or most of the 105 men might have returned to the ships. Nobody suggested that, with men aboard, one or both ships had been carried south, and that one of them had been abandoned in a desperate scramble, with men throwing everything into a nearby boat. Nobody suggested that the survivors had no intention of dragging that boat any great distance, only back into the water when the ice broke up.

McClintock also retrieved remnants of a blue jacket and a great coat, a clothes brush and a horn comb, a toothbrush, a sponge, some crested silver, and a prayer book called *Christian Melodies*, frozen hard, along with a Bible and a copy of an Oliver Goldsmith novel, *The Vicar of Wakefield*. Along the way, he also talked to an old Inuit woman who reported, "They fell down and died as they walked along."

Back on the *Fox* by the end of June 1859, McClintock and his men could only wait until the ice released them. They sailed on August 10 and reached London six weeks later. Together, they had charted eight hundred miles of coastline and completed the mapping of the northern coastline of the continent. They had found the only written record of the Franklin expedition to turn up in the nineteenth and twentieth centuries.

To Lady Franklin, who was travelling in southwestern France when he arrived in London, Leopold McClintock sent a letter summarizing his findings. He noted that Franklin himself had died on June 11, 1847: "I cannot help remarking to you what instantly occurred to me on reading the records. That Sir John Franklin was not harassed by either want of success or forebodings of evil." This was what Lady Franklin needed to hear. Her husband, having died months before any death march, stood personally absolved of cannibalism. Nor did he want for success! Jane Franklin could fill in the details herself. Leopold McClintock had brought her more than enough to create a legend, indeed a mythology, and to make of her husband an Arctic hero.

PART TWO

The Royal Navy Man

~

CHAPTER 7

Who Was This John Franklin?

∼

B orn in 1786, the son of a Lincolnshire shopkeeper, John Franklin
was essentially a product of the Napoleonic Wars—those five major
conflicts that raged around the world between 1803 and 1815, pitting
Napoleon's French Empire against an ever-changing European coalition.
Having become First Consul of France in 1799, Napoleon turned chaos
into order, creating economic stability and forging a powerful army. But
like many a tyrant before and since, he wanted a great deal more.

In 1803, when the first Napoleonic War erupted, John Franklin was
seventeen, sailing in Australia as a master's mate, and narrowly escaped
being taken prisoner by the French. The following January, he was serving
as a signalman on an East India Company ship that, through the captain's
genius bit of subterfuge, averted disaster after encountering five heavily
armed French warships. In October 1805, Franklin was almost deafened
while aboard the *Bellerophon* at the Battle of Trafalgar, a turning-point
victory that prevented the invasion of Britain.

By 1815, having seen action in the West Indies and at New Orleans,
Franklin was serving as first lieutenant aboard a fifty-gun frigate,
HMS *Forth*, when on land at the Battle of Waterloo, a coalition led by the
Duke of Wellington routed the French army and ended the Napoleonic

71

Wars. Even this turn of events played a major role in shaping the career of John Franklin, because suddenly the idea of maintaining a massive Royal Navy became impossible to justify.

The Admiralty set about cutting costs, slashing the number of men on active service from a high of 143,000 to around 23,000. Of all those not dismissed, one in four belonged to the officer class—more than 5,000 men. And 90 per cent of those, with no duties to perform, found themselves languishing at home on half pay—a subsistence-level income.

John Franklin was one of those officers. But he contrived to shift lanes and become an Arctic explorer. Certainly, most people know him as such. In addition to undertaking his famous 1845 voyage in search of the Northwest Passage, surely the act of an explorer, Franklin spent six years leading two overland expeditions in what was then Rupert's Land—the first from May 1819 to October 1822, which we are about to track, and the second starting in 1825.

Despite all this, that boldest of apologist-biographers, Andrew Lambert, insists that "Franklin was not sent to 'explore'" on his first overland outing but rather sent to establish navigational fixes for the Coppermine River and the coastline of the North American continent. Cleverly splitting hairs, and we shall soon see why, Lambert insists that Franklin should be assessed not as an explorer but as a navigator and a leader who had an extraordinary power to inspire. So he writes in *Franklin: Tragic Hero of Polar Navigation*. Such a reframing excuses Lambert from treating the two overland expeditions in any but the most cursory manner. And it enables him to ignore numerous inconvenient truths.

Picture John Franklin on June 16, 1819, a thirty-three-year-old Royal Navy lieutenant standing at a ship's railing watching Orkney recede into the haze of middle distance. Foul weather and thick fog would shadow the ensuing voyage for weeks. But as far as young Franklin could tell, his expedition was off to an acceptable start, all things considered. He would have been shocked to learn that in a biography of George Back, a twenty-first-century renaissance man—doctor, mountaineer, and historian Peter

Steele—would declare that "the whole concept, planning, and execution of Franklin's expedition was a mishmash." Popular historian Pierre Berton took a similar view.

The Admiralty's John Barrow had got clearance in February for a two-part extravaganza—one expedition to travel by land, the other by sea. He appointed the officers in April, leaving the leaders, lieutenants Franklin and Edward Parry, little more than a month to organize their itineraries. But to learn that no future explorer would undertake an overland trek like the one he faced without planning and preparing for at least one year—that would have left Franklin reeling in astonishment.

When he sailed from Greenhithe on May 19, 1845, John Franklin was fifty-nine. Some experts argued that Franklin was too old to withstand the rigours of an Arctic expedition.

The Royal Navy man did feel a certain embarrassment at hitching a ride on this Hudson's Bay Company vessel, the *Prince of Wales*, with five fellow naval men—his second-in-command, two midshipmen, and two able seamen. He would happily have traded places with Parry, who had recently sailed as leader of a proper two-ship expedition in the HMS *Hecla*. On the other hand, with so many officers out of work and collecting half pay, he was grateful to have this assignment.

Many observers, he knew, could not understand why Barrow had settled on him at all. The previous year, when he sailed as part of an expedition to achieve a passage to the far east by crossing over the North

Pole, he had commanded his own ship, the *Trent*, but sailed as second-in-command to David Buchan in the larger *Dorothea*. They had got as far as Spitzbergen or Svalbard, an archipelago just above 80 degrees that would become part of Norway after the First World War. The voyagers spent three weeks trapped in pack ice, slammed around by gale-force winds and storms, before limping home.

At roughly that same time, Parry sailed in his own ship as second to commander John Ross to discover a Northwest Passage farther south—an expedition also thwarted, but controversially. Parry challenged Ross's claim that, having sailed into Lancaster Sound, he had seen their progress blocked by a great wall of mountains. In truth, Ross saw an optical illusion or iceblink. Parry had rightly opposed turning back.

Logically, then, Barrow had given him command of a follow-up expedition through that same waterway. Commander Buchan, on the other hand, had made no questionable decision in their joint attempt to sail across the Pole. Given his seniority to Franklin, he might easily have been the one chosen to lead the overland expedition charged with exploring the Arctic coast and possibly meeting Parry. And so people wondered: *Why John Franklin?*

Certainly his naval record was impeccable, and marked him out as a lucky warrior. Born in April 1786 to a struggling shop owner in Spilsby, Lincolnshire, he was the fifth son and ninth of twelve children. He had gone to sea at age twelve, sailing on a merchantman that plied between Hull and Lisbon. Two years later, he joined HMS *Polyphemus*, a sixty-four-gun warship that carried the youth into the first in a series of life-threatening adventures. Early in April 1801, the ship engaged furiously in the first Battle of Copenhagen, which Vice-Admiral Horatio Nelson later described as the most savage and terrible of his hundred naval battles. On the *Polyphemus*, six men died and twenty-four were wounded.

Before sailing, Franklin had learned that one of his uncles, the celebrated navigator Matthew Flinders, was preparing a voyage of exploration to survey the coast of Australia. One of his aunts had married Flinders, who would soon sail in HMS *Investigator*, and Franklin wrote his parents that if he arrived home before his uncle departed, "I will thank you to use your interest for me to go." As it happened, they did precisely that. With the *Polyphemus* needing repairs, Franklin arrived back in England just in time to sail with Flinders in July 1801.

Soon enough, Franklin was winning praise from his uncle for his commitment to learning navigation. But in Australia, the aging *Investigator* began leaking badly. With the ship beached for repairs, carpenters warned that her timbers were dangerously rotted. Flinders pushed on sailing around Australia for eleven months, skipping stops for provisions. Five men died of scurvy. At Sydney, a board of officers pronounced the ship "not worth repairing in any country."

Ordered back to England, Flinders found another ship, the *Porpoise*. He chose twenty-two officers and men to sail with him, among them sixteen-year-old Franklin, now a master's mate. But the *Porpoise* foundered on a reef in Torres Strait, which runs between the northern tip of Australia and Papua New Guinea. The ship lost her masts and fell on her beam ends. After working through the night, the sailors found themselves on a sandbank roughly 900 feet long and 150 wide, where they managed to bring ashore supplies. They were on part of the Great Barrier Reef, some 200 miles from the nearest land and 750 miles from Sydney.

Having erected tents, the ninety-four shipwrecked men took inventory and determined that they had enough food to last three months. Best way forward: send a party to Sydney for help in a small, open, six-oared cutter. Franklin stayed put when, with thirteen men and food for three weeks, Flinders set out to sail south along the coast of Australia. Almost incredibly, he succeeded. He returned six weeks later with two government schooners and a merchant vessel. The three ships would now go separate ways, one each to Sydney, England, and China.

Flinders chose to sail straight to England on the *Cumberland* with two officers and eight men. John Franklin was not selected for this crew, which proved a stroke of luck. Flinders put in for much-needed repairs at Mauritius, a French-controlled island nation some 1,265 miles off the southeast coast of Africa. With the Napoleonic Wars underway, the French seized the ship and detained Matthew Flinders—not for a while, but for six years. Meanwhile, Franklin sailed to Canton (Guangzhou), a city northwest of Hong Kong, on the merchant ship *Rolla*. In January 1804, he embarked from there on the *Earl Camden*, a three-decker East India Company ship bound for England in a squadron.

Now he got caught up in one of the great episodes in merchant marine history. Under threat by five heavily armed French warships, Commodore Nathaniel Dance took the offensive, bluffing the aggressors into believing he was accompanied by powerful men-of-war. He not only drove them off but gave chase for two hours. Throughout this escapade, young Franklin was on duty as signal midshipman, flying the pennant of a rear admiral as part of the deception.

Back in England, Franklin enjoyed a six-week leave and then rejoined the war effort as a signal officer on HMS *Bellerophon*. In October 1805, after several months of blockade duty, that ship followed Lord Nelson into the Battle of Trafalgar off the southwest coat of Spain. The sailors fought off a boarding attempt while a second enemy ship blasted away at close quarters, destroying the *Bellerophon*'s main and mizzen masts. As signal officer, Franklin's duties included preserving the ship's flag. "Twice it was lowered by the enemy's shot," he wrote later, "but again speedily re-hoisted in triumph."

Franklin stood talking with a close friend when a sniper in the rigging of the French ship shot the fellow dead. Then, while he helped a marine sergeant carry an injured seaman below, the same rifleman shot and killed the wounded man. Franklin ducked just in time to foil an attempt on his own life. He then saw the ship's sergeant, who had vowed revenge, hit the sniper and knock him head first into the sea. He told Franklin, "I killed him at the seventh shot." The *Bellerophon* took possession of a Spanish warship but registered 28 dead and 127 wounded. Franklin escaped serious injury but, because of the noise of the guns, became slightly deaf. The official report noted that he "evinced very conspicuous zeal and ability."

Now came the war of 1812–14, in fact an extension of the Napoleonic Wars as both Britain and France sought to curtail each other's merchant shipping—including that with the United States. The British took to removing American sailors and pressing them into naval service. The Americans declared war and, in October 1812, invaded Upper Canada along the Niagara border—an invasion repelled by professional soldiers along with militia units and a First Nations contingent led by Tecumseh.

That same year, a twenty-six-year-old Franklin joined HMS *Bedford* as master's mate, then acting lieutenant. Two voyages to the West Indies interrupted blockading duties and the ship proceeded to Louisiana, where in December 1814 it took part in the Battle of Lake Borgne. Franklin was slightly injured during a landing, but a British victory led to an assault on New Orleans that ended in a decisive American victory. This battle occurred after peace had been agreed but not yet communicated to North America.

Back in England in May 1815, John Franklin transferred to a powerful fifty-gun frigate, HMS *Forth*. But then, on June 18, came the British victory at the Battle of Waterloo, which effectively ended the seemingly endless Napoleonic Wars. Now, suddenly, the idea of maintaining a massive Royal Navy became unthinkable. The Admiralty slashed the number of men on active service. At age twenty-nine, First Lieutenant John Franklin found himself subsisting on half pay—one of those officers singled out as expendable. For the next three years, as he entered his early thirties, Franklin stayed home in Lincolnshire, helping in his father's shop while growing ever more restless and frustrated. It is noteworthy, according to early Franklin biographer H.D. Traill, "as showing the natural bent of the born explorer, that during these years of inaction it was upon maritime discovery rather than naval warfare that Franklin's mind was fixed." His champion in the Royal Navy, his uncle Matthew Flinders, had died in 1814 on the very day he published a book about his six years of detention by the French.

Franklin was profoundly saddened—not just for his uncle's death, which was sad enough, but for all those who, like himself, had sailed with Flinders, and who might have benefited from the interest generated by the book. He expressed his dismay in a letter to the naturalist Robert Brown, with whom he had sailed on the *Investigator*—a man thirteen years older who was now emerging as one of Britain's leading botanists, thanks largely to studies he had conducted during their shared voyage to Australia. Brown had become a close friend of Sir Joseph Banks, Britain's leading scientist, who had sailed as a botanist with James Cook and had since become president of the Royal Society. Brown, who stayed at Banks's house when he visited London, assured Franklin that the Royal Navy would soon begin dispatching voyages of discovery. If the younger man was interested in exploration, Brown would put his name forward.

Franklin responded that he was keenly interested, "but I should hope, were an offer ever made to me, it would be accompanied by promotion. To embark on an expedition of that nature without some grounds for sanguine expectation, where an absence of five or six years may be calculated upon, and a total separation from any chance of improving your interest, is a most serious consideration; and perhaps on return, with a constitution much shattered, you may find the patrons and friends of the voyage either removed or unable to procure you the appointment you have anxiously sought."

Franklin did think to add that he would not be deterred should no promotion be forthcoming. But here, despite the ponderous writing style, we see that the man was not without ambition. Brown proved as good as his word. Another friend of Joseph Banks was John Barrow, second secretary of the Admiralty and the real decision maker in all things pertaining to the Royal Navy. Barrow often dined at Banks's home.

And so the appointments came about—first, command of the *Trent*, then leadership of the 1819 overland expedition: Franklin spoke to Brown, who spoke to Banks, who spoke to Barrow, who gave the appointment to

Franklin. Not that Banks was all-powerful. For example, in 1817, he had advocated appointing the outstanding whaling captain William Scoresby to the 1818 expedition that John Ross ended up leading in search of the Northwest Passage. The son of a wealthy whaler, superbly educated at Edinburgh University—in natural philosophy, chemistry, meteorology, and the polar regions—Scoresby had also spent eighteen years at sea, seven of them as an ice master.

Three years younger than Franklin, he had devised a "marine diver" to take deep-sea temperature readings (warmer than those on the surface) and invented "ice shoes" for walking across the pack. He had published scientific papers about ice and spearheaded an 1806 voyage that reached a latitude above 81 degrees in the eastern hemisphere, a record that held for twenty-one years.

Scoresby was completing his masterwork, *An Account of the Arctic Regions and Northern Whale Fishery*, which would be hailed in the *British Dictionary of National Biography* as "the foundation stone of Arctic Science." His 1817 letters to Banks about ice breaking up early off Greenland awakened Barrow, through Banks, to the possibilities of Arctic exploration—a way to employ naval men. Trouble was, Scoresby scorned the idea that an Open Polar Sea existed around the North Pole, a notion that the self-educated Barrow foolishly held dear and never relinquished. And when Banks invited Scoresby to his home and introduced him to the second secretary, Barrow rudely dismissed the whaling captain, telling him to submit any proposals through proper channels. Then he turned on his heel and walked out.

Barrow preferred to appoint creatures of the Royal Navy—men whose careers he could control. And early in 1819, Lieutenant Franklin remained a good bet. Never mind that, as Peter Steele would write, the deeply religious Franklin was overweight, out of shape, and completely without experience in trekking, canoeing, or hunting. Never mind all that.

John Barrow had become interested in geomagnetism and the shifting of the magnetic poles, and this provided an important secondary motivation for the expedition. Aware of the unreliability of compass readings near the north magnetic pole, Barrow surmised that in 1771, English fur-trade explorer Samuel Hearne—a very different former Royal Navy man—might have misjudged the latitude he had reached on the Arctic coast. To ascertain the position and direction of the coastline eastward from that location, Barrow wanted "an officer well skilled in astronomical and geographical science, and in the use of instruments." In this area, Franklin had shown competence.

Not only that but appointing Franklin after receiving a recommendation from Banks would repair any damage to that relationship caused by his mistreatment of Scoresby. And Barrow would make up any scientific shortfall by appointing, as second-in-command, the Scottish naval surgeon John Richardson, a doctor who had also studied botany and minerology at Edinburgh.

As for the junior officers, Barrow appointed two midshipmen in their early twenties—George Back, tough and active; Robert Hood, bookish and romantic. Barrow chose them largely because, in this age before photography, they were both talented artists, and he wanted a visual record of the Arctic landscape. Two able-bodied seamen rounded out the contingent that sailed with Franklin—five men in all. The lieutenant had instructions to keep detailed meteorological and magnetic records as he travelled, and he was relieved to learn that one of his midshipmen, Robert Hood, excelled at this.

For the rest, John Franklin would have to improvise. The Admiralty, with no experience mounting overland expeditions and no appreciation of the challenges involved, proposed that the lieutenant should draw logistical support from the two fur-trading companies active in Rupert's Land, which from 1670 to 1870 encompassed the vast northern territories encircling Hudson Bay. In London, representatives of the Hudson's Bay Company and the North West Company, ferocious competitors in fur-trade country, promised to assist the expedition in every way possible.

Franklin would hire experienced fur-trade voyageurs, rent boats and canoes from the HBC or the NWC, add a few expert Indigenous hunters, travel northwest to the mouth of the Coppermine River, and then make his way east along the Arctic coast of the continent, eventually into the northern reaches of Hudson Bay. How hard could it be? With luck, he might meet up with Edward Parry, who would sail west into Lancaster Sound and then proceed south. Franklin left London on May 23, 1819, eleven days after Parry. The hope was that, in tandem with Parry's voyage, this two-pronged exploration would solve the riddle of the Northwest Passage.

CHAPTER 8

Voyage *to* York Factory

~

Midshipman Robert Hood begins his journal with the departure from Gravesend of three Hudson's Bay Company supply ships. He describes how, on May 23, 1819, as one of six Royal Navy men, he sailed with a couple of dozen other passengers on the three-masted *Prince of Wales*, accompanied by two smaller vessels. The ships sailed up the east coast of England as a storm came on, covering no more than 130 miles before putting in at Great Yarmouth to wait it out. The navy men, Hood among them, went ashore to "provide ourselves with some necessaries."

But let's meet Robert Hood, the most evocative writer on the expedition. Born in 1797 in Bury, Lancashire, eight miles north of Manchester, he was the second son of a Protestant minister. He saw enough of the clergy growing up that he had no wish to join. His father worried that he was not sufficiently robust for a naval career, but at fourteen, the determined youth joined the Royal Navy. For one year, starting in August 1811, he served as a midshipman on the HMS *Imperieuse*. From October 1815, he did the same on the HMS *Spey*. On both ships he diligently painted and drew, and now here he was, sailing on a voyage of exploration.

With the *Prince of Wales* sheltering at Great Yarmouth, the wind changed abruptly and Captain John Davison fired his guns, signalling his intention to depart and summoning everyone to return immediately. "Our companion, Mr. Back," Hood writes, "had unfortunately separated from us on particular business," but about that he adds no detail. Nor did any of the other journal keepers add much. The Royal Navy men hurried back to the ship—all except midshipman Back, who was engaged, Franklin wrote later, "upon some business at a house two or three miles from Yarmouth." The nature of this "business" would never be specified, but in a letter to John Barrow, Franklin justified leaving Back behind by explaining that Captain Davison wished to get through a narrow rough-water passage— the intricate "Cockle Gat"—before darkness fell, and "I could not under such circumstances request the master to detain the vessel."

Franklin left a note for Back suggesting that he journey by coach to the north coast of Scotland and then take passage to Stromness in Orkney, "which appeared to be the only way of proceeding by which he could rejoin the party." In fact, the young midshipman had managed to reach the dock at Caister, about four miles north of Yarmouth, in time to witness the passing of the *Prince of Wales* three hundred yards away. But when he tried to hire a boat to take him out, the owners quoted such an exorbitant fare that he could not pay it.

Hood wrote that Back had "applied to some boatmen to carry him on board, which might have been accomplished in a few minutes, but discovering the emergency of his case, they demanded 20 guineas as the price of his passage." As he had only fifteen, they refused to help. "The east coast of England," Hood added, "is infested by these wretches, who match their opportunity to second the strokes of misfortune, and prey upon the remnant."

George Back would not be denied. Hood writes that he "threw himself immediately" into a northbound coach. Over the next nine days, Back rode a series of coaches 660 miles through Edinburgh and Inverness to Thurso, on the north coast of Scotland, where he caught a boat that carried him 30 miles across the water to Stromness. The *Prince of Wales* reached Stromness on June 4 and Back arrived on the evening of June 9, just in time to join a dance celebrating the naval expedition at a local ballroom. He joined in the festivities, Franklin wrote, "and could not be prevailed upon to withdraw from the agreeable scene until a late hour."

At Stromness, the *Prince of Wales* took on fresh water from Login's Well. To those in charge of local Hudson's Bay Company operations, Franklin laid out his hiring plans. Factor George Geddes warned the young lieutenant that he would find it difficult, and indeed almost impossible, to hire boatmen and steersmen once he reached York Factory, on the west coast of Hudson Bay. That fur-trade hub was perennially short-staffed and would certainly be overly busy when he arrived. Not only that, but the herring fishery, which the previous year had needed sixty boats and four hundred men, had exploded to employ three hundred boats and twelve hundred men.

Geddes tried to help. First, he lent Franklin and his men one of his houses in which to do a final check on navigational instruments. He introduced Franklin to Reverend William Clouston with whose family Franklin visited almost daily. Franklin describes him as "the worthy and highly respected minister of Stromness," but he was also Church of Scotland minister for Sandwick, seven miles north. Orcadian historian Tom Muir tells me that Clouston was a popular preacher who "wrote one of the best accounts of the parishes that can be found in The Old Statistical Accounts of Scotland."

Geddes and Clouston posted notices in churches throughout Orkney, inviting interested boatmen to assemble at Geddes's house on June 14. A couple of dozen men did so but, Franklin writes, "to my great mortification, I found they were all so strongly possessed with the fearful apprehension, either that great danger would attend the service, or that we should carry them further than they would agree to go, that not a single man would engage with us." Several said they would consider the idea overnight, which Franklin found "extremely annoying . . . especially as the next evening was fixed for the departure of the ships."

In the end, encouraged by Geddes and Clouston, four experienced men signed on—but only after perusing the proffered contract and stipulating that they would travel no farther than Fort Chipewyan on the shores of Lake Athabasca, and so within charted territory. After that, they would be paid off and released to return home. To this Franklin reluctantly agreed.

Later, he wrote that he "was much amused with the extreme caution these men used before they would sign the agreement; they minutely scanned all our intentions, weighed every circumstance, looked narrowly into the plan of our route, and still more circumspectly to the prospect of return. Such caution on the part of northern mariners forms a singular contrast with the ready and thoughtless manner in which an English seaman enters upon any enterprise, however hazardous, without inquiring, or desiring to know where he is going, or what he is going about." Clearly, Franklin preferred old-fashioned English bravado, but the Orcadian alternative would prove the wiser approach.

Two centuries later, given what we know about the geography of the Canadian Arctic, it is easy to dismiss this overland expedition as hubristic and naive. But John Franklin was a Royal Navy man to the tips of his fingers, and as he departed the British Isles, having added four careful Orcadians to his expedition, he judged that English grit and Christian faith would enable him to overcome any difficulties. On June 16, 1819, Franklin stood on the deck of the *Prince of Wales* among his fellows, watching as the towering sea stack known as the Old Man of Hoy receded from view.

~

The three ships left Stromness at noon, and those on board soon found themselves sailing through northwest gales, heavy swells, thick fog, and relentless rain. As an experienced midshipman who had endured many a storm, Hood noted that "the first novelty that engages the attention in these northern latitudes is the continuance of daylight through the twenty-four hours. It occasions a contention between the desires of the mind and the body, which produces a certain degree of restlessness" until one manages to adjust.

When the ship found itself encompassed by "icebergs of great magnitude," the precise Hood took measurements. One was 62 feet high and 1,154 feet long. Another, a conical berg, rose to a height of 149 feet, indicating that it "could not have been less than 150 fathoms below the surface of the water." Hood noted that the heavy weather and heaving ship dampened the spirits of a number of passengers heading out to join Lord Selkirk's colony at Red River. They had not anticipated "these preliminary difficulties," he writes, "and early disappointment, however trivial, withers the fair flowers of expectation. For seasickness there is no relief, except sleep, which was prevented by continual noise, and rest precluded by perpetual motion. This situation is truly miserable; but it is too common to excite any commiseration."

The voyage became more exciting on August 7, 1819, when, at around 12:30 p.m., as the ship approached the notorious Hudson Strait in a heavy swell, the fog lifted just enough that Franklin and his men saw a terrifying sight. Standing on deck with his naval companions, he perceived that the rolling ship was driving toward a perpendicular cliff, a part of Resolution Island that towered more than a hundred feet in the air.

Before anyone could move, the ship struck a rocky underwater ledge projecting from the island. This knocked several passengers off their feet and jolted the ship's rudder out of position, rendering it useless. A small boat that had been hoisted over the side slammed against the cliff and was almost crushed. Sailors grabbed poles to keep the *Prince of Wales* from smashing into the rocks, and the ship skidded and shuddered in the shallows. A jagged peak loomed directly ahead. A crash seemed certain until, almost incredibly, another invisible rock banged the rudder back into place, a sailor turned the ship's wheel, and the ship slid past the cliff edge, scraping its side.

Water began pouring into the hold. Sailors manned both pumps but still the water rose. Captain John Davison trimmed the sails, caught a breeze, and angled the ship clear of the cliff. But now it ran along a massive iceberg attached to the island. The captain fired the ship's guns, signalling distress, trying desperately to attract the attention of the two consort vessels lost in the fog.

Franklin and his men, experienced sailors, feared for their lives. Their fellow passengers were terrified and crying. These included eighteen Scottish Highlanders bound for the Red River Colony, among them women and children who had never been to sea. They had rushed out on deck despite efforts to keep them below and out of danger should the masts be swept away. Later, Franklin wrote that "the ship was driven along the steep and rugged side of this iceberg, with such amazing rapidity, that the destruction of the masts seemed inevitable, and everyone expected we should again be forced on the rocks in the most disabled state."

Captain Davison blasted away with his guns, and the midshipmen told the partially deaf Franklin they could hear the answering guns of the *Eddystone*. That ship approached and its captain sent aboard carpenters and crew, together with a third pump. The men worked through the night and all the next day as the water in the hold rose to above five feet. When a sailor tumbled into it, he had to swim for his life.

About this near disaster, Robert Hood added evocative detail. Earlier that day, around 9 a.m., the *Eddystone* had got trapped in the ice and both the *Prince of Wales* and the *Wear* had sent boats to assist. A thick fog reduced visibility, but the sailors had previously seen land, and "we concluded that we were driving towards the entrance of Hudson's Straits." In this they could not have been more wrong.

Shortly after noon, the fog lifted and "the shore broke once more upon our view, at the distance of 50 yards. It consisted of two inaccessible rocks, of bare stone, with an iceberg between them. They rose almost perpendicularly, till their summits were lost in the fog." The ebbing tide "forced us rapidly towards them, and destruction, apparently so inevitable, stupefied our people with dismay."

One lifeboat was absent in use and the others were stored on board, almost impossible to access. "The strength that is supplied by terror" enabled the crew to put one boat over the edge as the *Prince of Wales* struck the rock. The boat narrowly "escaped being crushed, contrary to our expectations." The crash "unhinged the ship's rudder, which was replaced by the next blow." The tide again drove the ship toward the iceberg, but the boat took her in tow and, with the help of a light breeze, managed to avert catastrophe. Those on board had "little cause for congratulation," however, as the ship had sprung leaks in the stern: "Disaster had not yet done with us."

The current drove the *Prince of Wales* against an iceberg whose overhanging projections "threatened the masts and tore away part of the chains." The ship ripped past the grounded iceberg "with appalling noise, but less real danger than we had already incurred." The *Eddystone* appeared out of the mist with three boats towing her away from the rocks. The *Prince of Wales* "made signals of distress, which she answered by sending her carpenter, with what other men she could spare, and taking us in tow."

Sailors worked furiously but could not staunch the leaks. As night came on, "the wind increased to a heavy gale off the land." Around midnight, "we let go the tow rope, as we were involving the *Eddystone* in difficulties from which we derived no advantage." Captain Davison freed the sails, but the men could not leave the pumps to furl them. Ice wrecked the stern boat. Hood writes, "Buffeted in every quarter, the leaks gaining upon us, and the people overcome by fatigue, many had already given themselves up to despair. To them death itself appeared less terrible than a continuation of such painful labour."

By 6 a.m. on the eighth, the water in the hold was five feet deep. "The vigorous conduct of a few persons revived the hopes" of many. "Mr. Franklin's profession secured attention to his advice," and passengers took to working at the pumps and toiling with buckets. "Even the women would not be excluded, and they displayed surprising strength and alacrity in the execution of the tasks allotted to them."

These furious efforts kept the water from overflowing onto the deck. But at 3 p.m., preparing for the worst, Captain Davison decided to send the women and children over to the *Eddystone*. Hood revealed that "one man was dastard enough to conceal himself among them, and voluntarily class himself by his cowardice with those whose natural timidity sometimes renders them useless. He was sent back to meet the execrations of his companions."

By 6 p.m.—progress at last. In a last-ditch attempt to staunch the leak and save the *Prince of Wales*, the sailors cut away part of the ceiling near the sternpost. They slowed the rush of water by jamming felt and oakum between the leakiest timbers and nailing a plank over the worst-hit area. Having pumped madly, non-stop, for thirty-six hours, they hauled a sail, which Franklin described as "covered with every substance that could be carried into the leaks by the pressure of the water," and secured it by ropes on both sides. Almost incredibly, this worked. Soon the men were manning the pumps at ten-minute intervals. The women and children returned to the ship.

Lieutenant Franklin called all those on board into the main cabin, where he invoked the name of Jesus, read solemn prayers, and led those present in giving thanks to the Almighty, who had seen fit to deliver them from a watery grave. Then, feeling secure, his Christian faith vindicated, John Franklin sailed on. The way ahead lay clear of ice.

~

A few days later, on August 13, sixteen miles off the Upper Savage Islands, a group of Inuit men approached in kayaks, "according to their usual custom, to barter with the ships." Women followed in "large skin boats," or umiaks. Trading took place over the next few hours, and Hood attempts no detailed description. He refers to books by Lieutenant Edward Chappell and Abbé Guillaume Raynal, noting that "I am unable to add fresh interest to a subject which is almost exhausted."

Hood did remark that "the country is probably the most ineligible in the world for the residence of man, yet the ingenuity of its inhabitants is equal to their wants. With no other materials than skins, whalebone, and driftwood, they have constructed machines [kayaks] by the aid of which they can assume the faculties of another race of creatures in their own particular element; can vie with them in swiftness and trace them through all the mazes of their flight, with such admirable dexterity, that life seems to be imparted to the vehicle which obeys every impulse so readily. The world cannot produce an instance of such powers invested by art in the strength of a single man."

CHAPTER 9

Upriver *to* Cumberland House

~

The *Prince of Wales* reached York Factory on August 30, 1819. The voyage from Gravesend "had occupied three months and seven days," Robert Hood writes, "which was considered a very unusual length of time." Since the accident, the ship had never stopped leaking. When she was "hove down," her astonished crew found a large hole near the keel. Hood could only marvel: "The leak was stopped by means beyond our conjecture." The HBC superintendent, Governor William Williams, came out in a boat. With room for three, he brought Hood, Franklin, and Richardson "to the factory in a heavy storm of rain."

Back in England, senior figures from the Hudson's Bay Company and the North West Company had offered assurances about co-operating and assisting the expedition. But here in the north country, rivalry between the two fur-trading outfits was spiralling to a murderous crescendo. Each accused the other of ambushing and killing agents. On landing at York Factory, the naval men learned that four North West Company partners were being held here as prisoners to be brought to trial in England—not a good omen.

At this time, the early 1800s, the HBC was far smaller than the NWC. In 1814, according to Canadian scholar C. Stuart Houston, the

HBC had fur-trade earnings of 15,000 pounds, compared to the NWC's 48,000. In 1816, that ratio was 8,000 to 29,000. The HBC employed mostly English-speaking Protestants from Orkney, while the NWC relied upon Montreal-based Scottish Highlanders to manage a vast river network of French Canadian and Métis voyageurs.

Robert Hood, who kept the best record of this leg of the journey, began absorbing this history with a feeling approaching dismay. In 1809, Nor'westers had driven one HBC man from his post at Île-à-la-Crosse and burned the place to the ground. Two years later, working through the HBC, Thomas Douglas, Lord Selkirk, had gained control of 116,000 square miles in the Red River Valley (around present-day Winnipeg) with a view to creating a settlement of Scottish Highlanders who had been forcibly cleared from their ancestral lands.

The Nor'westers perceived the Red River Colony as a threat to the viability of their river network—and not without reason. As more settlers arrived, tensions between the fur-trade companies escalated. Obviously, this poisonous situation could only hinder the present expedition, which had been premised on fur-trade co-operation that now looked increasingly unlikely. Before leaving York Factory, John Franklin would consult with both HBC men and the detained NWC partners, then write an official disclaimer of sorts, which could be produced as necessary along the way, advising his officers to avoid taking sides in the fur-trade dispute.

Robert Hood described York Factory with no enthusiasm. Situated two hundred yards from the west bank of Hudson Bay and five miles from the mouth of the Hayes River, it consisted of "several wooden buildings enclosed by stockades or wooden spikes four or five yards in length, driven into the ground. The principal building is two stories high, with a courtyard in the interior." Officers and clerks occupied the upper apartments and their servants the lower. Other buildings were given over to stores and furs ready for export.

"The whole has the appearance of a temporary erection by shipwrecked seamen," Hood wrote, "and the resemblance may be carried farther in the occupations and varied garbs of its inhabitants, who seemed to be clothed in what they had snatched by chance from destruction." He noted the existence of "a barbarous wooden crane" at the pier and "three or four small field pieces" for making signals. Those who choose to live here, he added, "must shake off every lingering want which abundance has cherished . . . and learn to think that sufficient, the deprivation of which would be fatal."

Here at York Factory, Hood and his naval colleagues perceived that their expedition faced hurdles and challenges that their superiors back home had failed to anticipate. Consultations produced a consensus that the best way forward was to follow the traditional fur-trade route up the Hayes River to Cumberland House and then proceed north to the mouth of the Coppermine River and the Arctic coast, reprising much of the route followed by Samuel Hearne fifty years before. The strong-minded Hood alone had voted to sail north to Repulse Bay (Naujaat) and then travel inland eight hundred miles to the mouth of the Coppermine—a journey that would have solved crucial geographical mysteries but was rightly judged impractical for lack of provisions and a seaworthy boat.

∼

With their route decided, the navy men confronted more problems. At York Factory, nobody wanted to join their expedition. The HBC governor, Williams, Hood writes, "was greatly disappointed in the numbers sent to him by the ships, having demanded 100 and obtained 20. He could therefore only provide us with a steersman, in addition to our own six men." Hood spoke as one of four officers and two English seamen, John Hepburn and Samuel Wilkes. They would be assisted on this initial leg of the journey by the newly assigned steersman and the four Orcadians hired in Stromness.

With the steersman at the helm, the eleven men would beat upriver against the current in a shallow-draft York boat featuring a single mast and a square sail. It could carry no more than three tons, Hood writes, so the party had to leave more than half its equipment and supplies—"a quantity of bacon, balls, tobacco and powder, to be carried after us at a more favourable opportunity." With the occasional help of fur traders travelling in the same direction, the party had to transport a huge weight of supplies and instruments through rough waters and over portages. They faced a journey of almost 700 miles up the traditional river system to Cumberland House, which is situated 275 miles northeast of Saskatoon.

From Scotland, before the team sailed, the celebrated fur-trade explorer Alexander Mackenzie had warned that the expedition should not expect, in its first season, to get beyond Île-à-la-Crosse—wise words, since that site, decimated since he passed that way, lay almost 430 miles beyond Cumberland House. Unfortunately, the experienced Mackenzie said nothing about foodstuffs, and a settler recently arrived at Red River had written recommending bacon as a primary meat source—words not so wise.

Unfamiliar with pemmican, that lightweight, dried-meat staple of the voyageur diet, much less with hunting buffalo and caribou, the navy men had brought seven hundred pounds of salted pig, which on arrival at York Factory was already mouldy and inedible. Never mind. At noon on September 9, urged on by cheers and a nine-gun salute, the expedition set out for Cumberland House. Hood was the one who took most of the observations, computing distances and drawing maps. At sunset, the men landed on a small island, pitched their tent, and built a large fire. They spread their bedding on buffalo hides "and slept without molestation." The next day, at sunrise, they embarked. And now the going got tough.

As the journey progressed, Hood named several different rivers, all of which would later be considered part of the Hayes River. Beyond the reach of the Hudson Bay tide, the opposing river current grew stronger and the men had to track or drag the boat upstream, "harnessed to a line and carrying large sticks to support themselves." Hood noted that the cliffs stood one hundred feet high. Two days out, the river grew shallow and "we were frequently obliged to get out of the boat and lift it over the shoals." Hood marvelled at the brilliant autumnal hues of the poplar and tamarack: "The trees opened into avenues discovering spacious lawns beyond them, with an effect which we could hardly conceive was produced by accident."

Some HBC men who had left York Factory one day later (September 10) overtook the navy men and told them their boat was too heavily laden for the flats that lay ahead. "This we quickly experienced," Hood writes, "for it remained half the day aground in spite of the efforts of our whole party." The men found themselves fighting a current running seven miles an hour. Over the next couple of days, they struggled onward. Twice the tracking rope snapped and the current smashed the boat against the rocks.

As the HBC had been directed to assist the expedition, Franklin prevailed on those in passing boats to carry "a small portion of our cargo, resolving to leave more of the remainder" at Rock House, scarcely seventy-five miles out of York Factory. Hood noted that this stretch of river included sixteen portages, from twenty yards to a quarter mile long, where every voyageur carried two or three packages weighing between seventy-five and ninety pounds. At noon on September 17, the men reached Rock House, a three-sided construction open to the water. In the store they left sixteen packages containing sugar, biscuit, tea, rice, and portable soup—a dehydrated broth, then a staple for British sailors and explorers, that would keep for months. They "now had the satisfaction to find that the other boats could scarcely keep up with us."

The officers—Franklin, Richardson, and the two midshipmen—did none of the physical labour. But the party spent a day traversing two long portages, and Hood noted that "the fatigue sustained in this constant labour disheartens those who are engaged in it for the first time. But example and habit reconcile them to a life calculated only for beasts of burthen." In his view, "few acquainted with the profits of begging in England, would live in Hudson's Bay." He did not care for the "mixture of fat and meat called pemmican," which the HBC had made available, describing it as "nourishing but unpalatable, and in summer, often mouldy or rancid."

On September 23, after covering sixty miles in "nine days of unintermitting exertion," the men reached Swampy Lake and were able to sail there for a dozen miles. The next couple of days brought more portages, but also a brilliant viewing of the aurora borealis: "The whole sky was streaked with parallel arches." By the twenty-seventh, Hood was convinced that the difficulties of the portages "might be removed by making use of trucks or carts and taking a few" stones out of the channels. Indeed, he thought a road for horses might easily be made between York Factory and Cumberland House, with ferries established on the rivers.

A few years before, the HBC had tried without success to build a winter road along this route and, in 1828, would try and fail again. C. Stuart Houston would note in the 1970s that "such a route has yet to be built," and the same holds true today, in the twenty-first century. Much else also remains unchanged. Hood remarked, for example, that "the sandflies and mosquitoes ceased their persecutions, to languish a little longer in the heat of noon, and then resign their annual existence."

Arriving at Oxford House on September 28, Hood described it as being "built like the rest, of wood, and enclosed by stockades. These lonely dwellings are more widely scattered than the cities of Siberia . . . They were raised for the primitive object of shelter, and variety is only to be found in decoration and arrangement, here neither attempted nor desired." Here, too, for the first time, Hood encountered a small settlement of First Nations people (almost certainly Cree) who had pitched tents near the house. They were suffering "the dreadful ravages of the whooping cough, and the measles had filled them with lamentation and despair." This was all the result of contact with white explorers and settlers who, coming from Europe, had built up certain immunities over the centuries.

~

On September 30, the party arrived at two difficult portages called the Hill Gates. The Hayes River narrowed to a width of ten yards and roared for a mile and a half through steep granite rocks. This opened "a magnificent defile," Hood wrote, "which one would have thought too regular for nature but too stupendous for art." After passing Upper Hill Gate, the men crossed a lake and camped at the beginning of the half-mile White Fall Portage. On October 2, they began crossing to where the river split into three waterfalls. The north bank, Robert Hood noted, "is a steep cliff covered with trees; along the foot of it, large masses of rock have been heaped at different periods." On the south side, the stream was so narrow as to be impassible.

"Mr. Franklin was traversing the banks, between two of the falls," Hood wrote, "when he slipped from the edge of a rock and rolled down into a declivity 15 or 20 yards into the water." Hood gaped in horror. "The current was not rapid," he wrote later, "but the bank for a great extent continued too steep and slippery to afford him a firm grasp, and he was tantalized by sometimes touching the bottom, while he was, in spite of all his efforts, slowly approaching a fall."

What if Franklin went over that waterfall and died, broken on the rocks below? Robert Hood watched, terrified. Could the expedition continue without Franklin? What of the planning and preparation? What of the terrible voyage they had made across the Atlantic and the hard slog now underway? Hood had been dreaming all his life of an adventure like this one. Surely, it could not all be lost, rendered meaningless by a careless accident? Luckily, several men just finishing a portage spotted the flailing lieutenant and rushed to his rescue. "He had however reached a low point before their arrival," Hood wrote, "and they found him, half immersed in the water, quite exhausted by his repeated attempts to land."

Hood was shaken by having witnessed this near-fatal accident. In his journal, he sought to rationalize the mishap, noting that Franklin had been coughing before he fell, and was so severely afflicted with whooping cough "that it often threatened strangulation." He added the lieutenant's mind "was too eagerly bent on the service which he had undertaken to be relaxed by the attacks of this disorder, even with the auxiliaries of cold, wet, and indifferent provisions."

~

Franklin's accident, which would not be his last, resulted in a broken chronometer. But at their next fur-trade post, a resourceful HBC man would manage to repair it. Now, to Hood's relief, the men resumed their work. By evening they had finished conveying boats and cargo to the far side of the portage. And four days later, on the morning of October 6, the expedition reached Norway House—originally the site of a shanty used by a Norwegian road gang that had tried and failed to build that winter road.

Here the navy men chanced upon the eighteen would-be colonists with whom they had crossed the Atlantic. These Highland refugees had recently learned, and now told the sailors, that grasshoppers, famine, and disease had decimated the Red River Colony. Worse, in June 1817, during what they called the Massacre of Seven Oaks, Nor'westers had shot and killed the settlement leader, five of his officers, and fourteen farmers.

These new arrivals now regretted their decision to flee the Highlands, Hood wrote, and had "lost all desire to proceed." He judged that "the extermination of a colony is no ordinary offence against mankind. To blast in the germ the provision of future multitudes, to deprive poverty of an asylum from guilt, and industry of its last retreat, is a complication of crimes in those people who have affected it, in which the murderer's share is the least atrocious."

On the evening the expedition arrived, the colonists unwillingly set out on the next leg of their journey—though only "after venting their discontents," Hood wrote, "by beating and ducking their conductor and medical attendant, [then departing] before any account of their proceedings reached the house."

The next day, accompanied by HBC governor Williams, who had caught up with them, the navy men entered Lake Winnipeg, a massive lake on which "a moderate gale raises the waves so high that boats seldom venture far from the shore and are sometimes detained many days." Accordingly, the men decided to run all night as "the Aurora stole silently across the northern sky, fluttering in half-formed circles, and glowing with brilliant colours."

On October 8, gale-force winds forced the expedition to land on a small island. The following evening, during a brief lull, the men set sail but soon found themselves "driven by heavy squalls accompanied by hail at the rate of seven or eight miles an hour." They tried to land on another island, but the surf prevented this. At midnight, a squall broke the boat's yardarm, "and our companions [sailing with Williams] immediately disappeared" from sight, lost in the heaving waves. Another hour took them to the mouth of the Saskatchewan River, where they rejoined Williams and set up camp, having sailed eighty-eight miles non-stop.

The Saskatchewan River "runs with extraordinary noise and fury for three miles," Hood wrote, "round a long peninsula, fretted into a sheet of foam by the rocks which interrupt it." A mile-long portage took the men across the peninsula to a wooden bridge built by HBC men. At this location "the whole trade of the interior is detained two days," the problem being that each company claimed that carts left at the site to improve efficiency were being destroyed by men from its competitor. Williams revealed that this was where he had made prisoners of the Nor'westers the navy men had met at York Factory. "In this country," Hood remarked, "justice cannot act without force." The HBC men anticipated a retaliatory attack but "were spared the humiliating spectacle of the expected contention."

On October 14, bad weather drove the men ashore on an island so stony that they could not pitch a tent. But next morning brought a fair wind and the men crossed Muddy Lake. They entered one of the main branches of the Saskatchewan River and began "the most tedious and uninteresting part of our journey"—nothing but muddy banks declining to the water in long shelves. Four days out, they met a large encampment of Indigenous people attached to Cumberland House, all of whom hailed Williams as "father," a gesture he felt obliged to acknowledge by serving out drams of spirits. Now the men could track the boats more quickly because the mud along the water was frozen. Snow showers signalled the

departure of geese and ducks as ice reduced their means of subsistence.

The men battled "a current and a wind so strong that nothing but the certainty of being, in another day, blocked by the ice, could have induced us to persevere." They forced their way across the lake to within four miles of Cumberland House. The next day, in freezing cold, they tracked a river "choked by driving ice" to the entrance of Pine Lake, and there "distinguished our intended winter abode at the distance of three miles on the south side." By Hood's reckoning, the expedition had covered roughly 685 miles from York

Walter J. Phillips painted *Hudson's Bay Company York Boats at Norway House* in 1928. These boats, the workhorses of the HBC fur trade, were modelled on Orkney boats designed by Norsemen who colonized the northern reaches of Scotland in the eighth and ninth centuries.

Factory. The edge of the lake was frozen 200 yards from the beach, but at 10 a.m. on October 23, the men climbed a slope to Cumberland House. Built by Samuel Hearne in 1774—some forty-five years before—this dilapidated outpost consisted of a stockade that enclosed five rough-hewn log buildings. None of them offered much protection from the cold.

CHAPTER 10

Once *a* Prisoner *of* War

~

Except for the rugged George Back, who had survived five years of marching around France as a prisoner of war, none of the Royal Navy men took readily to rough-country trekking. C. Stuart Houston, editor of Back's journal, *Arctic Artist*, notes that his subject was more physically fit than his fellow officers. He was also more affable and communicative. Between the ages of thirteen and seventeen, while incarcerated during the Napoleonic Wars, Back learned to speak French fluently. He could laugh and joke with the voyageurs, and managed to commandeer one of them, Gabriel "Paul" Beauparlant, as his personal servant. But here is the real mark of Back's linguistic competence: he contrived to collect numerous songs of the voyageurs and later publish them in French and in translation.

George Back was born, a second son, on November 6, 1796, in Stockport, England, seven miles southeast of Manchester. In September 1808, shortly before he turned twelve, he went to sea aboard HMS *Arethusa* as a first-class volunteer. In addition to learning seamanship, navigation, and log-keeping, he studied sketching and painting with a senior officer. By November, the *Arethusa* was cruising the English Channel in search of French ships. It succeeded in taking a sixteen-gun privateer off

This portrait of George Back (print by Louis Haghe, based on a sketch by George Robert Lewis) captures his attractiveness. But the young artist-midshipman was also tough and resourceful.

the Isle of Wight. The following March, off the northern coast of Spain, Back stowed away to join a night-time "cutting out," or raiding party, that succeeded in taking control of an enemy ship. He was among those who ignored a recall signal and instead attacked a fort at Deba, a port on the Bay of Biscay. The raiders spent four nights plundering French trading vessels, and Back wrote, "We were becoming rich and comfortable in our new vocation."

Luck ran out on March 20, 1809, when a flood tide grounded the marauders. Sixty Frenchmen attacked. They killed eleven of fifteen British raiders and took four prisoners, among them thirteen-year-old George Back. So began his five-year stint as a prisoner in Napoleonic France—a fate less onerous than might be imagined. Kept first in a château in Deba, Back was marched twenty-five miles to Zumaya, then taken by boat to San Sebastián. Here the prisoners gained permission to roam the streets. French officers and bystanders responded sympathetically to the curly-haired Back, who stood only five feet tall.

At Bayonne, Back charmed a wealthy merchant, his wife, and their young daughter. According to biographer Peter Steele, the merchant "wanted to adopt Back and to continue his education until the end of the war." Back remained with his fellows and marched on through Bordeaux, eventually slogging almost seven hundred miles northeast across France to the citadel prison of Verdun. Here, most prisoners were well treated and allowed to wander within a radius of six miles, on condition that they appear two or three times a day for roll call.

Back became fluent in French. Ensconced in a house with several British midshipman, the youngest prisoner at Verdun, he learned to fish and swim, and to gamble, hunt ducks, and ride ponies. He and his friends drew credit from banks—money repaid by their parents—and began, he later confessed, "a course of extravagances altogether unwarrantable." One of his housemates kept a mistress.

In his journal, Back writes that by age fifteen, having tired of the endless revelry, he rented a room near the library. He was one of several prisoners who attended a day school run by two senior British naval officers. While studying mathematics, navigation, and seamanship, he also found time to sketch and paint, developing his natural gift. Occasionally, he backslid, associated with "dissolute characters," and watched while "every description of irregularity was openly committed without shame and without reproach."

Late in 1813, with Napoleon losing battle after battle, the French worried that prisoners at Verdun, just 250 miles from the coastal town of Calais, might try to join their British compatriots. To prevent this, suddenly they marched southwest toward Blois, some 280 miles away. Back travelled with an older friend and his family. One night, they camped beside a frozen river: "I have often thought since that it was a mild fore-hardening of what I was doomed to experience in after life, and truly I learned many useful manipulations which were turned to good account even in the icy North."

After marching to Guéret, another 125 miles south of Blois, the prisoners were released and told to go home. Early in 1814, now seventeen, Back made his way north. He boarded a chartered fishing boat at Dieppe, crossed the English Channel, and hurried to join his parents and siblings, now living in Spitalfields, London. He became "thrice happy in the comforts of home and the indulgent fondness of family"—but not for long.

In 1815, when the war ended and young naval officers were being laid off in droves, Back nabbed a posting as a midshipman on HMS *Akbar*. The ship was making for North America, where his fluency in French might come in handy. At one point, after the ship took French prisoners, he did serve the captain as interpreter. In 1816, after being paid off in Portsmouth, Back passed the requisite exams and became an Admiralty mate. The following March, he joined HMS *Bulwark*, a seventy-four-gun guardship. He spent his days drawing and reading, complained of "the constant bustle and uproar of a midshipman's mess," and gave thanks to a friend who lent him a cabin in the gunroom.

In his free time, Back taught French, worked at drawing and painting, and mounted a theatrical production. He painted scenery and held auditions to resolve "certain petty jealousies" about who should play whom. He did have trouble teaching some of the sailors to step around like ladies and also to curtsey, but the show, performed on the main deck, left the audience howling for more. This success probably had nothing to do with it, but when the Admiralty started looking for two midshipmen to serve on a Northwest Passage expedition, he was invited to interview and faced a half-hour grilling. Did he need time to reflect? He most certainly did not: "To one who like me had been nursed in some degree of hardship, the very idea of adventure or discovery was captivating beyond language to express."

~

On April 25, 1818, on HMS *Trent*, George Back sailed for the Arctic under Lieutenant John Franklin. The leaky old ship, sailing in tandem with HMS *Dorothea*, eventually reached the island of Spitzbergen, which extends above 80 degrees north in the Svalbard archipelago. But then the sailors encountered heavy ice and gale-force winds and spent thirteen days heaving and rolling while threatened by monster icebergs. Both ships were back in Deptford on October 22, having accomplished nothing.

George Back did, however, establish himself with Franklin as "a correct, zealous and attentive officer [who] was assiduously anxious to promote every aspect of the voyage . . . I consider Mr. Back to be much entitled to my approbation." The enmity between the two men, later widely recognized, had yet to emerge, and in 1819 Franklin welcomed Back as one of the two midshipmen appointed to his first Arctic Land Expedition.

In retrospect, their mutual dislike looks predictable enough. As many have remarked, and Peter Steele writes, Franklin "was deeply—even excessively—religious." Indeed, in 1823, his evangelical Christianity would so alarm his fiancée, the acclaimed poet Eleanor Porden, that she would threaten to call off their engagement. Early in that year, after Franklin suggested that he was showing commendable flexibility by writing a letter on the Sabbath, Eleanor wrote, "Pardon me if I say that I almost consider the wish of seclusion on that day as partaking of the same aberration of religious zeal which drove many of the early Christians to the deserts of Syria and Egypt. Did you pick it up in North America?"

Franklin beat a hasty retreat. But a few months after this exchange, he would send Eleanor personal correspondence from Lady Lucy Barry, the spiritual leader of a fringe group of evangelical Calvinists whose writings had brought him to "seeing the light." Eleanor was appalled. She perceived Lady Barry to be a fanatical Methodist bent on making a convert of Franklin and asked, "Has she succeeded?"

If Franklin expected to convert his fiancée to Barry's creed, Eleanor wrote, she felt duty bound to tell him that he would never succeed, and that it would be best to say farewell. She stood ready to break off the engagement, "unluckily so publicly known," rather than enter into "any future contest" on this subject. Franklin again backed down, declaring that he was not a Methodist, and adding that while he admired the zeal and goodness of Lady Barry's circle, he did not assent to their doctrines. In truth, he would never renounce his passion for the gospel of Jesus Christ.

Now, in 1819, George Back of course professed Christianity. But his five years as a prisoner of war in France had broadened his perspective on what that might mean. This explains what happened at Great Yarmouth, when while sailing for North America, the *Prince of Wales* put in to shelter from the storm. George Back went alone two or three miles up the highway to visit, he said, "a much-respected friend." Such was the story he told. Probably the straitlaced Franklin either heard or suspected that Back had gone to busy himself at a house of ill repute. Certainly, Franklin did not request even a twenty-minute delay for the sake of his midshipman.

As a result, the irrepressible Back spent the next nine days in a desperate journey north. He took the Northern Mail coach through Norwich and Newcastle upon Tyne to Edinburgh, where he hired a gig to Thurso and then, because the ferry was halted by bad weather, paid a notorious smuggler to take him across the wild Pentland Firth to Stromness. He arrived just in time for the bon voyage party.

The midshipman took the ensuing Atlantic crossing in stride, though he was touched by the suffering of the would-be settlers when the ship collided with icebergs off Resolution Island. The women, those "poor creatures," he wrote in his journal, "whose occupations were entirely on the shore and consequently were unused to such spectacles as they had just witnessed—uttered the most piteous exclamations—fearing the torments of sudden death or the more horrible state of certain starvation—the screams of the children and the agonizing looks of despair of the fathers—with the bustle and confusion of the seamen added an awfulness to the scene which will never be obliterated from my memory."

When the crisis was over, Back noted, Lieutenant Franklin "read prayers and returned thanks for the very providential manner in which we had been saved." What Back left unsaid, his biographer, Peter Steele, added: "One hopes [Franklin] also thanked the carpenters and crew."

CHAPTER 11

Second-in-Command

~

N ow came the landing at York Factory and the upriver slog. On October 23, when the men entered Cumberland House, none were impressed. But only one man instantly hated the place. For George Back, the stockade evoked too-vivid memories of his early days as a prisoner of war.

As winter came on, the Royal Navy men determined that even the best of the old log buildings offered little protection against the cold. One of the two able seamen, Samuel Wilkes, was not holding up well. Assigned to work alongside the four hardy Orcadian Scots, he proved unable to keep up. At the man's own request, Franklin sent him back to York Factory with some HBC workers. Of the navy men, that left the four officers and one able seaman, John Hepburn—all of whom now faced a subarctic test.

Franklin's second-in-command, Dr. John Richardson, found he did not mind the freezing weather. He preferred the dry cold, with temperatures as low as thirty degrees below zero, to the damp winter days of Britain. Richardson was well trained as a scientist yet remained a devout Christian. When he described Franklin as "steady, religious, and cheerful," he intended every word as a compliment.

Dr. John Richardson, whose portrait is provided by London's Wellcome Library, proved his mettle while serving as second-in-command on the First Arctic Overland Expedition.

Born in Dumfries, Scotland, in 1787, Richardson was the oldest of twelve children of a wealthy brewer and local politician. According to biographer Robert E. Johnson, his father was known for "the rectitude of his public and private life." A precocious child who started reading at age four, John went to school with a son of the poet Robert Burns, who moved to Dumfries in 1791. At thirteen he began an apprenticeship with his mother's brother, a doctor. When that uncle died, he continued his apprenticeship with another surgeon.

For the next seven years, he alternated between learning practical skills in Dumfries and studying science and medicine at the highly regarded University of Edinburgh. Medical courses included anatomy, surgery, chemistry, botany, and pharmacy. To these he added Greek and natural history, the last of which he studied with the renowned Robert Jameson, who later taught Charles Darwin.

In February 1807, recently turned nineteen, Richardson received both a licence from the Royal College of Surgeons of Edinburgh and a naval certificate that enabled him to take British Admiralty examinations in London. He passed with flying colours and then, through the influence of one of the Lords of the Admiralty—not incidentally a member of Parliament for Dumfries—he received a desirable first appointment as assistant surgeon to a frigate fitting out at Deptford, HMS *Nymphe*.

Now came seven years at sea, during which Richardson worked his way from assistant to ship's surgeon. In September 1807, the *Nymphe* called in at Copenhagen for repairs shortly after the British had bombarded the port in the Second Battle of Copenhagen and seized the Danish fleet. That action thwarted Napoleon's expansionary plans but destroyed more than a thousand buildings and, in addition to military casualties, killed 195 civilians and injured 768. Richardson wrote that it would be "difficult for one who has not been in Copenhagen to conceive the devastation which the shells and rockets have made. There is a whole quarter of the city completely destroyed, not a single house standing."

Over the next few months, Richardson volunteered to take part in at least two more raids and his captain commended his coolness and bravery up the line. He became senior assistant surgeon of the flagship *Hibernia* and then, at twenty-one, after being cited for devotion to duty and gallant conduct, acting surgeon of the seventy-four-gun *Hercule*. Starting in November 1808, Richard served as surgeon of HMS *Blossom*, a frigate-built sloop-of-war—"a complete frigate in miniature."

He described the officers as excellent companions: "Most of them are men of more knowledge and reading than I have met at sea before, and when we put our books together we have a very respectable library." Ironically, this led to problems. The ship's captain was an ignorant, insecure man whom the biographer Johnson describes as "suspicious and overbearing." When the junior officers were writing sonnets, he believed they were laughing at him. A malicious purser fanned this paranoid belief, causing him to arrest the first and second lieutenants and charge them with plotting mutiny. Because he needed the surgeon's services, he accused Richardson only after the ship docked.

A court martial cleared all three officers. Richardson wrote to his father that "the charges were so ridiculous, and my conduct proved to be so correct, that I was honourably acquitted without even the trouble of making a defence." The captain was subsequently dismissed from the *Blossom* and never given another ship. Of the purser, Richardson wrote, "he perjured himself several times and will be turned out of the service in disgrace."

Richardson remained on the *Blossom* under Captain Francis Beaufort, who had an excellent library, happily shared it with his officers, and later became the Admiralty hydrographer, or principal mapmaker. To Richardson, he would become a lifelong friend. In December 1809, the doctor wrote a long letter home describing his shipboard life. "At present I seldom get up before seven, in summer earlier, but whether sooner or later my time until eight is generally spent on deck. I breakfast at eight, visit the sick at nine, which with writing a list for the captain, and a daily report of each case for the Transport Board, occupies me until eleven. We dine at two o'clock, visit the sick again at six, and if any are confined to bed, or particularly ill, of course I do it often. At ten we generally go to bed; the intermediate time I usually spend reading or walking upon deck, as we have not even a pack of cards or backgammon board."

Richardson moved to HMS *Bombay*, a seventy-four-gun warship engaged in the blockading of Toulon, in southern France. In a letter to one of his brothers, who ran a farm in Galloway, Scotland, he described his situation: "My cabin is twenty-one feet long and seven broad . . . In that small space I have contrived to stuff a sofa, a dressing table, a chest of drawers, and bookcase containing upwards of a hundred volumes; besides, by means of a curtain, it is divided into two apartments, a dressing-room and a sitting-room." In another missive, he outlined his routine: "We live well, but drink only Mahon (that is, Minorca) wine, which is similar to a good claret, but not so strong . . . I believe no people indulge less in wine than officers of the navy, and, on board ship, they must be careful from a regard to their characters and situation, drunkenness never being pardoned at sea."

In the summer of 1812, granted leave after a long sea duty, the studious Richardson travelled between Dumfries and London, where he attended lectures on surgery and anatomy. The following April, he got his first experience of shipwreck when, while serving as surgeon aboard HMS *Cruiser*, the ship went aground on a reef off the coast of Sweden.

The ship lost her rudder and false keel, and the crew worked forty hours, throwing overboard all guns and shot, to eventually get the ship into port for repairs at Sheerness on England's east coast.

In November 1813, one month after Napoleon suffered a decisive defeat at Leipzig (a turning point in Europe), the ship was taken out of commission. Richardson went on half pay and resumed studying in London. He considered going into private practice but gained an appointment as surgeon to a battalion of Royal Marines then stationed in North America and engaged in that spillover from the Napoleonic Wars, the British–American war of 1812–14.

Richardson was on board a ship during the 1814 invasion of Washington but strongly disapproved, writing home that such predatory warfare "served to degrade the British character without materially injuring the enemy . . . In the late attack on Washington, our troops destroyed the few works of art which were found there, and were barbarous enough to burn the public library, so that our conduct will not bear to be compared with that of the half-civilized Russians, who, with infinitely greater provocation, respected the monuments of learning and of the arts, during their progress through France."

The humanitarian Richardson similarly deplored the pillaging of St. Marys, a town in Georgia where British troops attacked civilians, leaving only "after plundering it of almost everything of value . . . I do not know by what principle we deprive the unresisting inhabitants of their property, but so it is that everything under the denomination of merchandise is taken for the general account, and the greatest part of what remains is seized by private plunderers . . . Those who come last and find everything carried off by their predecessors generally break the windows."

After the Treaty of Ghent officially ended the war between the United States and Britain in December 1814, Richardson went on half pay and moved to Edinburgh, where he set to earn a doctor of medicine degree, the highest professional qualification then available. He received it in 1816 by writing and defending a thesis on yellow fever, then went into private practice in Leith, Edinburgh's main port. He married in 1818, but his wife would die, young and childless, while he was in the north country.

Early in 1819, Richardson learned that the Admiralty was preparing an overland expedition in search of the Northwest Passage. He had spent a great deal of time studying natural history with Robert Jameson, who recommended him to Sir Joseph Banks, who supported him to Sir John Barrow, who wrote on March 26, 1819, asking if Richardson could be ready to leave by the first week of May. Richardson said yes and spent his remaining spare time studying northerly minerals, plants, and animals. On May 23, under Lieutenant John Franklin, he sailed from Gravesend on the *Prince of Wales*.

~

At Cumberland House, where a few HBC men maintained a trading post, the expedition arrived unannounced. The newcomers set about finishing a half-built house within the stockades. Midshipman Robert Hood described it as "built of wood, the interstices being choked up with mud, and the roof boarded. The chimneys were made of stone, and the windows of moose skin parchment. Our tardy people were a month in completing it, and it proved rather too airy for this climate. We kept the chimneys in a constant blaze, notwithstanding which our pens and brushes were frozen to the paper ... We retained two of our men as servants, and permitted the rest to serve with the people belonging to the post, on condition that they should not interfere in the business of trade."

To his wife, after walking alone in the woods, Richardson wrote of entering a silence so profound that one could be startled by the cry of a bird or the splitting of a tree from the cold: "I have often admired the pictures our great poets have drawn of absolute solitude, but never felt their full force till now ... How dreadful if without faith in God!"

CHAPTER 12

Journey *to* Fort Chipewyan

~

A t Cumberland House, although he read voraciously and took observations daily, George Back grew increasingly restless. While out
trudging around in the snow, he almost injured him himself by stepping
on a spring-loaded fox trap. He got lost in the trees, eventually discovered
that he had walked in a circle, and vowed never again to enter the for-
est without a compass. By mid-December 1819, after two months at the
fur-trade post, Back was pressing Franklin to send him forward with an
advance party to hire guides, interpreters, and voyageurs for the big push
north. Neither Doctor Richardson nor midshipman Robert Hood—one
a naturalist, the other a bookish artist—felt any strong desire to test himself against the wintry wilds. For now, they would stay where they were.
But Franklin could hardly let a mere midshipman lead the way to Fort
Chipewyan.

Finally, on January 18, Back set out snowshoeing northwest with
Franklin, able seaman John Hepburn, and some Indigenous guides. They
slogged along while dogs pulled sledges piled high with trading goods.
They camped out each night, often at forty degrees below zero. The men
slept in a circle with their feet to the fire. Back noted that "if you wish to
avoid being frost bit it is absolutely necessary when once laid down under

your blanket and buffalo skin that you do not move one jot, though you may ache in every joint."

The departure from Cumberland House, John Franklin wrote, with two sledges and two carioles, occasioned "considerable grumbling from the voyageurs of both companies respecting the overlading of their dogs." Fifteen days of provisions filled the two sledges to overflowing. Franklin, Back, and Hepburn piled luggage into the carioles "instead of embarking in them ourselves." But even so, "the loads appeared to us so great that we should have been inclined to listen to the complaints of the drivers." Instead, they "left the matter to be settled by our friends at the fort [HBC fur traders] who were more conversant with winter travelling than ourselves."

Early in the journey, Franklin realized that food shortages might present a problem. Day two on the trail from Cumberland House, an Orcadian named Isbester caught up with the northbound party to bring some pemmican they had left behind. This Isbester, Franklin wrote, was heading out to find a group of locals who had not been heard from since October, knowing only that they had promised to hunt in a certain area. As per usual practice, he carried enough food to last until he expected to succeed—in this case six or seven days. Frequently, the hunters had followed the animals elsewhere and then snow covered their tracks. A few weeks before, Isbester had been placed in a "distressing situation . . . and passed four days without either himself or his dogs tasting food." He had resolved to kill and eat one of his dogs when "he happily met with a beaten track, which led him to some Indian lodges, where he obtained food."

A few days out of Cumberland House, a heavy snowfall prevented Franklin and Back from visiting an Assiniboine camp because they would not be able to go and return in the same day. A North West Company interpreter explained that these "Stone Indians" had been known to welcome visitors hospitably but then to follow, attack, and rob them. Not only that, but whooping cough and measles had recently killed about three hundred Cree and Assiniboine in the vicinity, and those at this location rightly blamed "some white people recently arrived in the country." The interpreter feared the survivors "might vent their revenge on us."

One night, according to his rough notes, George Back awoke feeling "an acute pain in my right foot—popped out my head and saw my right shoe and Buffalo skin on fire—made a sudden jump up to my knees in the snow . . . found our canteen upset—dogs very busy about it—butter tub just emptied—ran after the thief with a stick—cooled my foot and went to rest." Next morning, 8 a.m., he was again slogging north on pain-inducing, three-foot-long snowshoes. The party reached Carlton House on January 31, 1820, having travelled 240 miles in fourteen days—not a pace to write home about.

~

Situated on the Saskatchewan River sixty miles north of present-day Saskatoon, the HBC post at Carlton House featured a stockade that encompassed several buildings and square towers. The surrounding plains stood treeless, which George Back recognized as a "great inconvenience." Yet here the buffalo visited frequently, and he watched as "a lad of 15 went out on horseback with his gun, and in half an hour returned having dispatched two."

Back and Franklin travelled three miles by horse cariole to visit a North West Company fort, where they were welcomed with a volley of firearms. This outpost "consisted of several low houses surrounded by a high fence of posts with two watch houses at opposite angles." They spent the day "in gaiety"—a contrast to the atmosphere at the HBC fort—though they could not join the dancing "from the state of our joints." The place was "like a rabbit warren," Back wrote, and he thought that women "would never cease coming in . . . though the room was as full as it could be." A storm kept the navy men here overnight, and the next morning they returned to Carlton House through eight inches of snow.

The following day, accompanied by HBC officers, Back and Franklin set out by horse cariole to visit a First Nations encampment and buffalo pound. Back drove and tipped over more than once, "which with all my might I could not prevent." The encampment comprised seven tents in a clump of poplars near the compound. The people "had by this time been made acquainted with our mission" and received the two navy men as chiefs. In the largest tent, Back and Franklin distributed rum and tobacco and smoked the ceremonial pipe.

Back at Carlton House, which was occupied by ten HBC men, Franklin and Back heard an old Cree man say that the Assiniboine "spoke of killing all the white people" in their vicinity this year. Chief trader John Peter Pruden did not take this seriously, and everyone chuckled when the man added, "A pretty state we shall then be in without the goods you bring us."

Now came the northward slog to Île-à-la-Crosse—a journey of more than 250 miles through rolling country dotted with willow, poplar, and spruce. Both navy men claimed they no longer suffered from walking in snowshoes, with Back insisting that he was "in every measure more capable of undergoing fatigue than at the commencement." Somehow, Back had acquired the dedicated services of a voyageur named Gabriel "Paul" Beauparlant, a clever one-eyed man with whom he was learning to joke in *joual*, the colloquial French that had evolved in Quebec. Back occasionally broke into that language in his notes, incidentally expressing an easy camaraderie with voyageurs that would make him singularly effective.

At one point he wrote that, after being enlivened by a dram of whisky, "my Canadian . . . cracked his whip with as much spirit as any French Knight of the lash that ever mounted in post boots—ah! Paul said I—(for that was the man's name) thou art but a poor resemblance of thy namesake of old—True Sir, said he—*Il eut deux yeux—moi, je n'ai qu'un—mais j'en doute beaucoup si cet Monsieur dont vous parlez eut l'usage de raquette.* [True. He had two eyes, I have only one. But I doubt very much whether this gentleman of whom you speak knew how to use snowshoes.]"

As the expedition pressed on toward Île-à-la-Crosse, an Iroquois man joined the party. He was living nearby with some Cree while securing meat and furs for the North West Company. He travelled with the men to where he had cached some meat and urged them to stop and join him in feasting. Franklin judged the day scarcely begun and declined, "much to the annoyance of our Canadian companions, who had been cherishing the prospect of indulging their amazing appetites at this well-furnished store, ever since the man had been with us." The Iroquois man gave them a small supply and on they went.

The expedition rested for two days at Green Lake, where both fur-trade companies ran small trading posts that usually enjoyed an abundance of provisions. This season, Franklin wrote, "they barely had sufficient for their own support, owing to the [whooping cough] epidemic which has incapacitated the Indians for hunting." Dugald Cameron of the NWC warned that supplies would be scarce the next spring because "of the sickness of the Indians during the hunting season." Cameron undertook to have a supply of pemmican sent to Île-à-la-Crosse, where it could be picked up by Richardson and Hood.

On the next leg of the journey, despite the freezing cold, Franklin and Back travelled more comfortably than ever before as they had light carioles "which enabled us to ride nearly the whole day, warmly covered up with a buffalo robe." The Canadian voyageurs slogged on as usual. A musket volley welcomed them to the Hudson's Bay Company fort at Île-à-la-Crosse, where both Cree and Chipewyan gathered annually to play lacrosse. Heavy snow detained the travellers here. The men in charge of both company posts proved co-operative and helpful. The NWC man, John Clarke, had lived for years on the Mackenzie River and had once paddled almost to its mouth, where he encountered "Esquimaux" in great numbers. "They assumed such a hostile attitude," Franklin reported, "that he deemed it unadvisable to attempt any communication with them and retreated as speedily as he could."

According to George Back, Clarke described how on the Mackenzie one morning, when the morning mist began lifting, the travellers discovered a great number of Inuit on the bank opposite. The fur traders, who included NWC men, made signs of peace, but the Inuit "sent their women and children away, stripped themselves and launched their canoes, placing themselves in menacing attitudes." The fur traders made for an island and then for a far shore but repeatedly encountered Inuit "on the banks brandishing their massive weapons and by their shouts appearing to threaten the destruction of the inmates of the canoes." The traders "set sail and still using their paddles," retreated upriver. Several kayaks gave chase for twenty-four hours before "the unfortunate voyageurs" escaped, aided by a fair wind.

"I think there can be little doubt as to the intentions of the Esquimaux in this case," Back wrote. "But then I also am of the opinion that two strong and forcible reasons may be alleged for such conduct." First, he recalled "the melancholy catastrophe" of that area in 1799, when fur traders Duncan Livingstone and James Sutherland and their men were "murdered by the Esquimaux in the very act of distributing presents." The hostile Inuit may have thought Clarke's party was coming for revenge. Second, "they had just returned from a war party where they had killed many of their enemies—consequently were furious with success—and in default of seeing no one else, would in all probability have fought among themselves." Back thought to add that Clarke "apprehended no particular danger in our journey except from the Esquimaux—a circumstance well known before we left London."

Six years later, Franklin would forget this warning about these Mackenzie River Inuit, some of whom were related to Alaska-based Aleuts who had clashed with Russians in 1763–64. The Aleuts had responded to a series of atrocities by destroying four Russian vessels and killing almost two hundred men. The Russians then applied a scorched-earth policy in crushing the Aleut alliance. In July 1826, at the mouth of the Mackenzie, John Franklin would push on ahead where the wiser Clarke had read the signs and retreated. Franklin and Back and their few men would escape with their lives thanks only to the courage of an Inuk travelling with them—Tattannoeuck.

Now, from Île-à-la-Crosse, John Clarke travelled some distance with the expedition, offering advice and causing the voyageurs to set up camp paying "more attention to comfort and shelter than our former companions had done." The voyageurs were still going strong. On March 6, after travelling twenty-six miles, "they entertained till midnight with paddling songs . . . [requiring] very little stimulus beyond their natural vivacity to afford us this diversion."

∾

A week later, on March 13, 1820, the travellers arrived at one of the most important portages in fur-trade history. Portage La Loche, later called Methye Portage, extended twelve miles between the rivers that flowed east to Hudson Bay and those that ran west to the Mackenzie River Basin. Here George Back showed that, when he put his mind to it, he could evoke a scene not only with paints but with words. He writes that a traveller passing through nondescript countryside will be astonished on arriving at Portage La Loche:

> Breaking through the thick foliage of the pine and cypress—he
> stands at once on the summit of an immense precipice—and
> like one bewildered in some vast labyrinth, knows not how or
> where to fix his eye—The view is that of a valley some thousand
> feet beneath you, in length upwards of 30 miles—in breadth
> three or four—and in the centre a meandering river holds its
> course near, covered with snow . . . The valley is filled with trees
> of various kinds and adds a finish to the scene—the path on
> which you descend is so narrow, that without great care—you
> may be precipitated by one false step to certain destruction.

John Franklin wrote of how he and Back "had a very pleasant ride across [Methye Portage] in our carioles"—at least to the top. But the voyageurs had to stagger over rough terrain for a dozen miles while carrying canoes and ninety-pound packs. The westward descent required special exertion "to prevent the sledges from being broken in going down these almost perpendicular heights." The voyageurs released the dogs and guided the sledges, descending with "amazing rapidity" while throwing themselves this way and that to prevent crashes. "When we had arrived at the bottom," Franklin wrote, "I could not but feel astonished at the laborious task which the voyageurs have twice in the year to encounter at this place, in conveying their stores backwards and forwards."

After crossing Cascade Portage, the last on the way to Lake Athabasca, the expedition arrived at tents containing five Chipewyan families. The officers smoked the ceremonial pipe in the chief's tent, gave out some tobacco and weak spirits, and learned of a tradition that would later play a role in their own lives. The Chipewyan were poorly clothed, and a fur trader named Frazer, who had travelled with the team from Methye Lake, explained that they "had recently destroyed everything they possessed as a token of their great grief for the loss of their relatives in the prevailing sickness." This widespread practice, usually inspired by the loss of a near relative, involved cutting clothes and tents to shreds and destroying guns and other weapons.

Farther north, at Pierre au Calumet, a senior partner with the NWC, John Stuart, greeted the newcomers warmly. He had twice crossed the continent and had reached the Pacific via the Columbia River. He had not been north of Great Slave Lake but knew that the Chipewyan who lived to the north of the lake would be able to help. Stuart also said that at Fort Chipewyan, sickness had recently decimated the hunters, reducing those present to subsisting on fishing, which barely supplied their needs. He expressed "much doubt" about hiring experienced voyageurs to travel to the Arctic coast "in consequence of their dread of the Esqimaux." He said those who had driven off John Clarke had also destroyed a crew who canoed north under a man named Livingstone to open trading relations. Sobering revelations all.

~

Stormy weather, drifting snow, and gale-force winds slowed their advance, but Back and Franklin reached Fort Chipewyan on March 26, 1820. The fort stood on a rocky rise on the western tip of Lake Athabasca, some 140 miles north of present-day Fort McMurray. Back described it as "the most regular and best constructed establishment we have seen in the country. It is the depot of the North and capable of containing some hundreds of persons." North West Company traders from Great Bear Lake to New Caledonia (interior British Columbia) would come here every spring before travelling almost 1,700 miles to Fort William (today part of Thunder Bay). Fort Chipewyan differed from the other posts, Back noted, "from being more extensive and having (what is termed an observation) about the centre of the principal building."

Looking back over the "disagreeable circumstances" of the journey, John Franklin declared walking in snowshoes the worst, as it involved marching with a weight of two or three pounds "attached to galled feet and swelled ankles." Secondly, he hated the way the voyageurs treated their dogs with "wanton and unnecessary cruelty" while venting on them "the most dreadful and disgusting imprecations."

On the other hand, he enjoyed the social mirth of those same men when, stretched out before a large fire, they traded tales of their former travels. "At this time the Canadians are always cheerful and merry, and the only bar to their comfort arises from the frequent interruption occasioned by the dogs, who are constantly prowling about the circle and snatching at every kind of food that happens to be within their reach." Eventually, the dogs would provide comfort because they would lie down beside the men.

Fort Chipewyan as it looked to George Back on May 27, 1820. He described it as "the most regular and best constructed establishment we have seen in the country."

Franklin also appreciated "the hospitable welcome" accorded a traveller at every trading post, when he enjoyed "being disrobed even for a short time of the trappings of a voyager and experiencing the pleasures of cleanliness."

On arrival, Franklin found Fort Chipewyan impressive. The HBC fort, one mile away, was far less grand. Given the difficult political context, Franklin and Back erected a tent halfway between the two company posts and hammered out arrangements, "each to furnish so much according to their resources." To advance, they would need at least twenty men who would travel in "light canoes with one month's provisions." They would hire Indigenous hunters during the winter and build a wooden dwelling on their advice somewhere near the Coppermine River. A North West Company man would attend to organize the Canadian voyageurs—one who could also communicate with the "Northern Indians" in their own language.

While ensconced at Fort Chipewyan, George Back drew an arresting sketch of the site. To his brother Charles, he also wrote a paper-saving cross-hatched letter—one featuring two sets of writing, one written over the other at right angles. This missive of more than three thousand words—vivid but rough and ungrammatical—appears as an appendix to his journal. Having last written from Cumberland House, Back describes his "winter's voyage of 800 miles on snowshoes three feet long," accompanied by dog sledges conveying provisions including pemmican "pounded and formed into one solid lump . . . oftentimes a delicate mixture of filth and long hair."

Back describes the daily routine: harnessing the dogs, donning snowshoes, beating a track for the dogs, taking the pleasure of the evening tea and pipe, and settling into a buffalo skin to sleep. "You lay with your feet to the fire, and your head entirely covered not daring to look out and equally heedless about the Wolves which are constantly howling around you and make frequent excursions in search of prey."

In an oft-quoted passage, he continued: "There was a wide difference between Franklin and me—and he suffered every evil I have mentioned whilst mine was a slight chafing in the toes occasioned by the Snow Shoes—he had never been accustomed to any vigorous exertion; besides his frame is bulky without activity . . . however before we got to the end of our journey, Franklin recovered and was as lively as any."

The party worried about being set upon by Assiniboine, or "Plains Indians," as they called them, and Back wrote of "these rascals" with tongue in cheek: "When they meet a party of voyageurs, being always the most numerous—they inevitably rob them—strip them of their clothing—and if they are in a good humour, give you an old Buffalo robe as a substitute for your dress—but if they spear your dogs—you have no chance of escaping—this is of no consequence as one might as well be killed by an arrow as to be frozen to death—We did not meet them therefore I had not an opportunity of witnessing their kindness."

Back added that "nothing but French is spoken about here the men being all Canadians—in this I'm at home." He devoted several hundred

"Manner of Making a Resting Place on a Winters Night," drawn by George Back, engraved by Edward Finden.

words to extending fond memories and best wishes, and then thought to add a characteristic postscript: "I was not frost bit the whole winter—the whole party except myself was."

CHAPTER 13

The Great Mustering

~

J ohn Franklin and George Back would spend almost four months at Fort Chipewyan, planning and preparing the onward journey. From François Beaulieu, a Métis interpreter who later became a widely feared Yellowknife leader, they received directions—"which we afterwards found tolerably correct"—about how to reach the Coppermine River. In mid-April, the migratory birds started returning and the snow began to disappear from the hills and the frozen lake. Peter Warren Dease, the HBC man who would later explore the Arctic coast with Thomas Simpson, shared his considerable expertise about the north country.

An old Chipewyan Dene man, Rabbit's Head, turned up—a stepson of Matonabbee, who had, as a young man, descended the Coppermine with Samuel Hearne. Franklin wrote that Rabbit's Head "was positive [Hearne] had reached the sea, though he admitted that none of the party had tasted the water. He represented himself to be the only survivor of that party."

As May 1820 unfolded and the fur traders of both the HBC and the NWC became busy preparing their first brigades to carry furs to Hudson Bay, Franklin felt forgotten. To his tent halfway between the two posts, he invited the managers of both companies to a joint meeting on May 25 and received assurances of assistance. He then asked the two companies to provide eight men each and to supply whatever stores they could spare. Volunteers were slow in coming forward, and those of the HBC in particular "demanded a much higher rate of wages than [Franklin] considered it proper to grant."

On June 3, an NWC partner named Edward Smith arrived from Great Slave Lake bringing word that the principal chief of the Yellowknives, Akaitcho, had welcomed news of the expedition. Along with Willard Ferdinand Wentzel of the NWC, he and his men had agreed to lead the way north as guides and hunters. They would wait at Fort Providence, on the north side of Great Slave Lake, and were confident they could "obtain the means of subsistence in travelling to the coast." This news raised the spirits of the Canadian voyageurs, and two more NWC men signed on to the expedition that evening.

Franklin and Back visited nearby Fort Wedderburn, where the HBC's Colin Robertson said that despite his urgings and admonitions, his most experienced men were demanding higher wages to join. Eventually, six HBC men signed on, all of them said to be "active and steady." Franklin asked Robertson that the first brigade to return from Hudson Bay should bring forward the supplies he had left at York Factory and seventy-five miles upriver at Rock House.

In response to the scarcity of provisions, Franklin sent his voyageurs—three of them with wives—to a nearby lake where they could subsist by fishing. By June 9, the senior fur traders of both companies had departed southward with their canoe brigades. Franklin sent letters to Richardson and Hood back at Cumberland House informing them that food was scarce. He sent a letter north officially inviting Wentzel to join the expedition. He asked him to go to Fort Providence to reassure the waiting Yellowknives that he was coming. He had learned that he had best not go without "the articles . . . with which they expected to be presented on my arrival," which Richardson and Hood would bring forward.

In mid-June, as temperatures rose, Franklin complained of the swarming mosquitoes, which "tormented us so incessantly by their irritating stings that we were compelled to keep our rooms constantly filled with smoke, which is the only means of driving them away." On July 2, the HBC men presented the expedition with a newly built canoe measuring thirty-two and a half feet by four feet ten inches. Franklin marvelled at how "these feeble vessels of bark will carry twenty-five pieces of goods, each weighing ninety pounds," plus food and baggage for five or six men, the total amounting to 3,300 pounds. He noted that a bowman and a steersman guided the canoes through rapids and at the portages, and "these two men carry the canoe, and they often run with it, though its weight is estimated at about three hundred pounds," not counting the poles and oars, often left inside. Franklin tested the canoe on July 5 and, when a heavy gale arose, causing a great swell in the lake, declared it to be "an excellent sea-boat."

~

On July 13, at Fort Chipewyan, Franklin welcomed the arrival of Richardson and Hood, whose "zeal and talent" elicited his "highest approbation." Back in mid-January, when Franklin had set out northward from Cumberland House with George Back and John Hepburn, needing to hire guides, hunters, and interpreters, Richardson and Hood had stayed behind to take meteorological and magnetic observations, analyze the aurora borealis, describe the people and culture of the area, and collect minerals, flora, and fauna.

Also, they needed to await supplies forwarded from York Factory and elsewhere, and then to hire as many voyageurs as they could. Early in the year, they had had their own adventures. On February 10, wolves decimated fish sledges that were on their way to Cumberland House. These animals became ferocious, and one devoured a dog at the stockade gates. On the eighteenth, a wolf attacked two men, who fought it off with hatchets. Meanwhile, Richardson and Hood received a letter from Franklin indicating that heavy snow had made the trek north difficult and that he had frozen his fingers while taking observations for latitude.

By March, the snow lay three feet deep on the lakes and drifting confined the men to the stockade. Spring brought sunshine and temperatures above freezing. The Saskatchewan River began thawing and opened into a channel on April 5. One week later, swans, geese, and ducks began arriving in the area. Mid-month brought rains, rising temperatures, and a deluge of melting snow. Reports of vegetation at Carlton House, some distance west, inspired Richardson to visit and collect botanical specimens.

He and Hood had to delay their northward departure until June 13, when they finally had enough expert men to handle two canoes. They were dismayed that the two fur-trading companies could provide only two barrels of powder, a keg of spirits, two pieces of tobacco, and enough pemmican for just sixteen days. Richardson's canoe carried three Orcadians and three Canadian voyageurs, while Hood travelled with five voyageurs. Both craft were heavily laden. And now the sailors learned, as Hood wrote, "that canoes were not calculated to brave rough weather on a large lake." They were forced to land on the far shore, their cargo already saturated.

When the wind moderated, they crossed smaller lakes and camped near the mouth of the Sturgeon River. The Canadians called it La Rivière Maligne, or "the wicked river," because it presented a run of almost continuous rapids while dropping ninety-one feet in twenty-three miles. According to Hood, the Canadians showed great dexterity in propelling the canoes by paddling or using poles, in contrast to "the awkward confusion of the inexperienced Englishmen [Orcadians], deafened by the torrent, who sustained the blame of every accident which occurred. Any collision with a sharp rock or corner would damage the bark of a canoe, which then had to be repaired with a mix of gum, bark, and roots."

On June 19, the men landed at Otter Portage, where the river ran fast through large stones for half a mile. After carrying across most of the cargo, the men began tracking, or hauling the canoes, along the edge of the rapids. They got the first through, but the second overturned, throwing both bowman and steersman into the current. Richardson wrote, "Mr. Hood himself was the first to leap into the [original] canoe and incite the men to follow him and shoot the rapid to save the lives of their companions."

The men raced downstream to where the overturned canoe floated in a little bay. They saw that one man had struggled out onto the riverbank but the other, bowman Louis Saint Jean, had disappeared forever. They managed to repair the canoe, though not to recover two guns and a case of preserved meat. Hood wrote that this "early disaster deeply affected the spirits of the Canadians, and their natural vivacity gave way to melancholy foreboding, while they erected a wooden cross on the rocks near the spot where their companion perished."

Meanwhile, mosquitoes were driving the men to distraction. Hood described them as "a plague which had grown upon us since our departure from Cumberland House, and which infested us during the whole summer. We found no relief from their attacks by exposing ourselves to the utmost violence of the wind and rain. Our last resource was to plunge ourselves in the water."

The death of Louis Saint Jean left the travellers without an expert guide and bowman. On June 21, they borrowed a man who worked for Colin Robertson of the Hudson's Bay Company, and two days later, encountering the last brigades heading south, they managed to hire a replacement. This was fortunate as navigating the twenty-two miles of Black Bear Island Lake required an experienced pilot. On June 26, after traversing Knee Lake in a thick fog, the men fairly flew across Primeau Lake with a strong and favourable wind.

Two days later, on Lac Île-à-la-Crosse, heavy winds drove Richardson into a deep bay. When he reached the fort on the twenty-ninth, he found Hood already installed. Île-à-la-Crosse, roughly halfway to Fort Chipewyan, was the last notable fur-trade centre along the route. It marked the boundary between the southern and northern Indigenous Peoples, the Cree and the Chipewyan.

Here, some 450 miles west and north of Cumberland House, those in charge of both company forts provided the expedition with what supplies they could. Fortunately, Franklin had requested that ten bags of pemmican be sent here across the plains for their use. The party could transport only five of these, but John McLeod of the NWC agreed to send the rest via canoe to Methye Portage, by which point they would have eaten enough to take on the added weight.

At Methye Lake, also known as Lac La Loche, the men made separate portages of five and two miles, battling fallen trees and cold streams. "We should have been contented to immerse ourselves wholly [in these waters]," Hood wrote, "had the puddle been sufficiently deep, for the mosquitoes devoured every part that was exposed to them." On this subject, the midshipman was moved to eloquence. Having reached the Clearwater River, he described how "we had sometimes before procured a little rest [from the mosquitoes] by closing the tent and burning wood, or flashing gun powder within, the smoke driving the mosquitoes into the crannies of the ground. But this remedy was now ineffectual, though we employed it so perseveringly as to incur suffocation. They swarmed under our blankets, goring us with the envenomed trunks, and steeping our clothes in blood. We rose at daylight in a fever, and our misery was unmitigated during our whole stay."

While more than thirty subtly different species of mosquito occur in the region that now contains Saskatchewan and Alberta, Hood identified two main ones, the largest brown, the smallest black. They appeared in May, and in July were most voracious. "The food of the mosquito is blood," Hood writes, "which it can extract by penetrating the hide of a buffalo, and if it is not disturbed, it gorges itself so to swell its body into a transparent globe . . . The wound does not swell, like that of the African mosquito, but it is infinitely more painful, and when multiplied an hundred fold, and continued for many successive days, it becomes an evil of such magnitude that cold, famine, and every other concomitant of the inhospitable climate must yield the pre-eminence to it. It chases the buffalo to the plains, irritating him to madness, and the reindeer to the sea shore, from which they do not return till the scourge has ceased."

~

Methye Portage, twelve miles long, marked the Great Divide between rivers flowing west and north to the Mackenzie Basin and those running east to Hudson Bay and the Atlantic. On July 8, 1820, two voyageurs arrived at the camp, having brought forward ten bags of pemmican from Île-à-la-Crosse. The contents proved to be rotten. Richardson and Hood selected the two least mouldy bags and debarked, leaving the other eight on the beach. Four days later, at 9 p.m., the men landed on the banks of a small branch of the Athabasca River and set up camp near what turned out to be a nest of mosquitoes. They fled before daybreak. Assisted by a strong wind, the travellers crossed Lake Athabasca to Fort Chipewyan, arriving before noon on July 13. Like Franklin and Back before them, they had journeyed 860 miles from Cumberland House.

John Franklin wrote later that he and George Back "had the sincere gratification of welcoming our long-separated friends, Dr. Richardson and Mr. Hood, who arrived in perfect health with two canoes . . . The zeal and talent displayed by [these two] in the discharge of their several duties since my separation from them drew forth my highest approbation. These gentlemen had brought all the stores they could procure from the establishments at Cumberland House and Isle à la Crosse."

Alas, this meant they brought next to nothing. Franklin mentioned the mouldy pemmican received from the NWC and noted that voyageurs supplied by the HBC, "being destitute of provision, had eaten what was intended for us." *Did these men really need to eat?* Bottom line: Fort Chipewyan could not "furnish the means of subsistence for so large a party."

Richardson and Hood had brought just enough that, with what he was able to squeeze out of the two fur-trading companies, Franklin "rejoiced to find that . . . we had a sufficient quantity of clothing for the equipment of the men who had been engaged here, as well as to furnish a present to the Indians." He did not, however, have enough spirits, tobacco, or ammunition, this last essential for hunting and subsistence.

Richardson and Hood also brought ten men keen to join the expedition. Franklin discharged those who were less willing to continue north, among them the four Orcadians who had signed on to travel this far and no farther. Now the expedition comprised the four officers, that faithful English seaman John Hepburn, sixteen Canadian voyageurs, the Chipewyan wife of one of them, and two interpreters waiting to be added at Great Slave Lake.

On July 18, five days after the arrival of Richardson and Hood, the expedition set out northward from Fort Chipewyan in three canoes with enough food for a single day. Franklin reported that "this scarcity of food did not depress the spirits of our Canadian companions, who cheerfully loaded their canoes and embarked in high glee after receiving the customary dram . . . The crews commenced a lively paddling song on quitting the shore and sang until they had left behind all signs of habitation."

CHAPTER 14

Akaitcho Leads
the Way

~

By July of 1820, John Franklin and his First Arctic Land Expedition had penetrated deep into the territory dominated by the "Northern Indians," as Franklin called them. These Dene Peoples spoke Athabaskan and had long been rivals and sometime enemies of the Cree. They hunted and fished through most of present-day Northwest Territories, edging north into what is now Nunavut. Subgroups of the Dene included the Dogrib, Slavey, and Chipewyan, whose name derives from an Algonquian Cree word referring to the wearing of beaver-skin shirts with backs that narrowed to a point at the bottom, like contemporary tails. The Yellowknife, or "Copper Indians," as European settlers called them because they used copper tools, were the most northerly of the Chipewyan. Numbering about 190, they spoke a distinctive dialect and contested territories traditionally controlled by the Inuit.

Like the Cree, the Dene responded to the demands of the environment by functioning mainly as extended families. Local bands might include 6 to 30 hunters, or 30 to 140 persons. Such groupings were often culturally diverse because of intermarriages, adoptions, and the widespread stealing of wives from different communities. The remarkable eighteenth-century interpreter Thanadelthur, for example, had been born

Chipewyan and, in her teens, was taken prisoner by the Cree. She escaped to live among HBC fur traders at Fort York, from where she helped create a peace between the Chipewyan and the Cree.

North beyond the Chipewyan lands lay the treeless tundra dominated by the Inuit, who extended across the Arctic from Alaska to Greenland. The Cree called them "Esquimaux," meaning "eaters of raw meat." The Inuit constituted a single people, as Danish ethnologist-explorer Knud Rasmussen would demonstrate early in the twentieth century. The many different groupings could understand each other because they spoke related languages: Yup'ik in the west, Inuktitut in the east, and Kalaallisut in Greenland. The Inuit hunted caribou, but also fish and sea mammals such as seals, walruses, and beluga whales.

The Inuit of the far northwest were not friendly with the Dene, who were beginning to acquire European muskets and guarded their role as fur-trading middlemen. Such was the background against which the expedition set out for Fort Providence. On the Slave River, soon after leaving Fort Chipewyan, the travellers entered a rapids that, according to George Back, whirled the canoes "about in every direction." At seven they camped on a swampy riverbank, but then came a terrible thunderstorm, when "the rain fell in torrents and the violence of the wind caused the river to overflow its banks, so that we were completely flooded." When the rain ceased, attacking swarms of mosquitoes "induced us to embark . . . and pursue our voyage down the stream during the night."

Next morning, Back wrote, the party traversed "several shoots and rapids and after landing to breakfast on the last remnant of rotten pemican (for we had not a day's provisions amongst us)," resumed paddling. At the entrance to the Dog River, they halted and set out their fishing nets but caught only four small trout. Overnight, they added a solitary pike.

At Dog Rapid, two of the canoes smashed into each other so violently that one had its bow broken off and its bark split to the water's edge on both sides. Fortunately, this happened near shore and the voyageurs managed to repair the craft in two hours. Another accident happened at Little

Rock Portage, when the bowman slipped and dropped the canoe onto a rock, breaking it in two. This repair, which involved sewing the pieces together and covering the seam with pitch, took another two hours. On July 22, after rounding a bend, the men saw a buffalo plunge into the river and four of them instantly opened fire with their muskets. The great creature fell, "but not before he had received fourteen balls." Having secured the meat, the party "descended the stream merrily, our voyageurs chanting their liveliest songs."

The next couple of days found the men battling heavy winds. But on July 25, having travelled 260 miles from Fort Chipewyan, they reached the south shore of Great Slave Lake and nearby Moose Deer Island, which is about one mile in diameter. At the NWC post on the island, called "the Slave Fort," they received letters from Willard Wentzel, who was waiting on the north side of the lake at Fort Providence. A guide was still there, he reported, but the chief and his hunters had grown impatient and moved off a short distance for better hunting.

On Moose Deer Island, Franklin visited the HBC post Fort Resolution, which Back described as much inferior to that of the NWC. It consisted "merely of a dwelling house and a store with a few miserable stockades in the front to prevent the NW men from beholding what is going on." Together, the two fur-trade companies managed to provide the expedition with 550 pounds of provisions, along with three fishing nets, a single musket, and a pair of pistols. Here on Moose Deer Island in Great Slave Lake, Franklin engaged Pierre St. Germain, a Métis (Dene-French) interpreter fluent in English, French, and Athabascan. St. Germain knew his own worth, prompting Franklin to complain, "This man required three thousand livres Halifax [two and a half times the wage of the average canoe middleman], which we were obliged to give him as his services were indispensable."

Because of heavy winds, the men made their way to Fort Providence on the far north side of the lake by hugging the shore. Here, at this solitary NWC outpost, Franklin met Wentzel, originally from Norway, who spoke several languages. He also met a second interpreter, Jean Baptiste Adam, and an Indigenous guide. Wentzel had undertaken to recruit guides, hunters, and interpreters. He announced the arrival of the expedition to all and sundry by building a fire on the top of a hill. Before long a messenger brought word that Akaitcho, the Dene leader, would come the following day.

～

For the past decade, while functioning as paramount leader among the Chipewyan Dene, Akaitcho had led a band of about forty in trading at Fort Providence as meat provisioners—an arrangement that allowed them to retain a high degree of autonomy. Willard Wentzel counselled the importance of ceremony, formality, and respect for the seriousness of the occasion, and so the four naval officers donned their uniforms—the "remnants of our European apparel," as Robert Hood put it—and hung medals around their necks. Akaitcho and his companions had been hunting and fishing nearby, waiting impatiently for the expedition to arrive. On the afternoon of July 30, they landed below Fort Providence in several canoes.

Akaitcho debarked from the first of these. He wore a blanket over a white cloak. On landing, Franklin writes, "the chief assumed a very grave aspect and walked up to Mr. Wentzel with a measured and dignified step, looking neither to the right nor to the left at the persons who had assembled on the beach to witness his debarkation, but preserving the same immovability of countenance until he reached the hall and was introduced to the officers."

The name Akaitcho, translated as "Gros Pied" or "Big Foot," suggested that, like a wolf with big paws, the chief could range rapidly over long distances in the snow. Franklin wrote that he was considered a man "of great penetration and shrewdness." Born around 1786, he was now, like Franklin, in his mid-thirties. He was known among voyageurs and fur traders to have terrorized nearby tribes of Dogrib, Hare, and Slavey, stealing furs and women and killing those who opposed him.

At first meeting, Akaitcho strove to communicate dignity and significance. He smoked a ceremonial pipe, downed spirits, and commenced what Franklin called "his harangue," rehearsing the circumstances that had led him to this moment. Akaitcho rejoiced, Franklin reported, "to see such great chiefs on his lands; his tribe were poor, but they loved white men who had been their benefactors; and he hoped that our visit would be productive of much good to them." Franklin responded in the same vein, remarking that he and his men had been "sent out by the great-

Yellowknife Dene leader Akaitcho and his son as depicted by Robert Hood.

est chief in the world, who was the sovereign also of the trading companies in the country." They had come to search for a sea passage that would "enable large vessels to transport great quantities of goods more easily to their lands." He sought Akaitcho's assistance "in guiding us and providing us with food."

The Great Chief across the water hoped local hostilities would cease, Franklin said, "especially between the Indians and the Esquimaux, whom he considered his children, in common with other natives." Franklin then had to explain that he was too short of supplies to distribute much at the moment, but after completing the expedition and arriving at Churchill, he would remunerate Akaitcho handsomely with cloth, ammunition, tobacco, and iron materials, and forgive the band's debts to the North West Company.

The chief replied, Hood wrote, "that he would attend us with his young men to the end of our journey; that the white people had always been friendly to the Indians [who had previously] lived by snaring, and shooting deer with arrows, which means of obtaining food and clothing were not to be depended upon . . . That their distress had often been great, till the white people brought them guns and cloth." The Yellowknife leader acknowledged that his people "had long since made war upon the Esquimaux at the sea, but that peace was desired by his tribe more than war." According to Franklin, Akaitcho then added that "the Esquimaux had never met a stranger whom they did not find an enemy, and that they would probably regard us as such, at first."

The guides now used charcoal to sketch maps on the ground while debating the best route through a chain of two dozen lakes to the Coppermine River. One of the men, an older brother to Akaitcho called White Capot, said he had travelled with the Chipewyan hunter Matonabbee and the English fur trader Samuel Hearne fifty years before on their journey to the Arctic coast. Unlike Rabbit's Head, White Capot could not say for sure whether Hearne had reached the sea.

Akaitcho proposed a certain lakeside location for a winter base some three days' journey from the Coppermine, where they would find trees and plenty of wood for building. Franklin and his officers took the medals from around their own necks and gave them to Akaitcho and his lieutenants. To ten hunters who would go forward they gave cloth, blankets, tobacco, knives, daggers, and guns, along with a keg of weak spirits.

The Yellowknives stayed nearby so that the next night, they could attend a celebration being organized by the Canadian voyageurs, at which everyone would sing and dance. So it happened that on the evening of July 31, 1820, little more than two weeks after rejoining Franklin, Dr. John Richardson found himself at Fort Providence on Great Slave Lake, talking with Akaitcho. Someone had told the Dene leader that the English had brought a medicine man with magical powers. Akaitcho had a particular case in mind—the wife of Keskarrah, a fellow leader, who had an ulcer on her face. Richardson had to insist through an interpreter that he could treat conditions and sometimes ease suffering but could not work miracles.

The previous night, acting on the advice of Wentzel, Richardson and Franklin had overseen the pitching of several tents. They had raised a silk Union Jack flag above the tent they shared. Tonight, with the Canadian voyageurs taking the lead, people fell to drinking, drumming, singing, and dancing. Richardson was enjoying the festivities when the biggest tent, the one he occupied with Franklin, suddenly burst into flames and collapsed into a heap. As usual, they had placed some embers in the tent to smoke out mosquitoes. Fortunately, John Hepburn had been dozing inside. He had startled awake, grabbed a nearby box of gunpowder, and stumbled out into the open air just as the tent crashed to the ground behind him.

After the men had beat out the flames, Richardson encouraged everyone to resume dancing. He and Franklin wanted to avoid any idea that the tent fire might be an omen of things to come. Akaitcho waived off that worry but, as George Back reported, expressed concern that his people might be blamed: "My young men are not rogues that they should do this thing." He voiced his dismay that the flag had been burned, but Franklin assured him that the party had another.

Next morning, August 1, the Dene guides set out northward, promising to wait at the mouth of the Yellowknife River. The naval men had deliberately delayed, wanting not to excite cravings as they apportioned goods by laying them out the ground. The voyageurs packed the provisions into eighty-pound bales. Hood wrote that these included "a few unserviceable guns, eight pistols, 24 broad daggers, two barrels of powder and balls for 2/3 of that quantity . . . Our provision was two barrels of flour, two cases of chocolate, two canisters of tea, 200 dried reindeer tongues, and portable soups, arrowroot, and dried moose meat for ten days."

The guides now proposed a shorter route to the Coppermine than the one they had first suggested to Wentzel, explaining that they would find more reindeer along this track. To estimate how long the overall journey would take, Franklin wrote, they needed to see "our manner of travelling in the large canoes." He began to hope that he might have time before winter to make an explorative journey partway down the Coppermine, if not to the sea itself. At one point, when he mentioned possibly meeting a discovery ship under the command of Edward Parry, Akaitcho impressed him by asking "why a passage had not been discovered long ago, if one existed."

Franklin engaged another voyageur here at Fort Providence. This brought the existing complement to twenty-eight persons, including the four officers; Willard Wentzel and John Hepburn; and the two interpreters, Pierre St. Germain and Jean Baptiste Adam, whom Franklin identified as Métis but Chipewyan–French Canadian rather than Cree–French Canadian. The voyageurs included Joseph Peltier; two Belanger brothers (Solomon and Jean-Baptiste, or J.B.); Gabriel Beauparlant, who attached himself particularly to George Back; and Michel Teroahaute, who was Iroquois. There were also three children, not counted, and three wives of voyageurs, who came along to care for them and to do most of the cooking.

On the evening of August 2, the expedition debarked in four large canoes and a small one carrying women and children. The men were in high spirits, heartily glad to at last be on their way to the Coppermine River. The next afternoon, Akaitcho and his hunters and some additional Yellowknives joined the travellers: "We were soon surrounded by a fleet of seventeen Indian canoes," Franklin wrote, and in that company, the voyageurs paddled along the river.

The navy men discovered that, at the portages, they could not keep up with the Yellowknives, who needed to carry their small canoes across only once, while the voyageurs had to retrace their steps three or four times to transport all the cargo in their large canoes. "We soon perceived," Hood wrote, "that they had overcalculated our speed in supposing it possible for us to reach the source of the river in ten days."

Every day brought four or five portages. Akaitcho directed his men to assist the expedition at the portages, and Hood reports that they cheerfully complied. The man "exercised an authority over his band to which no chief among the Crees has any pretensions." He remained aloof from his followers, staying in a canvas tent with his two wives, "and carefully avoiding all manual labour." Two young men paddled his canoe—his son and a young Dogrib man he had adopted as his servant—or taken as his slave, depending on who you asked.

Akaitcho "narrowly watched all our motions," Hood wrote, "and made rational enquiries on subjects that excited his curiosity." At night, the men and officers divided into watches. The Chipewyan chief, "who suffered nothing to escape his observation, remarked that he should sleep without anxiety among the Esquimaux, for he perceived that no enemy could surprise us."

At three o'clock one morning, a mother's loud shriek signalled that a child had fallen seriously ill. George Back reported that people crowded into the tent, where some "commenced howling—some crying—and others tried to sing the child well—when Doctor Richardson went over and gave it some medicine which soon afforded relief." A good omen, surely.

During one conversation, George Back wrote, Akaitcho told him that "he had a great wish to see a ship, and wherever we went—he would accompany us—from this and many other circumstances we expected to reach the sea during the summer." This anticipation would give rise to disappointment.

Initially, to establish his importance, Franklin wrote, Akaitcho had his canoe paddled "by his slave, a young man of the Dog-Rib Nation, whom he had taken by force from his friends." When he thought he was out of sight, however, Akaitcho paddled too. After a few days, "he did not hesitate to paddle in our presence, or even carry his canoe on the portages."

Certain humbling truths began to emerge at Bowstring Portage, a trek of 1,300 yards over a rocky hill, where Franklin found "that the Indians had greatly the advantage of us in this operation. The men carried their small canoes and the women and children the clothes and provisions.

Once over, they would be ready to go. The men of the expedition, however, had to return three or four times to transport the heavy cargo."

On August 4, difficult portages caused more delays. Next day the expedition tackled five portages and camped at a sixth. The hard-working party had eaten everything but a few portable soups and a few pounds of preserved meat. Akaitcho suggested that Franklin supply some hunters with ammunition and send them forward. Other Indigenous hunters, also growing hungry, "decided on separating from us and going on at a quicker pace than we could travel."

Next day, the voyageurs beat their way over another mile-long portage. They camped and caught a few fish, George Back wrote, "but we had a very scanty supper as it was necessary to deal out our provision sparingly." He added, "The perpetual fatigue of transporting canoes across the portages had harassed the men considerably and having no other sustenance than bad dried meat—it is only surprising how they maintained sufficient strength to perform their daily labour."

On the morning of August 7, after finding the fishing nets entirely empty, the discouraged voyageurs "complained of being unable to support the fatigue to which they were daily exposed on their present scanty fare." If this continued, they feared that their strength would fail. George Back wrote, "The Canadians complained here of a want of provisions though they well knew—by having more—they must suffer for it hereafter. Still, they are of that gormandizing disposition as to be never satisfied without wallowing in profuseness, and as long as any part remains . . . they never cease grumbling till they get it. There are few circumstances more galling to the feelings than to be with a set of people over whom you have no immediate control—this was our case—and we were obliged to make an addition to their allowance."

That night at 2 a.m., the wind carried embers from the campfire to the surrounding moss. The men on watch acted quickly, but soon flames encircled the site, threatening to destroy canoes and baggage. The watchmen roused their comrades and, after what Back described as "half an hour's thrashing," the travellers managed to extinguish the fire. Next day, after traversing five difficult portages, "the men were quite exhausted with fatigue by five P.M." They set the fishing nets at the edge of a lake.

Back wrote that "the Indians had been starving for some days but the expectation of meeting the hunters who had advanced for the purpose of killing animals—seemed to sustain their drooping spirits." Franklin doled out some portable soup and arrowroot. The men relished this fare but found it "too insubstantial to support their vigour under their exhausting labour, and we could not furnish them with a sufficient quantity even of this to satisfy their desires."

Evening brought heavy rains, which lasted until 4 a.m. The men set out in "a very wet uncomfortable state" and, after portaging around two tough, stony rapids, camped at a lake that Akaitcho identified as providing good fishing. He himself went ahead to see how the hunters were faring and promised to build a signal fire if they killed any deer. Of the Chipewyan, only two remained with the expedition: Keskarrah and his wife, Birdseye, whose facial ulcer was being treated by Dr. Richardson.

The voyageurs caught only four carp but found a great many blueberries. On August 11, after catching and eating some trout, whitefish, and carp—enough for two hearty meals—the expedition resumed travelling. They met a Dene man who had spotted several fires, indicating a successful hunt. This energized the voyageurs, who started a long portage. Franklin and Back climbed five hundred feet to the top of what they called "Prospect Hill" and there found Akaitcho surveying the lands around. He pointed to the distant smoke of fires—more Dene people.

CHAPTER 15

The Indispensable St. Germain

~

In the first-ever history of Red River Settlement, *The Fur Hunters of the Far West*, colonist Alexander Ross devoted pages to paraphrasing an aging voyageur he had met while travelling in the 1830s. An abridged version of that long passage evokes the spirit of the Métis voyageurs who travelled with John Franklin—and that in particular of Pierre St. Germain: "I could carry, paddle, walk and sing with any man I ever saw. I have been twenty-four years a canoe man, and forty-one years in service; no portage was ever too long for me. Fifty songs I could sing. I have saved the lives of ten voyageurs. Have had twelve wives and six running dogs. I spent all my money in pleasure. Were I young again, I should spend my life the same way over. There is no life so happy as a voyageur's life!"

Born around 1790, St. Germain doubled as an interpreter, tripled as a hunter, and by 1820, commanded a wage two and a half times that of the typical canoe middleman. Probably he stood no more than five foot six, as taller men struggled within the confines of the heavily laden canoes. The Athabasca men, like those Franklin hired, resided permanently in the far northwest, in the *pays d'en haut*. They were masters of the birchbark canoe, that brilliant invention of the Algonquians. The best of the voyageurs knew how to repair the craft and could even transform a single *canot du maître*, or Montreal canoe, of thirty-five or forty feet into two *canots du nord*, each of them half that length.

Pierre St. Germain was one of the best. He had spent six years serving in the Athabasca District with the North West Company. In 1819, he transferred to the HBC and moved to Fort Resolution on Great Slave Lake, where he worked as an interpreter. In an 1821 letter, Hudson's Bay Company governor George Simpson would reflect the rivalry between the fur-trade concerns when he wrote, "St. Germain is out of a bad nest [the NWC] and I trust we shall soon be able to shake off this fraternity. I expect a few attached English half-breeds into the country next season and then we shall be more independent of N.W. renegadoes." That would come later.

On June 5, 1820, the HBC's senior man in the district, Colin Robertson, wrote Robert McVicar at Fort Resolution giving permission for St. Germain to join Franklin's overland expedition. Describing him as "an intelligent young man," Robertson wrote, "I have given up an excellent Chipewyan interpreter, St. Germain." McVicar had mixed feelings about releasing the man. He called St. Germain indispensable and noted that he could travel seemingly forever without so much as a blanket or provisions, relying on his skill as a hunter.

But McVicar also noted that St. Germain was strong-minded and given to revelry and strong drink. Case in point: On December 1, 1819, McVicar sent the voyageur on business from desolate Fort Resolution to Fort Wedderburn near the fur-trade centre of Fort Chipewyan, telling him to return promptly. St. Germain delayed his departure to attend New Year's celebrations and did not arrive back until January 20. "His long stay," McVicar wrote, "shows a complete contempt for the interests of the concern." Later, McVicar would write of "that scoundrel's machinations" and call him "a dangerous man."

Having gained permission to join the Royal Navy expedition, Pierre St. Germain drove a hard bargain with Franklin, who noted, "He is represented to be a most valuable man and bears an excellent character." Direct and forthright, St. Germain signed on for that hefty wage and came aboard at Fort Resolution on July 24, 1820. Five days later, Willard Wentzel and Jean Baptiste Adam joined the party at Fort Providence, but neither could rival St. Germain's fluency in French, English, and Chipewyan. His language skills, his abilities as a hunter, and his expertise in repairing birchbark canoes made him a natural leader among both the Dene and the Métis.

Paddling and trekking north, the hard-working voyageurs needed food. On August 13, at a location Franklin later called "Dissension Lake," they said that if they didn't get it, they would proceed no farther. Writing of his rejection of their ultimatum, Franklin adopted a tough but reasonable and even sympathetic tone—although without accepting any responsibility. Nor did he acknowledge that he had lost his temper and ended up roaring at the men. The twenty small fish caught that morning "furnished but a scanty breakfast for the party," he admitted.

George Back wrote that while the fish were being cooked, the Canadian voyageurs "who had been for some days past murmuring at their meagre diet . . . broke out into open discontent, and several of them threatened they would not proceed forward unless more food was given them." This conduct was "the more unpardonable," Franklin wrote, "as the men could see the fires of the hunters in the distance, where they could reasonably expect more food. I, therefore, felt the duty incumbent upon me to address them in the strongest manner on the danger of insubordination, and to assure them of my determination to inflict the heaviest punishment on any that should persist in their refusal to go on, or in any other way attempt to retard the Expedition."

Franklin justified his hard line by explaining that the Canadian voyageurs invariably tested the limits of "every new master" and would "continue to be disobedient and intractable" if he did not nip their complaining in the bud. He had to admit, however—and here we have the retrospective sympathy—"that the present hardships of our companions were of a kind which few could support without murmuring, and no one could witness without a sincere pity for their sufferings."

George Back would more vividly depict how Franklin quelled the revolt. He described how at about 10 a.m., "a mutinous spirit displayed itself amongst the men." Indeed, "they refused to carry the goods any farther, alleging a scarcity of provisions for their conduct." In response, Franklin snapped. He told the men, "we were too far removed from justice to treat them as they merited, but if such a thing occurred again he would not hesitate to make an example of the first person who should come forward by 'blowing out his brains.'"

Back added that "this salutary speech had a weighty effect on the weather cock minds of the Canadians—who without further animadversion returned quietly to their duty." As for the "first person" Franklin had in mind, everyone understood he was referring to Pierre St. Germain, who had emerged as the de facto leader of the voyageurs. After quelling this "apprehended insurrection," Franklin wrote, "we went forward until sunset."

Seven portages later, the men set up camp and joyfully welcomed the arrival of four Dene hunters bringing the meat of two deer. This would be enough to last only through the next day, yet "instantly revived the spirits of our companions." Franklin added that they "immediately forgot all their cares." Over the next while, the hunters provided enough food and the men "worked extremely well, and never again reflected upon us as they had done before, for rashly bringing them into an inhospitable country where the means of subsistence could not be procured."

∿

When the expedition reached Grizzly Bear Lake, St. Germain went hunting with Akaitcho and his men. This party returned bringing meat, having left still more "en cache." While the women prepared this over a slow fire, another successful hunt produced a total of seventeen deer—enough meat to get the party to Winter Lake, their destination. Akaitcho said he wished to absent himself for ten days to hunt and provide clothing for his family.

Franklin writes that he sent "St. Germain to accompany [Akaitcho], that his absence might not exceed the appointed time." Far more likely, given the recent altercation, the interpreter simply announced that he was going hunting with Akaitcho.

In his narrative, which obviously he was writing for a British audience, Franklin offers an aside meant to undermine the expertise of the Dene chief and assert his own superior wisdom. He writes that before leaving, Akaitcho "warned us to be constantly on our guard against the grizzly bears, which he described as being numerous in this vicinity, and very ferocious. One had been seen this day by an Indian, to which circumstance the lake owes its appellation. We afterwards learned that the only bear in this part of the country is the brown bear, and that this by no means possesses the ferocity which the Indians, with their usual love of exaggeration, ascribe to it. The fierce grizzly bear . . . is not found on the barren grounds."

In fact, grizzlies are most certainly found in that area. Today, four or five thousand grizzlies inhabit the Northwest Territories, the highest concentration in the mountains west of the Mackenzie River. Compared with other bears, grizzlies range widely, the males often covering more than two thousand square kilometres—and of course they roamed in this area during Franklin's time. The lieutenant tended to believe he was right when he was wrong.

On August 19, 1820, Franklin reached the east end of Winter Lake. He and his fellow officers climbed the nearby hills, gazed around, and judged the prospect of spending several months in this vicinity less than agreeable. Trees were few and their wood less than ideal for building. Next morning, the men paddled to the west end of the lake and crossed a river to its north bank, and there "the Indians recommended that the winter establishment be erected." The trees were numerous, and some were thirty or forty feet high—far larger than they had looked from a distance.

The site "possessed all the advantages we could desire," Franklin wrote, and the officers decided to build their big house at the top of a riverbank with "a beautiful prospect of the surrounding country." That afternoon,

Franklin wrote, "we read divine service and offered our thanksgiving to the Almighty for his goodness in having brought us thus far on our journey; a duty which we never neglected when stationary on the sabbath." The men built a fire on the river's south bank to signal their arrival to the distant Akaitcho. Alas, they lost control in the wind, the fire spread, and "we were completely enveloped in a cloud of smoke for the three following days."

On the morning of August 25, Franklin noticed early signs of winter—small pools freezing over and a wedge of geese flying south. That afternoon brought a heavy fog. Franklin put some of the voyageurs to work cutting wood for a storehouse, others to fetching meat. The English seaman John Hepburn had gone hunting that morning and failed to return. Two hunters went searching but failed to find him. To Franklin's relief, searchers would finally locate him on the twenty-seventh. He had got lost in the fog and had been wandering ever since, having eaten only a partridge, some berries, and part of a deer he had shot. After a hearty supper, he retired, slept soundly, and "arose next morning in perfect health."

Meanwhile, on the afternoon of the twenty-fifth, Akaitcho arrived back at Winter Lake with fifteen deer—far fewer than anticipated. By way of explanation, Pierre St. Germain said the chief had learned of the death of his brother-in-law and "had spent several days in bewailing his loss instead of hunting." Franklin found this unacceptable. He made no effort to hide his displeasure—indeed, his outrage. But evening would bring a worse development: the "refusal by Akaitcho to accompany us in the proposed descent of the Coppermine River."

CHAPTER 16

The Dene Leader's Question

~

S tarting in August 1820, soon after they left Fort Providence, Franklin and Akaitcho found themselves increasingly at odds. During their first meeting, late in July, Akaitcho believed and declared that before winter came on, he would accompany the expedition on a scouting sortie to the mouth of the Coppermine River. Through August, however, during the journey to Winter Lake, the Dene leader got a good look at how Franklin and his men travelled.

At Winter Lake on August 25, when Akaitcho returned from hunting, Franklin sent Willard Wentzel to communicate "my intention of proceeding at once" to the mouth of the Coppermine River. Akaitcho sent word that he wanted to discuss that and invited Franklin to his tent. When the navy man arrived, the Dene leader began by stating that trying to descend the Coppermine at this time of year "would be rash and dangerous."

The weather had turned cold, leaves were falling, geese were flying south. Winter was upon them. A short distance north, where the land was without trees, travellers would be unable to build fires. From here at Winter Lake, a party would need forty days to reach the mouth of the Coppermine. Meanwhile, ice would block the river and, as the deer had already left the area, travellers would suffer for lack of food. Such a journey would threaten the lives of all who went. Akaitcho would neither go himself nor permit his hunters to go.

Most of this information came, necessarily, through Pierre St. Germain, and Franklin could not help wondering if the interpreter had encouraged Akaitcho to take this position. He responded angrily that at Fort Providence and again while travelling, Akaitcho had presented a different scenario—that before winter arrived, he and his men would accompany the expedition to the mouth of the Coppermine. The chief, unflappable, answered that winter was arriving early and he "had been unacquainted with our slow mode of travelling." Franklin answered that the naval officers had instruments that revealed the state of the air and water and that winter was not so far advanced as Akaitcho claimed. The party could return at first sign of a change. Also, because they would leave baggage behind, the men would travel much faster than previously.

Franklin wrote that Akaitcho "appeared to feel hurt that we should continue to press the matter further and answered with some warmth: 'Well, I have said everything I can urge to dissuade you from going on this service, on which, it seems, you wish to sacrifice your own lives, as well as the Indians who might attend you.'" Franklin insisted that he did care about safety and survival. But he wanted at least to visit the river, to see its situation and size, and to witness from its banks an imminent eclipse of the sun.

This subtle assertion of superiority—"we know things you don't"—irritated Akaitcho. Running out of patience, he responded "with more temper" than previously. He had lived all his life in this country and knew what he was talking about. Why wouldn't this man listen? He would explain no more. Through St. Germain he told Franklin, "I have said all I have to say. It seems that you do not mind losing your lives or the lives of any of my men who go with you. After all I have said, if you are still determined to go, some of my young men shall join the party. It shall not be said that we permitted you to die alone after having brought you here. But from the moment my young men embark in the canoes, I and my relatives shall lament them as dead."

Franklin jumped up and stormed out of the tent. After watching him leave, Akaitcho sent Wentzel after him to say that he and his men had better things to do than go charging down a river to their deaths. They had to procure deerskins to make winter clothes for themselves and the voyageurs. Since his advice was deemed worthless and his presence useless, he would supply Franklin with some winter provisions and then return to Fort Providence with his hunters. He would have no more to do with this expedition.

For Franklin, this last communication inspired second thoughts. He talked with Richardson, Back, and Hood. They shared his disappointment but cooled his outrage. They had to accept that Akaitcho was essential— not only to their future success, but to their survival through the winter. Franklin had hoped to communicate with Inuit on the coast and to determine when the sea might be clear of ice. But he had to admit that the weather was changing in ways that gave him pause.

By morning Franklin had abandoned hope of venturing immediately down the Coppermine to the coast. In his narrative, writing as a stalwart naval officer, he would remark that "had the chief been willing to accompany us with his party, I should have made the attempt." Franklin's officers agreed unanimously that they could not try to reach the ocean this season "without hazarding a complete rupture with the Indians." They proposed a shorter scouting sortie, with George Back and Robert Hood setting out as soon as possible in a light canoe to determine the route and distance to the Coppermine.

Franklin wrote that he informed Akaitcho "of our intention to send a party to the river, and of the reasons for doing so, of which he approved, when he found that I had relinquished the idea of going myself." George Back echoed this, noting "a proposition was then made to send a party on foot to the Copper Mine River, which was agreed to." Interestingly, Robert Hood indicated that instead of telling Akaitcho about the scouting plan, they "gave the chief and his hunters some ammunition and clothing" and sent them off to retrieve meat from several deer that John Hepburn had cached. "We did not choose to acquaint the chief with the measure we had taken, till after its execution."

Either way, the Dene leader also sought to repair relations by asking questions about the eclipse Franklin had mentioned. He brought some hunters who, as if prompted, expressed astonishment that the white men would know when precisely it would happen. They remarked, Franklin reported, "that this knowledge was a striking proof of the superiority of the whites over the Indians." Akaitcho discerned what Franklin wanted to hear and played him like a fiddle.

Years later, in Van Diemen's Land, the naval officer would be lulled into a dangerous complacency by fawning and flattery, while a clear-eyed friend perceived that certain "government officers read him in a moment and were delighted to find the measure of his foot so easily." There, his friend would try to awaken Franklin to the manipulative insincerity of his interlocutors, but "it was like trying to force a piece of barley-sugar out of a child's mouth."

So it was with Akaitcho at Winter Lake. Franklin himself had noted that the Yellowknife leader "often surprised us by his correct judgment of the character of individuals amongst the traders or of our own party." Now the leader and his men feigned attentiveness while Franklin, that devout Christian, "took advantage of this occasion to speak to them respecting the Supreme Being, who ordered all the operations of nature, and to impress on their minds the necessity of paying strict attention to all their moral duties, in obedience to his will."

As an evangelical Christian, Franklin saw no parallel between his own unquestioning faith in a benign, all-powerful Christian God—one who had sent his only human-born son to bring salvation to believers by dying on a cross—and Dene mythologies. He would ridicule these last in his official narrative when writing of Fairy Lake River, noting that "the Northern Indian fairies are six inches high, lead a life similar to the Indians, and are excellent hunters. Those who have had the good fortune to fall in with their tiny encampments have been kindly treated and regaled on venison."

On the morning of August 29, 1820, the scouting party set out for the Coppermine River: George Back, Robert Hood, Pierre St. Germain, eight Canadian voyageurs, and one Dene hunter. Akaitcho and his men turned to establishing their own winter camp, leaving two hunters with Franklin, Richardson, Wentzel, and the voyageurs who were still building Fort Enterprise.

Akaitcho and Franklin had both stepped back from outright confrontation. But these early indications of trouble between them, historian Richard C. Davis writes, "foreshadowed many of the difficulties Franklin encountered in the following year." They established "a pattern of misunderstanding . . . that affected how these two leaders worked together in future." In his introduction to Franklin's journal, the Canadian scholar observes that the British expedition leader derived his authority from his "superiors," not from those he led. A code of discipline, complete with the possibility of corporal punishment, kept his subordinates obedient. Akaitcho, on the other hand, led his men "by virtue of his personal successes in his life and of the beneficial results of this success for his followers." He led as "first among equals" because people chose to follow him. If anyone grew disenchanted, they could leave and follow another Dene leader. This difference would play itself out in many ways.

~

In mid-October 1820, with everyone ensconced at Winter Lake, Akaitcho reported that Nicholas Weeks, the North West Company man in charge of Fort Providence, had spoken dismissively of the expedition. Weeks asserted that Franklin and his officers were not "the officers of a great King," he explained, but "merely a set of dependent wretches whose only aim was to obtain subsistence for a season in the plentiful country of the Copper Indians." The fur-trading companies had supplied the expedition with some goods out of charity, Weeks had said, but Franklin would never be able to reward the Dene for the work they did.

Akaitcho sought clarification. Furious, Franklin repudiated the complaint. He pointed out that Wentzel—with whom the Dene had long worked—had pledged the support of the North West Company and that some debts had already been remitted. Now, as Akaitcho well knew, the expedition was in the process of bringing two Inuit interpreters from Churchill—an expensive proposition and a clear indication of their intentions. Franklin proposed to write immediately to the NWC's senior trader and did not doubt that Weeks would be chastised.

The Dene leader left satisfied, though troubled by niggling uncertainty. And early in February 1821, when he received what Franklin called "further unpleasant reports concerning us from Fort Providence . . . , his faith in our good intentions was somewhat shaken." Akaitcho complained that Franklin was supplying too little ammunition and so was diminishing him in the eyes of his people. He was the leader. Why was he not better treated? At Providence, Weeks had refused to honour some notes Franklin had given to his hunters.

The Royal Navy man immediately sent Akaitcho powder and shot and a keg of diluted spirits, along with his strongest assurances of respect. Meanwhile, a widespread food shortage was putting pressure on both leaders. Akaitcho had arrived with forty followers and subsequently recognized his cultural obligation to welcome an influx of another sixty Yellowknife people affected by the prevailing scarcity. At some cost to their relations, Franklin persuaded Akaitcho to vacate Fort Enterprise with most of his people and to establish a campsite nearby.

Even so, food deriving from the annual caribou migration lasted only until March 23, 1821, when Franklin was forced to begin dispensing the pemmican he had reserved for travelling along the coast. On March 30, at Fort Enterprise, Franklin showed Akaitcho the charts and drawings he was sending to England, which outlined his intentions. The Indian chief expressed his pleasure and noted that although he had heard "a vast number of idle rumours" during the winter, he was now confident about moving forward.

Franklin called for an early departure and stressed the need for provisions. Akaitcho promised to urge his hunters into action and, in response to questioning, said he "would accompany the expedition to the mouth of the Coppermine River." If Franklin did not there encounter some Inuit, Akaitcho would continue "for some distance along the coast." The Dene leader said he was anxious to make peace with the Inuit and asked that, if Franklin met any Dogrib on the Coppermine, "we should use our influence to persuade them to live on friendly terms with his tribe."

Akaitcho's desire for peace emerged out of a history of mutual hatred and retribution. Two years from now, in 1823, a large party of Dogrib would attack and kill thirty-four Yellowknife people led by Akaitcho's friend and fellow leader Long Legs. Now, in mid-April of 1821, despite rationing, most of the pemmican was gone. Several Dene families, among them women and children, remained at Fort Enterprise. Franklin had asked them repeatedly to join Akaitcho at his campsite, but they were mostly sick or infirm and receiving medicines from Dr. Richardson. Franklin obviously kept them on short rations because they cleared the snow off nearby campsites from the previous autumn "to look for bones, deer's feet, bits of hide, and other offal." Although aware of the widespread hunger, Franklin complained to Akaitcho that his hunters had shared some of their recent kill with "several families of old people" who had arrived at their camp. In his view, that food should have been reserved for the men of the expedition.

Meanwhile, as early biographer H.D. Traill writes, "the long confinement in the prison of a northern winter" was testing everyone. "Upon a man of Franklin's deeply religious temperament, its effect may be easily anticipated." In a long letter to his sister, now Mrs. Wright, Franklin decided to write not of the comings and goings at Fort Enterprise—and certainly not of the starving Dene—but of his "present sentiments on religion." The excerpt that follows comes from a much longer document. Before beginning, Franklin wrote, "I would humbly offer my grateful thanks to Almighty God that the peculiar circumstances of my situation, arising from want of society and full occupation, have led me to seek consolation from the perusal of religious books"—and especially the Holy Bible. Judging from some of his language, he was perusing the King James Version.

> To this sacred volume I have applied for grounds of hope, comfort, and support, and never in vain; I am fully convinced that therein, and therein only, can be found the treasures of heavenly love and mercy. I have been amazed at the state of ignorance under which I laboured with respect to its blessed contents. Neither the order, connection, or regularity of God's mercies to the Jews were known to me. Consequently, His goodness and the grandeur of the deliverances vouchsafed to them were not duly appreciated by me. But an attentive perusal of His Holy Word, with fervent application for His assistance, will open all these mysteries to the inquiring mind, and lead you through them to see the mighty work of redemption by the death of His Blessed Son for all mankind . . .
>
> Surely that heart must be awfully impenitent which can read the recital of His sufferings unmoved or without feeling a sincere desire to repent and pray fervently for that heavenly grace which He faithfully promised to all who firmly believe on Him and seek to do His will . . . [How are those who sin to be saved?] Christ, who died for the salvation of sinners is the way, the truth, and the life. Whoso cometh unto Him in full purpose of heart shall in no wise be cast out. Can anything be more cheering than these assurances, or better calculated to fill the mind with heavenly impressions, and lift up the heart in grateful adoration to God? This is the commencement of the Christian joy which, if it beget a live faith that worketh by love, producing the fruits of obedience, will lead to everlasting life.

John Franklin saw no contradiction between his pieties and prayers and his attitudes toward the hungry Dene. Later, he did note that when the navy men saw the Dene gnawing pieces of hide and pounding bones and boiling them to extract nourishment, they regretted their "inability to relieve them, but little thought that we should ourselves afterwards be driven to the necessity of eagerly collecting these same bones a second time from the dunghill."

To gain the support of Akaitcho, Franklin would have had to adapt to the practices of the Indigenous Peoples, as Samuel Hearne had done fifty years before while travelling with Matonabbee. Franklin proved unwilling to do this—and, as a fervent Christian, was probably unable. Given the realities of Royal Navy culture, the lieutenant could hardly abandon or postpone his expedition because he faced challenges. On the other hand, Akaitcho could see no sense in risking his life and the lives of his men on a coastal journey that would almost certainly end in disaster. He could not understand it. *What was wrong with these white men? Why could they not listen?*

PART THREE

Haunting *the* Land

CHAPTER 17

The Gjoa Haven Mystery Box

~

W ait, what? Unearth a logbook from the lost Franklin expedition? A detailed, day-by-day accounting of the worst catastrophe in Arctic exploration history? Why, that would be a transformative discovery—the ultimate. So I find myself thinking as I wander around Gjoa Haven looking for Louie Kamookak. Late August 2010. The Victory Point Record remains the only meaningful piece of paper recovered from the disaster.

In 1859, it's true, Leopold McClintock turned up a few pieces of paper and a seaman's certificate belonging to Henry or Harry Peglar, a petty officer on HMS *Terror*. But the hard-to-decipher "Peglar papers" consist mostly of newspaper clippings, fragments of poetry, and snippets of reminiscence about visiting southern ports. Nobody expects them to shed any light on the fate of the Franklin expedition. Forget that.

But a logbook or diary written as the catastrophe unfolded? Now we are talking Holy Arctic Grail. I have just finished interviewing Wally Porter, spokesperson for an Inuit family that claims to know the location of logbooks from the long-lost expedition. Nor is this just another unsupported rumour. Acting on the insistence of one of their Elders, the Porter family has convinced government archaeologists to dig up those purported logbooks from beneath a seven-decade-old cairn near the centre of town.

Unearthing those logbooks seems a long shot. And yet ... such a find is certainly conceivable. Not only that. Some outside experts are already convinced. Conservators will arrive from Ottawa in a few days to demolish the cairn while a CBC-TV crew records the moment for posterity. Where is Louie Kamookak when I need him? A couple of young guys have told me he is out on the land. At a time like this, how can that be?

Two hours ago, life was simpler. I stood on a hill overlooking Gjoa Haven and gazed out at the bay that Norwegian explorer Roald Amundsen described in the early 1900s as "the finest little harbour in the world." I had arrived by ship with Adventure Canada and come ashore in a Zodiac. As the visiting resource historian, together with a local guide, I had led a dozen passengers up a rough path to a recently refurbished site dedicated to Amundsen. At the top of the hill we found a wooden memorial, a few old boats, mostly from the Hudson's Bay Company, and some new plaques. These had been erected since 2007, when I last visited Gjoa Haven. From atop the hill, I could see our ship, the *Clipper Adventurer*, standing at anchor half a mile offshore.

∼

Half an hour later, back in town, a passenger takes me aside. She tells me that, while visiting the hamlet office, adjacent to the museum, she got talking with a liaison officer, an Inuk named Wally Porter. He told her that the logbooks from the long-lost Franklin expedition were about to be excavated from a cairn. What? This sounds crazy. But not so long ago, I was earning my daily bread as a journalist. Spent two decades at big-city dailies. No way I can turn my back on a tip like this. I head for the hamlet office.

Wally Porter is an articulate man in his mid-forties. He plays me an audio tape made by his grandfather, George Washington Porter II. He tells me that some months ago, David F. Pelly, a well-respected Arctic historian, interviewed several Porter family members. He shows me the report Pelly submitted to the Nunavut government—an impressive-looking ten

The Gjoa Haven Mystery Box

or twelve pages. Now the government is sending a team of archaeologists to excavate the cairn for logbooks. CBC-TV is sending a crew from Yellowknife. The Porters have agreed that any documents will not be examined at the site but flown to a federal government conservation office in Ottawa.

At this point, I begin to ask myself, What if? After all, unlikely is not *impossible*. Porter won't let me have Pelly's report but agrees to show me the cairn. I climb onto the back of his three-wheel ATV and we drive a few hundred yards along the dusty road. The cairn stands roughly six feet high, solid with rocks and cement, and bears a plaque commemorating William "Paddy" Gibson, a long-dead inspector of the Hudson's Bay Company. Grandfather of Louie Kamookak.

All along, still skeptical, I have been scratching notes. At the cairn, I begin to succumb. What if the Porter family's oral history is correct? What if the excavation of the cairn turns up logbooks? As the only writer on the spot, I have the inside track. The international headlines will change my world. And then, why not: I write a blockbuster narrative drawing on what the logbooks reveal. Maybe I should stay and find out? Look out! Suddenly, I'm a literary superstar.

So that is how it happens—how a veteran journalist gets caught up in a vision of big-time book deals and movie rights going for millions. I ask again after Louie Kamookak. Wally shrugs and reiterates that he is "out on the land." Given my friend's obsession with all things Franklin, I find this incomprehensible. Maybe he doesn't want to witness the destruction of his grandfather's cairn? That I can understand. But what about the logbooks? Those, surely, he would want to see.

Looking out at the harbour, I wrestle indecision. Maybe I should stay in Gjoa Haven for a few days to witness the excavation. But Louie's absence makes me nervous. *Let's think this through.* To stay would mean breaking my contract with Adventure Canada. And since no documents will be examined on site, what could I learn by remaining? I have already taken Wally Porter's phone number. Back on the ship, to ensure that the story "belongs" to me, I rough out a yarn datelined Gjoa Haven, Nunavut.

After arriving home in Toronto, and before I file the story, I telephone Louie Kamookak. Things become clearer. I incorporate his comments. The story I write, published first in the *Montreal Gazette* (September 3, 2010), is picked up by newspapers across Canada. I lead by declaring that the search for the logbooks of the ill-fated Franklin expedition—the Holy Grail of Arctic exploration history—has taken on new life. An Inuit family based in Gjoa Haven, the only settlement near the spot where the 1845 expedition got trapped in the ice, is promising to unearth those logbooks on Saturday.

Now comes the nut graph. I describe how searchers have been yearning after the logbooks since the 129-man expedition led by Sir John Franklin disappeared into the Arctic while searching for the Northwest Passage. The expedition got trapped in ice at the northwest corner of King William Island, roughly one hundred miles from Gjoa Haven. Starting in April 1848, 105 sailors endured a horrific march down the west coast of the island before succumbing to scurvy, starvation, and lead poisoning. The final survivors resorted to cannibalism. So goes the standard reconstruction.

Now pick up from the present-day interview. Descendants of George Washington Porter II, a Hudson's Bay Company manager, say they will excavate the logbooks from beneath a cairn in the centre of Gjoa Haven (population 1,100). Wally Porter says his grandfather arrived there in 1927 to work for the Canalaska Trading Company, which in the late 1930s was absorbed by the Hudson's Bay Company.

The cairn was erected in 1944 to commemorate William "Paddy" Gibson, a Hudson's Bay Company inspector who had died in a plane crash two years before. By the late 1950s or early '60s, the cairn had deteriorated. Porter's grandfather buried the Franklin documents beneath the cairn when he rebuilt it about then. In 1984, just before he died, he told his son Chester about the Franklin logbooks. Chester Porter shared that secret with family members just a few months ago.

More historical context: Down through the decades, historians have speculated that the Inuit on King William Island discovered logbooks. But until now, the story has been that they scattered the pages to the wind. The oral history relayed by Wally Porter suggests that, while the Inuit discoverers could not decipher the handwritten log, they knew they had found something valuable. Porter says his grandfather acquired the documents from a Roman Catholic priest based in Gjoa Haven. He sealed them in a metal container and then reburied them under the cairn beneath a marble stone that had been left by Roald Amundsen.

Roald Amundsen in June 1899, photographed by Daniel Georg Nyblin. By proceeding through Rae Strait, he became the first voyager to sail through the Northwest Passage from the Atlantic to the Pacific (1903–1906).

If unearthed in readable condition, the logbooks might answer questions about how and why the first two dozen men died relatively early in the expedition. They might contain details about Franklin's death and burial (whether on land or at sea). They might explain why the final survivors trekked south rather than east toward a known cache of food, or point to the location of the still-missing ships.

Time for a caution. I note that the Porter family's claim has its skeptics. Having spoken to Louie Kamookak, I relay what he has told me. He said that in the 1980s, he interviewed the two men who rebuilt the original cairn. He believes the excavation will turn up old trading-company documents. End of first article.

After the excavation, I file a follow-up article that also runs nationwide (September 6). After recapping as necessary, I report that an old wooden box has indeed been excavated from beneath the cairn and is being flown unopened from Gjoa Haven to Ottawa. By now, I have also contacted and spoken with historian Kenn Harper, who lives in Iqaluit and has spent months researching the Porter family claim. He predicts that the box—which measures 14.5 by 11 by 6.5 inches—will contain records left in 1905 by Roald Amundsen during the first-ever navigation of the Northwest Passage.

Harper explains that Eric Mitchell of the HBC, the senior man in the territory, dug up the Amundsen records in 1958, along with George Washington Porter II. The two men found documents first discovered in 1927 by Gibson, an HBC inspector who reburied them. He wrote in *The Beaver* magazine of finding Amundsen records, which included a signed photograph of Georg von Neumayer, a German scientist who sparked the Norwegian's interest in the north magnetic pole.

I check in again with Wally Porter, who insists that we wait and see. We wait and wait. On September 30 I publish a third newspaper article revealing the "final answer" to the mystery box. I have again touched base with Louie Kamookak. Before the excavation, he says, he wrote several letters to the Nunavut government insisting that the cairn hid no Franklin documents: "I told them there was nothing there. But they didn't listen."

He suggests that I contact the Prince of Wales Northern Heritage Centre in Yellowknife. I telephone the museum and write the final "reveal." The wooden mystery box, just opened in Ottawa, contains no items related to any Arctic explorers whatsoever. Officials from the Canadian Conservation Institute say the box contains only bits of cardboard, pieces of newspaper, and what appears to be tallow mixed with sand and rocks.

I quote Louie Kamookak, who explains that in the 1970s, another HBC man dug up the Neumayer photograph while yet again repairing the cairn. He says that this man, whose name he forgets, worried about deterioration. He took the photo to Yellowknife, where it ended up at the Heritage Centre. Someone in the archives there confirms to me that they do indeed have the Neumayer-signed photograph in their Nunavut collection. An inscription on the back reads, "Best wishes for success in exploring the North Magnetic Pole, to his friend Roald Amundsen."

In Gjoa Haven, Wally Porter interprets a cairn erected in 1944 to commemorate William "Paddy" Gibson, an HBC man who had died in a plane crash two years before. The cairn was demolished a few days later in a search for Franklin expedition logbooks.

So ends the saga of the Gjoa Haven mystery box—clearly not with the bang for which I was hoping. And yet, while I am reminded to be careful when interpreting oral history, I wonder anew if maybe my friend Louie isn't on to something. Maybe I should be paying closer attention to the elusive John Franklin.

CHAPTER 18

Hunters, Interpreters, Eyewitnesses

~

Appreciative laughter erupted among passengers sitting in the darkened lounge of the *Ocean Endeavour*. We were watching the docudrama *Passage* and had just seen Inuk statesman Tagak Curley roll his eyes, sigh loudly, and shake his head in frustration. He was struggling to teach the actor playing explorer John Rae how to build an igloo. The 110-minute film, based on my book *Fatal Passage*, marked a move to plan B. On this voyage, *Into the Northwest Passage*, we had intended to visit Grise Fiord on Ellesmere Island, Canada's northernmost civilian settlement. In the 1950s, the Canadian government relocated three Inuit families there to assert sovereignty over the area. Now, in 2016, the population stood at about 165 people, mostly descendants of those displaced from northern Quebec.

Stormy weather had prevented our landing at Grise. The waves had already overturned one Zodiac, throwing an experienced Adventure Canada staffer into the water near shore. He had been helping to deliver some gifts to the community. One dunking was all it took. We would not be landing any passengers today. Having crossed Davis Strait from Greenland, we did manage to clear Canadian customs by bringing aboard two officials. After lunch, instead of going ashore, we shifted to viewing this film, in which Rae emerges as a champion of the Inuit and Charles Dickens stands revealed as ... something else.

Toward the end of the film, Tagak Curley—who was now voyaging with us—elicits an apology from a great-great-grandson of Dickens for the celebrated author's racist accusations against the Inuit. Earlier in the day, drawing on personal experience as an elder statesman, Curley had given a talk on the evolution of Nunavut, tracing the complex political negotiations that settled the Inuit land claims agreement and then the boundaries of the new territory. But my favourite among his presentations was one he called "Tulugaq's Expedition."

Most Arctic aficionados know it as Frederick Schwatka's Expedition, so right away you could see what he was getting at. In Inuit mythology, Tulugaq was the creator of light. But Curley spoke, rather, of a flesh-and-blood Inuk. In 1879, Tulugaq was living on the west coast of Hudson Bay just north of Chesterfield Inlet when American explorer Frederick Schwatka arrived to search for information about the sailors of the lost Franklin ships.

Schwatka brought two men who would write books about the expedition—William Henry Gilder of the *New York Herald* and Heinrich (Henry) Klutschak, a German artist and surveyor who had emigrated to the US in 1871. But the man who kept the party fed and flourishing was the Inuk Tulugaq, a little-known figure who emerges in accounts of the expedition as singular and irreplaceable. He was the man who made the expedition happen. A superlative dogsled driver, he was above all a peerless hunter. When the party located a herd of caribou, Tulugaq shot and killed eight—four more than the next best hunter.

Eight times, during this year-long Arctic odyssey, and according to those who wrote about it, Tulugaq killed two caribou with a single shot. At one point, according to Klutschak, the Inuk was set upon by a pack of thirty wolves. He leaped onto a high rock and, knowing that wolves will halt any attack to consume their own dead, "with his magazine rifle began

Crossing Simpson Strait in kayaks. This sketch of Frederick Schwatka and his party, drawn by Heinrich Klutschak, appeared in *The Illustrated London News* in 1881.

providing food for the wolves from their own midst." While they were distracted, he made his escape.

Tulugaq's courage and skill register most memorably in his dealings with polar bears. At Cape Felix, the northernmost tip of King William Island, Tulugaq used his telescope to locate a bear on the ice roughly five and a half miles away. He hitched up twelve dogs and, with one man and a youth, set off at a furious pace. When he drew within about 550 yards of the polar bear, the creature turned and fled, making for open water.

Tulugaq had already unleashed three dogs. He freed three more, and finally the bear had to stand and fight to keep six dogs at bay. From twenty-five paces, Tulugaq fired one shot after another, but the bear, which stood more than ten feet tall, scratched at his head, whirled, and came charging at him. Tulugaq's third shot hit the bear in the heart and brought him down. The hunter dug his first bullet from the bear's head. Despite the close range, Klutschak writes, "it had not penetrated the bone but had been completely flattened."

Not long afterward, when the expedition had finished searching Terror Bay and had travelled more than fifty miles south, Tulugaq took a dog team to retrieve some goods left behind at the previous night's campsite. While travelling, he spotted three bears and gave chase as they fled for open water. As they reached it, Tulugaq shot and killed all three with five shots. To take their hides, he then led the woman who was his travelling companion in hauling the bears out of the water, each weighing at least eight hundred pounds. "For Tulugaq," Klutschak writes, "nothing was impossible—except transporting the skull of an Inuk." That he would not do.

On another occasion, Tulugaq spotted a large piece of driftwood in the water. He took some dogs to help him fetch it but, unusually, left his rifle behind. Near the shore, he chanced upon a large female polar bear with a cub three or four months old. He freed all his dogs and pelted the mother to separate her from her cub. With the dogs at her heels, she took to the water, and Tulugaq used his knife to dispatch the cub. "Apart from its tenderness," Klutschak writes, "the cub's meat had a particularly piquant taste, and we greatly regretted that the old bear had not had twins."

Tulugaq was also remarkable for his good humour, his willpower, and his perseverance, and when Klutschak writes of sadly parting from him, he freely admits that "for a full year we had been indebted to this man for the fact that the execution of our plans had proceeded so well."

~

As crucial as hunters like Tulugaq were to overland expeditions, interpreters were arguably more important still. They were the ones who asked the questions and relayed the answers. We have already met William Ouligbuck,

Taqulittuq, also known as Tookoolito, posed in western clothing for this photograph by Giles Bishop in New London, Connecticut, in 1875. After serving as a guide and interpreter for Charles Francis Hall, Taqulittuq lived for some years in nearby Groton, where she and her three children lie buried in Starr Cemetery.

who enabled John Rae to determine that the final survivors of the 1845 expedition had trekked south along the west coast of King William Island, many of them "driven to the last resource—cannibalism—as a means of prolonging existence." Ouligbuck's father, also William, had worked with both Rae and John Franklin.

In the search for the lost 1845 expedition, two more interpreters would prove indispensable—Taqulittuq and her husband, Ipiirvik (both of whom have been recognized as National Historic Persons). Born near Cumberland Sound in 1838, Taqulittuq was the younger sister of Eenoolooapik, an adventurous Inuk guide who talked Scottish navigator William Penny into taking him to Scotland, where he resided for several months. At fifteen, inspired by his example, Taqulittuq convinced an English whaling captain to bring her and her new husband to England. There, over the next two years, she mastered the English language and even met Queen Victoria.

In November 1860, Taqulittuq was back at home on the east coast of Baffin Island when she heard that an American explorer—Charles Francis Hall—had arrived on a ship called the *George Henry* and desperately needed an interpreter. She boarded the vessel, introduced herself, and astounded Hall with her fluency in English. She and Ipiirvik began working with Hall as guides and interpreters.

Hall was an ex-blacksmith and printer who had no Arctic experience and no qualifications to lead an expedition but who believed himself called by God to locate survivors from the Franklin expedition. Together, Taqulittuq and Ipiirvik would transform him into a significant figure. In the mid to late 1860s, they travelled with Hall, chasing one false lead after another. Finally, in April 1869, supported by a party of hunters, they reached the west coast of Boothia Peninsula.

There, they interviewed some Inuit who had personally encountered Franklin expedition survivors trekking south, and others who had later discovered dead bodies. From them, Hall acquired several relics, among them a spoon bearing Franklin's initials and part of a writing desk. He and his party had crossed Rae Strait to King William Island, and in the south, on one of the Todd Islets, they found a complete skeleton. Later, Hall would send this to England, where recent forensic studies indicate that the remains are those of Harry Goodsir, physician and scientist on the Franklin expedition. His bones showed no signs of scurvy.

But the real significance of this expedition can be found in the accounts that Taqulittuq elicited from eyewitnesses. These stories, preserved in notebooks, were published in 1879 in *Narrative of the Second Arctic Expedition Made by Charles F. Hall*. They constitute the single most extensive archive of Inuit testimony about the Franklin expedition. Hall was not a clear thinker, nor was he a good writer, but with the help mainly of Taqulittuq, he did collect and compile an encyclopedia of material that vindicated John Rae's reports of cannibalism and anticipated the 2014 discovery of *Erebus*.

Here we encounter horrific tales whose details are so vivid as to be incontrovertible, including references to human flesh cut to facilitate boiling in pots and kettles: "One man's body when found by the Innuits [*sic*] flesh all on & not mutilated except the hands sawed off at the wrists—the rest a great many had their flesh cut off as if some one or other had cut it off to eat."

Some Inuit spoke of finding numerous bodies in a tent at Terror Bay on the west coast of King William Island. One described a woman using a heavy sharp stone to dig into the ice and retrieve a watch from the body of a corpse: "[The woman] could never forget the dreadful, fearful feelings she had all the time while engaged doing this; for, besides the tent being filled with frozen corpses—some entire and others mutilated by some of the starving companions, who had cut off much of the flesh with their knives and hatchets and eaten it—this man who had the watch she sought seemed to her to have been the last that died, and his face was just as though he was only asleep."

Taqulittuq relayed some gruesome stories, among them tales of finding bones that had been severed with a saw and skulls with holes in them through which brains had been removed "to prolong the lives of the living." She also interviewed In-nook-poo-zhe-jook, John Rae's most articulate informant. After talking with Rae and then learning of Captain Leopold McClintock's visit to the region, this hunter had personally explored King William Island. Hall described him as "very finicky to tell the facts . . . In-nook-poo-zhe-jook has a noble bearing. His whole face is an index that he has a heart kind & true. I delight in his companionship."

Later, the capricious Hall would write that In-nook-poo-zhe-jook "speaks truth & falsehood all intermingled," though as Canadian mariner David Woodman suggests, In-nook-poo-zhe-jook "probably never intentionally told Hall a falsehood." At Erebus Bay, this Inuk had located not only a pillaged boat—the one Hobson and McClintock had ransacked for relics—but a second boat, untouched, about one thousand yards away. Here, too, he had discovered "one whole skeleton with clothes on—this with flesh all on but dried, as well as a big pile of skeleton bones near the fireplace & skulls among them." Bones had been broken up for their marrow, and some long boots that came up as high as the knees contained "cooked human flesh—that is human flesh that had been boiled."

All this Taqulittuq relayed. Late in the twentieth century, while researching Inuit accounts for what would become his book *Unravelling the Franklin Mystery: Inuit Testimony*, Woodman perused Hall's unpublished field notes. In them, he found testimony elaborating on stories about a shipwreck at the location McClintock had called Oot-loo-lik, which Hall transcribed as Ook-joo-lik. According to a local Inuk named Ek-kee-pee-ree-a, the ship "had 4 boats hanging at the sides and 1 of them was above the quarter deck. The ice about the ship one winter's make, all smooth flow, and a plank was found extending from the ship down to the ice. The Innuits were sure some white men must have lived there through the winter. Heard of tracks of 4 strangers, not Innuits, being seen on land adjacent to the ship."

A woman named Koonik told Taqulittuq about the finding of a dead white man on a ship. She reported that several Inuit "were out sealing when they saw a large ship"—all very much afraid except a man named Nuk-kee-che-uk, who went to the vessel while the others went to their igloo. He looked around, saw nobody, and stole a few things before rejoining the others. "Then all the Innuits went to the ship and stole a good deal—broke into a place that was fastened up and there found a very large white man who was dead, very tall man. There was flesh about this dead man, that is, his remains quite perfect—it took 5 men to lift him. The place smelt very bad. His clothes all on. Found dead on the floor—not in a sleeping place or berth." This, of course, is one reason searchers expect to find dead bodies on one or more of the ships.

Taqulittuq asked Koonik if she knew "anything about the tracks of strangers seen at Ook-joo-lik?" Some other Inuit had mentioned "walking along the tracks of 3 men Kob-loo-nas & those of a dog with them . . . says she has never seen the exact place."

Thanks to Taqulittuq, Charles Francis Hall gathered a wealth of new information. But he lacked the analytical and imaginative abilities required to develop a coherent revision of the "standard reconstruction" that had evolved from the findings of Rae and McClintock and the one-page Victory Point Record, according to which all the surviving men had fled the two ships in 1848.

~

Early in the 1870s, with the help of Hall, Taqulittuq and Ipiirvik set up house in Groton, Connecticut. Ipiirvik revisited the Arctic several times as a guide while Taqulittuq stayed in Groton, working as a seamstress and caring for their daughter, a fragile child. When the girl died at age nine, a pining Taqulittuq fell into declining health. Ipiirvik was with her when, at thirty-eight, she died on December 31, 1876. She was buried in Groton.

Her death meant that Ipiirvik was living alone two years later when the American Geographical Society chose a thirty-one-year-old army officer, Frederick Schwatka, to lead yet another search for records from the lost Franklin expedition. Over the next two years, as guide and main interpreter, Ipiirvik would play an essential role in unearthing still more Inuit testimony.

Schwatka and his five men spent the winter of 1878 near Daly Bay, north of Chesterfield Inlet on the coast of Hudson Bay. There they met Tulugaq, the hunter whose contributions are outlined above. On April 1, 1879, the expedition set out to scour the west coast of King William Island. Now the expedition encompassed fifteen men, three sledges, and forty dogs. Over the next year, while relying on an Inuit diet and travel methods, this party reached their target destination while accomplishing the longest sledge journey then on record: 2,709 miles.

The expedition spent the summer searching the area from the mouth of the Back River to Cape Felix at the northern tip of King William Island.

They found bones and rel-
ics that would in winter have
been covered by snow. William
Ouligbuck had joined the
party, and journalist William
Henry Gilder would verify
what John Rae had asserted—
that Ouligbuck spoke all the
Inuktitut dialects fluently, and
that he "spoke the [English] language like a native—that is to
say, like an uneducated native."

In short, two outstanding
interpreters enabled Schwatka
to add an extraordinary amount
of priceless Inuit testimony—
William Ouligbuck Jr., who
had made his reputation while
working with John Rae, and
Ipiirvik, who along with
Taqulittuq had gleaned the eye-
witness accounts reported by Charles Francis Hall.

The hunter-interpreter Ipiirvik, also known as Ebierbing, photographed by G.W. Pach.

At Terror Bay on King William Island, where in 2016 the *Terror*
would be found, and at Starvation Cove on the mainland near Chantrey
Inlet, Schwatka located more remains and evidence of cannibalism. With
Ipiirvik and Ouligbuck, he elicited eyewitness accounts whose importance
has emerged only recently. Thanks to those interpreters, he gleaned tales of
Inuit entering an abandoned ship and of papers being distributed among
children and blown away by the wind.

Given the 2014 discovery of the *Erebus* at Oot-joo-lik (in Wilmot
and Crampton Bay, off Grant Point and the Adelaide Peninsula), today we
recognize the special relevance of the stories told by an Inuk man named

Puhtoorak. Now sixty-five or seventy, Puhtoorak saw the ship while it lay frozen in ice during the autumn of 1851 or 1852.

According to Gilder, Puhtoorak had only once seen white men alive. As a boy, while fishing on the Back River, "they came along in a boat and shook hands with him. There were ten men. The leader was called 'Tos-ard-e-roak,' which Joe [Ipiirvik] says, from the sound, he thinks means Lieutenant Back. The next white man he saw was dead in a bunk of a big ship which was frozen in the ice near an island about five miles due west of Grant Point, on Adelaide Peninsula. They had to walk out about three miles on smooth ice to reach the ship."

Around this time, which Gilder estimated to be 1851 or '52, Puhtoorak saw the tracks of white men on the mainland. "When he first saw them there were four, and afterward only three," Gilder writes. "This was when the spring snows were falling. When his people saw the ship so long without any one around, they used to go on board and steal pieces of wood and iron. They did not know how to get inside by the doors and cut a hole in the side of the ship, on a level with the ice, so that when the ice broke up during the following summer the ship filled and sunk.

"No tracks were seen in the salt-water ice or on the ship, which also was covered with snow, but they saw scrapings and sweepings alongside, which seemed to have been brushed off by people who had been living on board. They found some red cans of fresh meat, with plenty of what looked like tallow mixed with it. A great many had been opened, and four were still unopened. They saw no bread. They found plenty of knives, forks, spoons, pans, cups, and plates on board, and afterward found a few such things on shore after the vessel had gone down. They also saw books on board and left them there. They only took knives, forks, spoons, and pans; the other things they had no use for."

Klutschak, working with Ipiirvik, told much the same story. He wrote that Puhtoorak "was one of the first people to visit a ship which, beset in ice, drifted with wind and current to a spot west of Grant Point on Adelaide Peninsula, where some islands halted its drift." According to

Puhtoorak, then, the ship did not sail to its final location but was carried there while frozen in the ice. Klutschak notes that "on their first visit [in the autumn] the people thought they saw whites on board; from the tracks in the snow they concluded there were four of them."

He reiterates how, the following spring, when the whites were gone, the Inuit "found a corpse in one of the bunks and they found meat in cans in the cabin." He said "the body was in a bunk inside the ship in the back part." The Inuit also found "a small boat in Wilmot Bay which, however, might have drifted to that spot after the ship sank." That boat might also have been left by sailors making a final bid to escape overland.

In Schwatka's rendition, the Inuit found the tracks first of four white men, and later of only three. Puhtoorak "never saw the white men. He thinks that the white men lived in the ship until the fall and then moved onto the mainland." When he went on board the ship, Puhtoorak "saw a pile of dirt on one side of the cabin door showing that some white man had recently swept out the cabin. He found on board the ship four red tin cans filled with meat and many that had been opened. The meat was full of fat. The natives went all over and through the ship and found also many empty casks. They found iron chains and anchors on deck, and spoons, knives, forks, tin plates, china plates, etc." Ipiirvik reported, and Schwatka wrote, that Puhtoorak "also saw books on board the ship but the natives did not take them. He afterwards saw some that had washed ashore."

This narrative, which resembles one communicated by Taqulittuq to Charles Frances Hall, takes on added credibility as Parks Canada found the *Erebus* almost precisely where Puhtoorak said it was. Without Ipiirvik, who did most of the translating with Puhtoorak, none of the white men would ever have gleaned a word about the *Erebus*. And without the accounts they relayed, which identified a general location, that ship might never have been found.

And all of this reminds me of 2014, when news broke that Parks Canada had discovered a ship in that southern field of search. Franklin aficionados went online and began guessing: Was it *Erebus*? Was it *Terror*?

Everyone guessed *Terror*, almost to a person, and sometimes offered reasons. But then Louie Kamookak came online and wrote one word: *Erebus*. And of course he proved correct. Later, when I asked how he knew, he smiled and opened his hands as if in presentation: "Inuit oral history."

CHAPTER 19

The Peter Bayne Complication

~

B ut we have come this far and have yet to report on the Inuk and the whalers—Supunger, Peter Bayne, and Patrick Coleman—whose stories bear directly on Louie Kamookak's quest for the Franklin vault. In the spring of 1866, Supunger, a young Inuk from Pelly Bay, relayed his story to Charles Francis Hall through Taqulittuq. Four years before, Supunger and his uncle had been travelling along the coast of King William Island, searching for things that had "once belonged to the white men who had died" in that vicinity.

Near the north end of that island, they came across a large tupik, a sealskin or caribou-skin tent, that had been collapsed. A "little way inland," they found a skeleton of a white man partly eaten by wolves. Nearby, they found a stick, pillar, or post standing erect, immovable, with a broken part on the ground. "But what attracted their attention the most," Hall wrote, "was a stone or rather several large flat stones lying flat on the sandy ground & tightly together." After a struggle, they managed to loosen one of these stones and lift an edge just enough "that they could see that another tier of large flat stones firmly & tightly fitted together was underneath." This second layer discouraged further efforts.

At Hall's request, Supunger used a knife on the snow to indicate the shape and size of the spot covered by flat stones—a rectangle measuring four feet by two. The pillar of wood, planted to one side, stood four feet high. When Supunger said the stones were so tightly placed that no water could get between them, Hall wrote that Taqulittuq "said to me with a joyful face, 'I guess I can tell just what that is for—for papers!' And, said I, I think so too." Supunger reiterated that the stones looked "as if they were tied together," and Hall concluded "that the stones were laid in cement & that they cover a vault of the precious documents of the Franklin Expedition or the greater part of them."

Left to Right: Taqulittuq, Charles Francis Hall, and Ipiirvik. This illustration first appeared as the frontispiece to Hall's book *Arctic Researches and Life Amongst the Esquimaux* (1865).

Supunger reported that, not much farther north, they found numerous graves, a big pile of clothing, and "a great many tin things" (canisters). Using John Rae's map, Supunger pinpointed the location as the long bay south of Victory Point. He and his uncle tried a second time to raise one of the flat stones. They succeeded and "found a hole of the depth from the feet up to the navel & of a length more than a man's height & wider than the width of a man's shoulders & this was all nicely walled with flat stones placed one above another, flatwise. In this vault they found a clasp knife, a skeleton bone of a man's leg & a human head (skull)." Some wild animal had apparently dug a hole into the vault and ransacked it, leaving water and mud inside and a partly clothed human skeleton nearby. None of this came to light until 1991, when David Woodman perused Hall's original journals and published *Unravelling the Franklin Mystery*.

Our second "vault story" from the 1860s, that of the two whalers, did not become public knowledge until 1931, when Canadian Major Lachlan Taylor Burwash published a comprehensive report in Canada's *Western Arctic* magazine. In 1866, friendly Pelly Bay Inuit who were travelling with Supunger warned Charles Francis Hall that people living farther west were dangerously protective of their hunting grounds. The explorer retreated to Repulse Bay and Rowes Welcome, where often whalers spent the winter to get an early start on their hunt. Hall hired five well-armed men to provide protection for a trek to King William Island. Two of the men, Patrick Coleman from Dublin and Peter Bayne from Nova Scotia, went north to cache supplies near Committee Bay. Bayne later shared his story with George Jamme, a mining engineer who kept silent about what he had been told until Bayne's death in 1926.

About sixty miles north of Repulse, travelling with an Inuit family, Bayne and Coleman encountered and camped with another small party of Inuit who had been heading south. Bayne, an excellent marksman, made friends with the strangers by sharing meat from a recent hunt. The Elder of the group responded with an eyewitness account of having seen the two Franklin ships trapped in the ice off King William Island. Some of the Inuit camping with him had gone out to the ships and had talked with Franklin. Many of the sailors came ashore and camped for the summer in one big tent and several smaller ones.

This Elder had talked with their leader (probably Captain Francis Crozier), and sometimes the white men hunted with the Inuit and shot seals, ducks, and geese with their guns. "Some of the white men were sick in the big tent," Jamme reported, "and died there; and were buried on the hill back of the camp." Also, "one man died on the ships and was brought ashore and buried on the hill near where the others were buried." He was "not buried in the ground like the others, but in an opening in the rock, and his body covered over with something that, 'after a while was all the same stone.'"

This man told Bayne that he was out hunting seal at the time of the burial but heard about it from his companions. Bayne realized that these statements about "the white men coming ashore, and of their hunting with the natives, and their camping there and the description of the camp, and some of the men being sick and dying and being buried ashore, and of the funeral from the ships and the guns being fired, were all new and important. Bayne says that Coleman was even more strongly of [this] opinion than himself, and the latter became quite excited over the matter."

The Inuk Elder described where the men were buried, and "Bayne figured the camp to have been about a fourth of a mile back from the beach . . . that it was situated on a flat-topped mound near the base of a low ridge; that the crest of the ridge was not very wide and was formed of projecting rocks; and that the slope on the other side faced the southeast." Bayne also learned "that there were several cemented vaults—one large, and a number of small ones; the natives thought that these latter contained only papers, for many papers were brought ashore—some blew away in the wind, but others were buried."

Bayne and Coleman invited their new Inuit friends back to camp to relay their story to Hall. The American had recently left on a wild goose chase, however, so the Elder told the story to all who remained. When Hall got back, he reprimanded Bayne and Coleman for their actions. An altercation ensued and Hall shot Coleman, who died fourteen days later. The other four whalers left on the first ship, and Hall, who wrote nothing about this in his journals, explained the shooting by saying Coleman had become threatening and mutinous.

~

Over the years, some Franklin aficionados have proven skeptical of the Supunger and Peter Bayne stories. But Tom Gross of Hay River (recently retired to Kaslo, British Columbia) says that in March of 1994, responding to those stories, he made his first search expedition with Louie Kamookak, travelling to Cape Felix at the north end of King William Island. At the time, Gross was managing the Northwest Territories Housing Corporation, whose jurisdiction then included Nunavut. The men had met in 1993, introduced by the manager of the Gjoa Haven Housing Association, where Louie had recently started work. "We hit it off right away," Gross told me in an email. "He shared the story of his great-grandmother Hummahuk and I told him about Bayne and Supunger."

With his research, Gross has added intriguing detail to the early stories. In April 1913, Peter Bayne—then sixty-nine—bought a schooner and proposed to sail it to King William Island, where along a twenty-mile stretch of western coastline he expected to find the Franklin vault. Three years later, an article in the *Spokesman-Review*, a Spokane newspaper, announced his imminent departure—but then came no further news. Before his death in 1926, Bayne shared his Franklin vault story with George Jamme, who later passed it along to T.W. Jackson, a Vancouver judge. Jackson tried to sell it to the Canadian government for $25,000 but eventually accepted $1,000. In 1930, Major Burwash investigated the area around Victory Point but found nothing.

The 1994 trip from Gjoa Haven to Cape Felix, organized to resolve the Bayne mystery, was one of three that Gross made with Louie Kamookak. Two years later, Louie "was to drop [him] and four sled dogs off at Port Parry"—at the northeast corner of King William Island. "But his snow machine broke down halfway up. George," Gross reports, "Louie's father, came to the rescue and ended up taking me the rest of the way to the old mission house."

In the fall of 1999—not long after Louie, Cameron, and I erected the John Rae memorial plaque—Louie and Tom Gross made a final trip together. Again they drove north on snow machines and camped at Port

Parry during the fall fishing season. They then travelled across the top of the island to Victory Point, Gross says, and stopped at the cairn: "Louie handed me a camera and said, 'Take my photograph,' and before I knew it like a big bear he climbed up on the cairn. I think that picture ended up in the Canadian Geographic building in Ottawa." The two men explored the area and then returned to Gjoa Haven.

During an exchange of emails, Gross told me that he travelled with many Inuit over the years and Louie was an especially great travelling companion. "I never saw him get mad or upset. If things broke he simply tried to repair them and move on." As a young man, Gross lived in Holman Island (Ulukhaktok), so he and Louie shared "wonderful stories not only about Franklin but also about hunting and travelling and just growing up in a small northern community."

All told, Tom Gross has undertaken more than forty search expeditions—at least one each year since 1994 and sometimes two. Travelling mostly by ATV (he bought his own in 2004), Gross did three trips alone and the rest with various partners, including five with author David Woodman. Between 1992 and 2004, Woodman led nine expeditions, among them both sonar and magnetometer searches.

Gross designed his searches "based on Inuit testimony that documents sites relating" to the last Franklin expedition. These stories, collected by Charles Francis Hall (1866) and Captain Peter Bayne (1868), "describe a similar burial site consisting of a cemented stone underground vault or several vaults. Furthermore, they both report that one was larger than the others and that it contained human remains while the smaller vaults contained papers." Gross located the Franklin campsite at Cape Felix and concluded that it "was a land-based magnetic observatory." He also found other sites containing artifacts and boat planking, and "seven stone marker cairns located over several miles along the western shore."

Franklin's men built these in the spring of 1847, he believes, while surveying the western shore of King William Island. Each cairn consists "of about a dozen stones placed on top of large erratic boulders a short distance from the shore." While some mysteries around the expedition may never be resolved, Gross believes searchers "may locate the burial site spoken of" by the Inuit. The idea of a vault site "is logical from the perspective of the expedition. The security that stone and cement would provide, until a recovery expedition could return to recover them, would have been a well-thought-out and doable task in the summer of 1847."

The Victory Point Record, he notes, includes "a few obvious mistakes, in terms of the dates entered, and if we consider that there may be some other errors, perhaps the document might read very differently." The note was clearly written in a state of some duress on the frozen shore, and without the usual care. "Finally, could we attribute these errors to the fact that both Captains Crozier and Fitzjames were succumbing to the illness that had already claimed the lives of nine other officers?"

These considerations led Gross to conclude in 2009 that "the Victory Point document was misleading us." Having spent many years "going around in circles," he basically took that record "out of the mix and started looking for the vault further south towards Erebus Bay." In 2015, Gross added aerial surveying to his search techniques and, judging from a list he provided me, has now undertaken at least a dozen of those. Meanwhile, he brought aboard Russell S. Taichman, an associate dean for research at the University of Michigan School of Dentistry, who leads research on how bone marrow functions in both health and disease states. In 2017, the two published a nineteen-page "comparative analysis of the Supunger and Bayne testimonies related to the Franklin expedition." Gross notes that the two stories contain discrepancies that suggest that "there are actually two burial sites, located over thirty miles apart."

The site reported by Bayne "is the burial vault of Sir John Franklin and the crew members who perished between September 1846 and August 1847." He now thinks the Supunger site is the burial vault either of Francis Crozier or of Lieutenant Graham Gore, who was third in command of the *Erebus*, after Franklin and Fitzjames. Nearby human remains are probably those of sailors who died between September 1847 and

April 1848, before the major abandonment of the ships. Since 2011, Gross has focused on Erebus Bay as "the location of the Peter Bayne story."

In the summer of 2022, Gross undertook two search expeditions, including one with a team from the National Geographic Society. That outing brought some success and is the subject of a documentary film under development. "We never found the vault this summer," Gross told me, "but let's just say that things turned up where I hoped they would. I plan to keep looking next summer and now that I am retired can spend longer in the field."

Like Louie Kamookak, Gross remains convinced that "the Franklin crew went to great lengths to keep him and the expedition records safe. I am also very sure that the vault will be found within the next few years. Maybe not by me, but hunters are now heading out further and further looking for game. And depending on the snow conditions, the site can be visible in winter. Everyone uses GPS now so if found it can be marked and relocated."

This much is certain: any discovery of logbooks or journals will make international headlines.

CHAPTER 20

What Do We Know *for* Sure?

~

The Arctic eureka moment came one gorgeous September afternoon in 2014 after the chance discovery on a tiny island of a heavy U-shaped piece of metal and a wooden scuttle or deck-hole cover. These weather-worn objects turned up in Wilmot and Crampton Bay, roughly 95 miles southwest of Gjoa Haven on King William Island. Identifiably Royal Navy in origin, could they have come from one of Sir John Franklin's ships?

Underwater archaeologists Jonathan Moore and Ryan Harris, leading a Parks Canada investigation from a nearby vessel, responded by laying out a new search grid in the area, near where they themselves had investigated in 2008, 2010, 2012, and 2013. Others had been hunting in this "Oot-joo-lik" area for decades, notably David Woodman, acting on the Inuit oral tradition frequently referenced by Louie Kamookak.

On September 2, 2014, Moore and Harris established their new electronic lines the usual 150 metres apart. They put a sidescan sonar unit or "towfish" to work "mowing the lawn" up and down these lines, sending images back to the sonar screens they sat watching on their vessel. They had scarcely begun the day's work when *Eureka!* the image of a ship began to emerge from the sonic waterfall on one of the screens. "That's it!" Harris cried. "That's it!"

189

What a moment! Following an international search that had lasted almost 170 years, they had located Franklin's flagship, HMS *Erebus*, sitting just eleven metres beneath the surface. Well-earned kudos went to Moore and Harris and those working with them on the survey boat Investigator; to archaeologist Douglas Stenton and pilot Andrew Stirling, who had turned up those artifacts on that tiny island; and to Louie Kamookak, the very incarnation of Inuit oral history.

John Geiger, Chief Executive Officer of the Royal Canadian Geographical Society, called Louie "the last great Franklin searcher." He added, "Louie brought a particular perspective, and that perspective was to listen to the elders, to listen to the oral tradition." Louie was thrilled and called the discovery "bigger than the Titanic." But later, to a writer for Up Here magazine, Louie clarified his view of the search for the lost ships: "That's not my mission. I'm looking for Franklin."

On September 3, 2016, precisely two years and one day after the finding of *Erebus*, a team from the Arctic Research Foundation found the *Terror* off southwestern King William Island after acting on a tip from an Inuk crewmember. Sammy Kogvik, also from Gjoa Haven, told operations director Adrian Schimnowski that a few years earlier, while out hunting on the ice of Terror Bay in winter, he had chanced upon what appeared to be a protruding mast. He kept the find secret because, after snapping photos, he lost his camera and so lacked proof.

The team entered Terror Bay and soon located the *Terror* sitting on the ocean floor twenty-four metres below the surface. Although not authorized to do so, Schimnowski sent a remotely operated vehicle into the ship through an open hatch. The ROV entered cabins and explored the food storage room, where on shelves it located plates, one tin can, and two wine bottles. The ship's three masts were still standing, most hatches were closed, and everything was neatly stowed. Experts surmised that a few remaining crew closed down and abandoned the *Terror*, then boarded and sailed the *Erebus* forty miles south to where she was found.

Either way, the discovery of the two long-lost ships speaks to the greatest mystery of Arctic exploration: What happened to the Franklin expedition? We know now that its demise was more complex and protracted than anybody had realized. In 2014, I was one of the first writers to respond to the finding of the *Erebus*. That December, writing in *Canadian Geographic* magazine, I hailed it as the Discovery of the Century. In retrospect, I see that I got carried away. Since then, others have weighed in and I have had occasion to reflect. Drawing on all these, I will catch us up to where we are now.

The finding of the two ships vindicates both Inuit oral history and those explorers who ventured into the Arctic to record it. For Canadians, most of whom live along the US border, the discoveries mean we have to rewrite a foundational myth that underscores our national identity as a northern people. In 1854, as we have seen, John Rae worked with William Ouligbuck and relayed Inuit testimony that many of Franklin's men had starved to death while trekking south, and that some of the final survivors had been driven to cannibalism.

In the mid-1990s, archaeologist Margaret Bertulli and physical anthropologist Anne Keenleyside investigated a grisly discovery in Erebus Bay. They analyzed more than four hundred bones, the remains of at least eight men. Using an electron microscope, they discovered cut marks on ninety-two bones—marks easily distinguished from animal tooth marks and even marks made by stone tools, occurring "in a pattern consistent with intentional disarticulation." In short, the survivors had dismembered the bodies and carved away the flesh.

Today's Royal Navy, as represented by historian Andrew Lambert, has finally acknowledged the overwhelming evidence of cannibalism. Lambert's 2009 biography, *Franklin: Tragic Hero of Polar Navigation*, is disingenuous in reframing Franklin and insisting that he not be assessed as an explorer. But it does open with a prologue that vividly describes how sailors from the *Erebus* and *Terror* "began butchering and eating their comrades."

Back in Victorian England, five years after Rae's evidence exploded like a bombshell, Leopold McClintock returned from King William Island having found skeletons and a one-page record left in a cairn by expedition officers. Today, most analysts take the view that this "Victory Point Record" has been accorded too much weight. It did reveal that after spending the winter of 1845–46 at Beechey Island and there burying three men, Franklin sailed southward into Peel Strait. In September 1846, his ships got trapped in pack ice off Cape Felix at the northwest corner of King William Island. On June 11, 1847, Franklin himself died. Over the next several months, many others died. Total loss: nine officers and fifteen crew.

Drawing on the Victory Point Record, McClintock articulated the so-called standard reconstruction. The starving crews, he wrote, abandoned the *Erebus* and the *Terror* in April 1848. "The survivors, under Crozier and Fitzjames, numbered in all 105; they proceeded with boats on sledges to the Great Fish River. One of their boats was found by us, untouched by the Esquimaux, and many relics brought from her, as also obtained from the natives of Boothia and the east shore of King William Island."

Today, thanks to the discoveries of both *Erebus* and *Terror*, most experts believe that while some men trekked south in 1848 along the coast of King William Island, others returned to one or both ships. Thanks to overland searches and Inuit testimony, we know that in Terror Bay, some men erected a large hospital tent to accommodate—and perhaps to segregate—the deathly ill. Journalist Henry Gilder, travelling in 1879 with Schwatka, wrote that according to a woman named Ahlangyah, "There were dead bodies in the tent, and outside some lay covered over with sand." Nearby she saw two graves, and also a scattering of "knives, forks, spoons, watches, many books, clothing, and blankets."

In 1923, ethnologist-explorer Knud Rasmussen collected stories and found bones and skulls at Starvation Point on the Canadian mainland: "There, exactly where the Eskimos had indicated," he wrote, "we found a number of human bones that were undoubtedly the mortal remains of members of the Franklin expedition." Subsequent discoveries, such as those of remains found fifteen miles west of Starvation Cove in 1926 and 1936, suggested that instead of marching south in a single body, those later survivors travelled in smaller groups.

In 1931, William Gibson found the remains of four skeletons on one of the Todd Islets just west of Gjoa Haven. Also, on an islet in nearby Douglas Bay, he found the remains of seven men and buried them beneath a large stone cairn. Four decades later, a Northwest Territories government employee organized a multi-member search expedition. In 1972, Bob Pilot and a few others created the Franklin Probe, which undertook several ambitious sorties. Pilot was obsessed with finding not Franklin's ships but rather his grave, which he believed was located on King William Island. Like Louie Kamookak and Tom Gross, he regarded this quest as "the true Franklin search."

In the early 1980s, a forensic anthropologist, Owen Beattie, discovered and analyzed some skeletal remains from King William Island. They showed evidence of scurvy and such high levels of lead as to suggest lead poisoning. In 1984 and 1986, Beattie excavated three early-expedition graves at Beechey Island, where bodies had been buried in permafrost. His most significant discovery, as described in *Frozen in Time*, which he co-authored with John Geiger, was that the three men had indeed suffered from high lead levels, although this had not killed them.

Beattie theorized that lead poisoning, contracted from the solder used to seal cans of preserved food, affected the entire expedition. Its symptoms include anorexia, weakness, fatigue, anemia, paranoia, and irritability, which matched certain Inuit tales of disoriented sailors. But some researchers were skeptical that lead poisoning played a major role in what happened. Others argued that if it did, the lead probably came from the ships' water pipes.

In April 2014, three British scientists—Keith Millar, Adrian Bowman, and William Battersby—published a statistical analysis in *Significance* magazine, repudiating the idea that most of Franklin's men died of lead poisoning as too simplistic. They argued that a combination of factors killed the sailors. Further scientific analyses of bone samples support this view. And in his introduction to *May We Be Spared to Meet on Earth*, American scholar Russell Potter exonerates the tinned foods, stating that neither lead poisoning nor botulism caused the expedition's breakdown.

The *Erebus* turned up far to the south of where, supposedly, everyone abandoned it. And that brings us again to David Woodman, who in 1991 challenged the standard reconstruction with *Unravelling the Franklin Mystery*. Woodman created an alternative scenario, which now stands corroborated in many particulars, by sifting through Inuit accounts as gathered by explorers. After analyzing the Inuit testimony, Woodman argued that the Victory Point Record indicated only what the surviving sailors intended to do, not what they did.

Thanks to the finding of *Erebus* and *Terror*, we can see that Woodman was essentially correct. He suggested that in 1848, with Franklin dead, Captain Francis Crozier set out with the bulk of the remaining men for the mouth of Back's Great Fish River, nine hundred miles away. Most of these men returned to the ice-locked ships. Some of them were aboard the *Erebus* as it sailed or was carried south by ice to Wilmot and Crampton Bay, an area known to the Inuit as Oot-joo-lik. Woodman suggested that a large group of sailors abandoned that vessel in 1851, before it reached its final resting place. Some Inuit hunters met this party of men, weak and starving, slogging south along the west coast of King William Island. These were the men In-nook-poo-zhe-jook described to John Rae. A few sailors—probably four, according to Puhtoorak—remained aboard the ice-locked ship until early 1852.

All this leaves us still with the question of root cause. Why did this expedition end in catastrophe? The Victory Point Record tells us that by 1848, nine officers and fifteen seamen had died. That represents 37 per cent of officers and 14 per cent of crew members. Historians have scratched their heads: *Why such disproportionate numbers?* Researchers have spent vast amounts of time and energy inquiring into the deaths of the first three sailors, whose graves remain on Beechey Island. But what if those three passings were anomalies, exceptions that tell us nothing about subsequent

Underwater archaeologist Jonathan Moore excavates in area 44J of the wreck of the *Erebus* on September 4, 2022. Here, on the lower deck, we see a wash basin and a sleeping berth.

illness and loss of life? Perhaps the other twenty-one men—nine officers, twelve sailors—died by some other cause.

And so the search continues. During the 2022 field season, Parks Canada divers retrieved 275 artifacts from the wreck of the *Erebus*. Along with table settings, a lieutenant's epaulettes, and other personal effects, they brought up what archaeologist-diver Ryan Harris described as "probably the most remarkable find of the summer." In the pantry, he "came across a folio—a leather book cover, beautifully embossed—with pages inside." It had a feather quill pen tucked inside the cover. The pages may contain an inventory of stores or food supplies, which could reveal more than one might think. How many casks of salted bear meat, for example, remained on board at such and so a date? As we went to press with *Searching for*

Franklin, conservators were working on the folio. If they can decipher even mundane scribblings, that will constitute a breakthrough. It will prove that, when divers retrieve logbooks or journals from within either of the wrecks, conservators will be able to provide transcripts—and those on-site reports should answer most remaining questions. Don't be surprised if they corroborate a new theory, advanced later in this book, about why the expedition broke down.

CHAPTER 21

The Second-Worst
Disaster

~

While seeking the root cause of the final Franklin catastrophe, I felt driven to investigate the second-worst disaster in Arctic exploration history—at least if we judge by number of deaths. I speak of the Jens Munk expedition of the early seventeenth century. True, Munk was Danish and played no role in Britain's great imperial enterprise of the nineteenth century, much less the decades-long search for two long-lost ships. And his expedition sailed in 1619—fully two centuries before John Franklin's first overland misadventure.

But I also remembered an article from a decades-old edition of *The Beaver* magazine. I dug it out and realized that the Munk expedition was not just relevant but central to my quest for answers. This will take some explaining. Jens Munk was a veteran navigator who secured backing from King Christian IV of Denmark for a low-cost expedition in search of the "Strait of Anián," or the Northwest Passage. On May 9, 1619, he sailed out of Copenhagen with two ships. The *Unicorn*, a frigate, carried forty-eight men, and the sloop, *Lamprey*, sixteen.

Delayed in Norway and then by a storm-tossed Atlantic crossing, Munk reached the west coast of Hudson Bay on September 7. Despite high winds, snow, hail, and fog, he guided the *Unicorn* through rolling breakers and anchored in the mouth of what came to be called the Churchill River. Two days later, the *Lamprey* arrived.

In the exhausted latecomers Jens Munk discerned the early symptoms of scurvy. "I caused the sick men to be taken ashore from the ship," he wrote, "and there we found still some cloudberries, gooseberries, and others which in Norway are called cowberries and crowberries. And I caused thereto a good fire to be made each day for the sick, whereby they were refreshed, and thereafter came speedily to health again."

Early on the morning of September 12, after a two-day snowstorm, "a large white bear came down to the water's edge," Munk wrote, "where it started to eat a beluga fish [whale] that I had caught the day before. I shot the bear and gave the meat to the crew with orders that it was to be just slightly boiled, then kept in vinegar overnight. I even had two or three pieces of the flesh roasted for the cabin. It was of good taste and quite agreeable."

One week later, after consulting his officers, Munk sailed the two ships upriver as far as possible. By October 1, he had secured both vessels. He moved a lot of gear ashore and placed the ship's cannons in the empty hold, where they would be out of the way. To simplify cooking arrangements, he ordered all the men to eat their meals on the *Unicorn*. And he had protective breakwaters built.

On October 7, Munk travelled upriver in a small boat, bringing "all manner of small items with me in the hope that we would meet some natives, and that by giving them gifts we would become better acquainted with them, but we didn't see a soul." This was because the Cree who visited the area in summer followed the animals inland as winter came on.

Munk started rationing wine on October 10, though he let the men drink as much beer as they wished. He organized the posting of sentinels, the fetching of wood, the burning of charcoal, and the melting of snow for water. Soon men were hunting every day. They set traps, built small blinds, and ventured into open country to hunt hares, ptarmigan, and other birds.

On November 21, Munk writes, "we buried a sailor who had been ill for a long time." This would prove to be a harbinger of worse to come. On December 12, one of the two surgeons died: "We had to keep his body on the ship for two days because the frost was so severe that no one could get ashore to bury him." On Christmas Eve, Munk gave the men "some wine and strong beer, which they had to boil as it was frozen." They celebrated "the Holy Christmas Day solemnly, as is a Christian's duty, with a goodly sermon and a mass." Over the next few days, the men played games to amuse themselves. "At the time," Munk writes, "the crew was in good health and brimming with excitement."

Frozen into the ice, the men found ways to endure the cold, the dark, the blizzards. The downward spiral began on January 10, 1620, four months after Munk shot the polar bear. The priest and the remaining surgeon, Munk writes, "took to their beds after having been ill for some time. That same day my head cook perished. And then a violent illness spread among the men, growing worse each day. It was a peculiar malady, in which the sick men were usually attacked by dysentery about three weeks before they died."

At Churchill, through December and early January, healthy men continued to hunt and provide for the rest. But by January 21, thirteen men were down with the mysterious illness, among them the sole remaining surgeon, "who was mortally ill by then." Munk pleaded with that man "if there was not some medicine in his chest that would cure the men, or at least comfort them. He replied that he had already used every medicine he had with him, and that without God's assistance he was helpless."

Two days later, one of the mates died after an illness that had confined him to bed for most of the last five months—indeed, shortly after the arrival at Churchill. That same day, "the priest sat up in his berth and preached a sermon, the last one he was ever to deliver in this world." By February 16, Munk writes, only seven men "were healthy enough to fetch wood and water and do whatever else had to be done on board."

In March, the cold became so severe that men hesitated to go ashore even to fetch food or water. A kettle burst when the water inside turned to ice. Occasionally, someone would shoot a few ptarmigan. Some of the men "could not eat the meat," Munk writes, "because their mouths were so swollen and inflamed with scurvy, but they drank the broth that was distributed amongst them."

Soon, "most of the crew were so sick that they were both melancholy to listen to and miserable to behold." Illness was raging so violently "that most of those who were still alive were too sick even to bury the dead." Munk examined the contents of the surgeon's chest but could make no sense of what he found: "I would also stake my life on the opinion that even the surgeon did not know how those medicines were to be used, for all the labels were written in Latin, and whenever he wished to read one, he had to call the priest to translate it for him."

Munk went ashore, collected berries, and distributed them among the men. But his "greatest sorrow and misery" began as March ended, "and soon I was like a wild and lonely bird. I was obliged to prepare and serve drink to the sick men myself, and to give them anything else I thought might nourish or comfort them." By April 3, almost nobody could get out of bed, "nor did I have any men left to command, for they were all lying under the hand of God." By now, so few were healthy "that we could scarcely muster a burial party."

Munk writes that he "felt abandoned by the entire world, as you may imagine." Later in April, as the weather improved, a few men crawled out of their berths to warm themselves in the sun: "But they were so weak that many of them fainted, and we found it almost impossible to get them back into bed." Men continued to die. The living were "so weak that we could no longer carry the dead bodies to their graves but had to drag them on the small sled that was used for hauling wood."

Occasionally, even now, someone would shoot a grouse or a goose. But by May 10, only eleven men remained alive, all of them sick. When two more died, Munk writes, "only God can know the torments we suffered before we got them to their graves. Those were the last bodies that we buried." Now those who died remained unburied on the ship.

By late May, only seven men lived. Munk writes, "We lay there day after day looking mournfully at each other, hoping that the snow would melt and that the ice would drift away. The illness that had fallen upon us was rare and extraordinary, with most peculiar symptoms. The limbs and joints were miserably drawn together, and there were great pains in the loins as if a thousand knives had been thrust there. At the same time the body was discoloured as when someone has a black eye, and all the limbs were powerless. The mouth, too, was in miserable condition, as all the teeth were loose, so that it was impossible to eat."

Alone among the symptoms, this last sounds like scurvy. Soon only four men remained alive on the ship, "and we just lay there unable to do a thing. Our appetites and digestions were sound, but our teeth were so loose that we could not eat." Dead bodies lay scattered around the ship. On June 4, believing he was about to die, Munk wrote a note requesting that "if any Christians should happen to come this way, they bury my poor body in the earth, together with the others that are lying here." He asked that his journal be sent to his "most gracious Lord and King . . . in order that my poor wife and children may obtain some benefit from my great distress and miserable death."

On June 9, having crawled out on deck "wrapped in the clothing of those who were already dead," Munk was astonished to see two crewmen walking around on land. More than two weeks before, on May 21, "we had beautiful clear sunshine; and I and three others, though with great difficulty, went on shore, where we made a fire and anointed our joints with bear's grease." By this time, surely, eight months after arriving, grease from the first polar bear Munk shot would have been expended—suggesting that one or more bears had since been shot and eaten.

Returning to the *Unicorn*, according to biographer Thorkild Hansen, two of the men were too weak to board and floundered back to shore. Munk thought they would soon be dead. But now they crossed the ice to the ship and helped him ashore. With them, Munk took to sheltering "under a bush on shore, where we built a fire each day."

Whenever they found "any green thing" growing, they would dig it up and suck the juice out of its main root. The weather grew warmer and, slowly, the three began to recover. They reboarded the *Unicorn* and found nobody living. They retrieved a gun and returned to shore, where they shot and ate birds. From the *Lamprey* they took a flounder net that enabled them to catch trout.

Slowly, the three survivors recovered. From the *Unicorn* they threw decomposing bodies overboard "because the smell was so bad that we couldn't stand it." Then, battling a plague of blackflies, and as ice began clearing from the bay, they stocked the smaller *Lamprey* with enough food to reach home. Finally, on July 16, 1620, Munk writes, "we set sail, in the name of God, from our harbour."

Such was the navigational skill of Jens Munk that he guided the sloop through fog, ice, gale-force winds, and the swirling currents of Hudson Strait, then across the storm-tossed Atlantic Ocean. On September 22, Munk reached Norway and "our joy was so great we could not hold back our tears." Sixty-four men had arrived at Churchill. Only three had survived. For more than two hundred years, this Arctic disaster remained the worst ever. But what does it have to do with our multifarious search for Franklin? To that we shall return.

PART FOUR

The True Believer

~

CHAPTER 22

The Resolute Back

~

Why in October of 1820, with winter coming on, did John Franklin send George Back on a 550-mile snowshoe journey from Fort Enterprise to Fort Chipewyan? For the record, John Franklin explained that the expedition needed provisions and, among his officers, Back was the best rough-country traveller. The irrepressible midshipman himself wrote that he volunteered to undertake the journey. But a crucial contributing factor, deliberately omitted from every written account, was that Back and Robert Hood had got embroiled in a jealous wrangle over a young Chipewyan woman the navy men called Greenstockings.

None of them mention this in their journals. But in August 1851, three decades after the fact, English sailor John Hepburn revealed the truth. While trapped in the Arctic ice aboard the *Prince Albert*, searching for Franklin's lost ships, he told his confidant, the French officer Joseph-René Bellot, that the two young midshipmen had threatened to kill each other but that he, Hepburn, had managed to intervene.

This drama unfolded soon after the arrival at Fort Enterprise. Back and Hood had been getting along well enough. Back writes of the scouting sortie that Franklin put him in charge: "We were to visit the river and if not pressed for time were to go downstream two or three days so as to

determine the nearest route to it from our house for the purpose of transporting the goods over in the spring." They were to be absent no more than
a fortnight and to return if the temperature should fall below forty degrees
Fahrenheit or any of the crew got hurt or sick. Back set out with Hood and
seven voyageurs, one Dene guide, and the multi-talented interpreter Pierre
St. Germain.

Back writes that "our guide knew but one route, and that very imper-
fectly." Hood elaborates, noting that "the guide told us, to our infinite
surprise, that he was totally ignorant of the route to the Coppermine River,
having been there only once with other Copper Indians, who had set out
from a different place." On day one, the party tackled five portages ranging
between 250 and 1,000 yards. The next day, after the men had paddled
some distance in their large canoe, the guide said they should stop and
proceed on foot.

They stashed the canoe and some provisions among a few dozen pines,
and St. Germain insisted on erecting a pole with a piece of bark attached to
it, on which in charcoal he "delineated a rude sketch" of a man and a house.
This was to tell any passing First Nations hunters that "whites were near" in
hopes that they would leave these things unmolested. Back adds, as if with
a twinkle in his eye, that St. Germain "did not rely implicitly on the magic
of said piece of bark, for shortly after I saw him pealing the moss up" and
hiding the canoe and provisions.

Over the next several days, carrying tents, a few blankets, and some
pemmican, the men marched northeast through a range of hills intermixed
with swamps and lakes. One night, during a snowstorm, the wind blew
down their tents. Hood wrote that "the gale brought with it, from their
northern haunts, long flights of geese, stretching like white clouds from
the northern to the southern horizon, and mingling their ceaseless screams
with the uproar of the wind among the hills."

On September 3, 1820, the men reached the Coppermine River,
though to Back the body of water looked initially "rather like an extensive lake." This was Point Lake, a sixty-mile-long broadening of the

Coppermine River. The men tracked it north and west, killing enough deer to keep themselves fed. On the seventh, they set out on their return journey. They arrived without incident late in the evening of September 10 and found Willard Wentzel alone in charge.

The previous day, Franklin and John Richardson had set out with a few men on a separate scouting exploration. The doctor later described this as "a pedestrian excursion to the Coppermine River, under the guidance of an old Indian named Keskarrah and accompanied by John Hepburn and [the voyageur] Semandrie, who carried our blankets, cooking utensils, hatchets, and a small supply of dried meat." This party arrived back on September 15, having taken what George Back agreed was a shorter, more treed, and overall "better route than ours." So—no trouble yet between Back and Hood.

Meanwhile, the voyageurs assigned to building winter quarters under Wentzel had been hard at work. The men moved into it near the beginning of October—though not, as Back writes, before "the mud that formed a part of the roof had been several times washed through by some heavy showers of rain." The log house was fifty feet long and twenty-four broad and divided into four apartments: "two at the east end, one at the west, and a large hall in the centre." Later, the men added a small kitchen measuring thirteen by sixteen feet. Great numbers of deer roamed past this house, Back writes, "which by the way I must not forget to say was now distinguished by the appellation of 'Fort Enterprise.'"

He notes that "our ammunition and clothing were entirely out, and as we expected some at Slave Lake [Fort Providence/Moose Deer Island], which was to have been conveyed there by the canoes of both companies, I volunteered my services on the occasion to go in search of it." Franklin supports this rendition, noting that Back "had volunteered to go and make the necessary arrangements for transporting the stores we expected from Cumberland House and to endeavour to obtain some additional supplies from the establishments at Slave Lake." In what looks like a retrospectively created order, made to justify Back's continuing onward from Slave Lake,

Keskarrah (right) and his daughter, nicknamed Greenstockings, as drawn by Robert Hood in 1821. Hood and George Back almost fought a duel over the young woman.

Franklin adds that if acquiring more goods proved impossible, Back was to proceed to Fort Chipewyan.

This official version of events elides the trouble that erupted between the two midshipmen as October began, when they almost came to duelling over the daughter of Keskarrah. Greenstockings, as they called her, now fifteen or sixteen, had already had two husbands—not unusual in that time and culture. Keskarrah had stayed on at Fort Enterprise after the other Dene left for their own winter quarters because Dr. Richardson was treating his wife, Birdseye, for a facial ulcer that was eating away at her nose. Greenstockings stayed to help care for her mother.

The only record of what then transpired turned up three decades later, when Bellot exchanged shipboard confidences with Hepburn. In his journal, Bellot discreetly leaves the names blank. Filling them in, and translating from the French, the reference reads as follows: "Mr. Hepburn tells me that George Back and Robert Hood had a quarrel one day about an Indian woman and were to fight a duel; but he overheard them and drew the charges of their pistols at night."

The faithful Hepburn no doubt alerted Franklin, who sought to defuse the situation by sending one of the two midshipmen south. George Back donned snowshoes and struck out on October 18, 1820, accompanied by Wentzel, two voyageurs (Gabriel Beauparlant and Solomon Belanger), and two Dene hunters and their wives, one of whom brought a child. Back writes that "the walking was extremely bad" owing to rough ground, large stones, and melting snow. On day four the party crossed Dissension Lake, roughly one-third of the way south to Fort Providence. The hunters killed enough deer to keep the party in food, but by October 23 they had remaining only eight balls of ammunition. Provisions were running low when, on the twenty-seventh, one of the women made a hole in the ice on a lake and "caught a fine Jack," or male salmon. The Dene declined to partake, Back wrote, "from the idea as we afterwards learnt, that we should not have sufficient: 'We are accustomed to starvation,' said they, 'but you are not.'"

Cold and hungry, the party beat on through thick woods and deep snow. One of the Dene broke through the ice on a river but "escaped with a sound ducking." On October 31, having arrived at the entrance of the Yellowknife River, Back climbed a hill and, to his surprise, there encountered Akaitcho. The next day, some of the Dene made a raft and ferried people across the river three at a time. On November 2, after twice breaking through ice along the edge of Slave Lake, the travellers arrived at Fort Providence.

~

Here George Back met an apprentice clerk, Nicholas Weeks, who had joined the North West Company in 1816 and was now in charge of this post. Weeks told him that in addition to letters and packets for the different officers, "only 5 of 16 pieces had been brought for us, and they were at the Hudson's Bay establishment on Moose Deer Island and consisted of the most useless articles."

Weeks said he had received orders not to supply the expedition with anything. But George Back had met Edward Smith, the NWC partner who was Weeks's superior, and "could not by any means credit this last assertion." Weeks added "a confused account of everything that had occurred respecting" the expedition. This infuriated Back, who now wished to proceed as soon as possible (when the lake froze) to Slave Fort and, if necessary, south to Lake Athabasca. He meant to find out more about "the cool and negligent manner in which the expedition had been treated" and to acquire more ammunition and provisions.

By November 9, Back had sent the voyageur Solomon Belanger back to Franklin at Fort Enterprise, along with a hunter and his wife. Belanger carried the letters and packets and a hundred balls of ammunition that Back had wheedled out of Weeks. He arrived at the headquarters on November 23. Back had also got hold of a private letter written by James Leith, the senior partner of the North West Company in the Athabasca District. It said that the HBC had forwarded some expedition packages as far as Lake Winnipeg, where that company had asked the NWC to transport some of them. Leith said he refused because the NWC canoes were already too deeply laden: "I could not think of throwing away the Company's property for to embark that of others." He blamed the HBC for making promises it could not keep.

Back notes that his previous long residence at Fort Chipewyan "had given me some insight in the manners of the traders." Leith's letter "wore a rather discouraging aspect," but he could not consider it official and he "determined to have an éclaircissement," or clarification, as soon as the lake froze and he could travel. To Franklin, Back also quoted a missive from the HBC's George Simpson, referring to that gentleman as a "senior clerk" although Simpson had charge of Fort Wedderburn and the entire

Athabaska District. Simpson wrote that five pieces had been sent to Slave Lake and insisted that he would "be happy to render the expedition any assistance in my power . . . and trust you will command my best services on all occasions." This gave Back reason to hope that he might have no problem acquiring much-needed provisions farther south.

On November 23, while Back was at Fort Providence, some Dene arrived there "with reports rather detrimental to the expedition." Back refuted these and wrote to Franklin. He accused Weeks, the NWC man in charge of the fort, "of having given directions to the Indians not to supply us with provisions—he said he *might* have done so—but *if* he had it was not without orders." Back was furious: "Afterwards, he [Weeks] confessed the whole was fabricated by himself and that it was the only offense he had been guilty of—so much for the faith of this person . . . whom I now considered as a slanderous and malignant vagabond replete with hypocrisy and a discredit to all society."

George Back's previous report to Franklin had prompted the latter to fret that "Weeks's inconsiderate foolish reports among the Indians . . . might prove highly injurious to the members of the expedition." He was clearly drawing on Back, who had described Weeks in very similar terms.

CHAPTER 23

The Immovable Simpson

~

O n December 7, 1820, with Great Slave Lake finally frozen over, George Back left Fort Providence with Wentzel, Paul Beauparlant, and two other voyageurs who said they had orders from Mr. Weeks "not to return with anything belonging to the Expedition." On the afternoon of December 10, this party reached the NWC fort on Moose Deer Island, where the friendly Edward Smith was in charge. That evening, Back visited the nearby HBC post and, from Robert McVicar, learned that the reports had been "but too correct—there being only five pieces for us there."

The next day, to his great disappointment, he determined that these included three kegs of adulterated rum, one of flour, and a mere thirty-five pounds of sugar, instead of sixty. Missing were the anticipated ammunition and tobacco, "the two most essential requisites." McVicar and Smith blamed each other's company for the absence of these and other supplies. George Back immediately made "a suitable demand on both parties, and though their connected list did not furnish half of what was required," he felt that they both contributed all they could spare—especially McVicar, "who in many articles gave me the whole of what he had."

As George Back was packing goods to send north, the interpreter Pierre St. Germain arrived from Fort Enterprise with three men. They had

At Fort Enterprise in May 1821, Robert Hood sketched the interpreters Tattannoeuck and Hoeootoerock. The English called them Augustus and Junius.

come to guide two Inuit interpreters, Tattannoeuck and Hoeootoerock, who had just arrived at Moose Deer Island from Fort Churchill, more than 620 miles away. Back and the others, struggling to pronounce the names correctly, took to calling them Augustus and Junius. The experienced Tattannoeuck, now in his twenties, had been raised in a settlement two hundred miles north of Churchill and had worked as a Hudson's Bay Company interpreter for four years. He had recently married and begun a family. George Back, who stood around five foot six in height, described both Inuit as "short of stature but broad and well-built—apparently good natured, and seemed perfectly acquainted with the purpose for which they were intended." Elsewhere, he specified that Tattannoeuck was "five feet one inch high but extremely strong and well made, as is Junius [Hoeootoerock]."

Not incidentally, Pierre St. Germain carried letters from Franklin referring to the "diabolical reports said to be propagated by Mr. Weeks." Smith of the NWC was just as surprised as Back "and positively denied having given any orders to Mr. Weeks relative to the expedition, except that he should assist it as far as his means would permit." Realizing that Weeks had gleaned his negative reports from the Dene, Back puzzled over "the channel through which the reports had flowed, for our best interpreter pretended total ignorance of the whole affair." Back thought "the ambiguity of his answers savoured strongly of falsehood," indicating the lack of trust that at this point existed between him and St. Germain.

It may well be that the interpreter had assessed the rough-country capabilities of Franklin and his crew, believed the expedition was doomed, and inadvertently let this slip in the wrong company. It seems far less likely that, anticipating disaster, he deliberately started rumours among the Dene. This matter was not as trivial as it looked, Back wrote, "for the contagion had expanded itself to such a degree amongst the loquacious and fickle-minded Indians—that our vital interest was connected with it—and had I not fortunately succeeded in procuring a few goods, the Expedition could not have proceeded beyond its present situation."

Even so, Back could not acquire enough at Slave Lake and so "determined to go on to the Athabasca and search the dispositions of the Gentlemen there." Smith doubted that anything could be spared at Fort Chipewyan. He noted that goods had never been carried so far during the winter season and added that the same dogs would never be able to haul sledges both ways. The journey would take sixteen days, the provisions would grow mouldy, and by slogging forward on snowshoes, Back would suffer "a great deal of misery and fatigue to no purpose."

Rejecting all this, George Back left Fort Resolution on December 23 with two men—the man he called his "servant," Beauparlant, and an unnamed voyageur—and two dog teams hauling sledges. Wearing snowshoes, the men pounded south on Christmas Day through cold and deep snow. Toward evening on the twenty-sixth, Back took a bad fall while turning to look at a distant hill. The exhausted dogs thought he had paused "for the purpose of beating them [and] took the excellent precaution of running the sledge over my snowshoe and upsetting me—and then trotted away as fast as they could go." He ended up "sunk two feet in snow with a fine view of the zenith [and] suffered severe discipline about the toes from the strings or thongs of the snowshoes."

Back righted himself, then carried on despite sore knees and swollen ankles. His companions suffered frostbite in the face, and the dogs struggled in the snow. By December 29, the dogs' feet were raw and the men had to drag and steer the sledges themselves. Back had intended to sketch several memorable waterfalls but now found them frozen solid. "When a person can just prevent himself from freezing—he has no great relish even for the finest views."

Beauparlant, whose face "was much lacerated by the frost . . . complained bitterly of the cold while passing amidst the rapids." Then, on reaching the upper part of the river, "he vented his indignation against the heat—'*mais, c'est terrible!*' said he, to be frozen and burnt in the same day—the poor fellow who had been a long time in the country regarded [frostbite] as the most severe punishment that could have been inflicted on him, and would willingly have parted with a quarter of his wages rather than that disgrace had happened—for there is a pride amongst old 'voyageurs' which considers freezing oneself as clownish—and only excusable in a 'Pork Eater' or a peasant just come from Canada."

On January 1, 1821, still suffering in his knees and ankles, Back sent the other men on ahead "and followed at a slow pace, actually dragging the snowshoes after me. It was only by dint of perseverance that I crept on at all." The next day at noon, having started at 5 a.m., the party reached Fort Chipewyan. Where Edward Smith had predicted a journey of sixteen days, Back had taken ten days and four hours, which he proudly described as "the shortest time the distance has been performed in the same season of the year."

The two men in charge of this NWC establishment, George Keith and Simon McGillivray, were astonished to see him. New Year's celebrations were in full swing, and Back decided to wait until "this scene of debauchery was over" before making "any demand." He went immediately to Fort Wedderburn, the HBC post where George Simpson was in charge, and delivered letters from John Franklin. Simpson was more surprised even than the NWC partners, for he had heard that Franklin and his men had already been "speared by the Esquimaux."

Back returned to the comfort of Fort Chipewyan. Over the next few days, he and Simpson exchanged letters. Back apparently viewed Simpson as just another HBC clerk in a wilderness fur-trade post. In fact, at age twenty-nine, well connected to the leadership of the HBC, Simpson had been sent across the Atlantic to end the fur-trade war with the North West Company, which was bad for business, and to unite the rivalrous companies. He was tough, smart, active, ruthless, racist, and misogynistic. To Simpson an Indigenous wife was just "a bit of brown." After some years in Rupert's Land, using an intermediary, the man infamously evicted his country wife, Margaret Taylor, from her home at Red River Settlement. Taylor had given birth to several of his children, but Simpson had married his teenage cousin and was bringing her out from England. Canadian author Peter C. Newman dubbed him "a bastard both by birth and by persuasion."

Yet he was a well-connected hard case, and before 1821 was out, Simpson would be governor of the HBC's northern district. By 1825, he would in effect be British viceroy of Rupert's Land—a position he would hold for the next thirty-five years. He became known as a rough-country traveller, though unlike John Rae, for example, he relied on Canadiens and Iroquois voyageurs to do all his paddling for him. With their indispensable assistance, Simpson would become known as the first person to circumnavigate the world by land.

Born in the Scottish Highlands in 1792, he cared little for Englishmen like John Franklin or George Back. On January 3, 1821, George Back requested supplies from both fur-trade companies, specifically ammunition, tobacco, spirits, guns, flints, axes, files, and clothing. He stressed "extreme necessity" and wrote that unless the expedition received these goods, it "must be arrested in its progress." From the partners of the NWC, he received a "most satisfactory" response and an avowal that their "inclinations to render assistance to the Expedition remain unshaken."

George Simpson, on the other hand, responded that he was "unable to comply with your demand, the few articles specified in the enclosed list excepted." The most significant items on that short list—which Back describes sarcastically as "rather compendious"—were ten axes, fifty gun flints, and four new guns. Simpson added that "any further assistance I may be enabled to render this season entirely depends on the arrival of supplies expected in a few weeks hence from a distant establishment."

Back wrote again to Simpson, he explained in his journal, "urging him to make an addition to his former list—telling him that, the officers (not to mention the men) were destitute even of the most common articles of dress—and that I could not persuade myself he would permit me to quit that department—without providing at least for their exigencies—I trusted he would comply with my desire—were it only for the reputation of the [Honorable Hudson's Bay Company and not let this] be recorded as a solitary instance, where both parties had not equally contributed to our wants."

Simpson remained icy and immovable. He regretted "his inability to administer to our wants in any shape"—and observed "that the H.B.C. has done more for the expedition than was expected or required" by Lieutenant Franklin. On January 5, having seen loaded sledges arrive at Fort Wedderburn, Back wrote a third time "and requested that he would mention in direct terms whether it was really his intention to make any further addition to the supplies—as I should consider any deviation as mere equivocation."

In this increasingly testy exchange, Simpson replied that "any promise of further assistance depended on his receiving the expected supplies from Îsle-à-la-Crosse." Those supplies had not come and "the arrivals you allude to have no connection with the Goods expected from Îsle-à-la-Crosse, and your conjecture that [the sledges] 'were not all empty'—is perfectly just, but I presume you will give me leave to know the purposes for which they are intended."

In his journal, Back described this last sentence as "highly improper." Clearly, Simpson had received goods, but as they had not come from Îsle-à-la-Crosse, "I could not have them—what was this but equivocation?" The next day, the HBC packet arrived from the specified post but without any supplies. After packing up the stores provided by the NWC, Back began preparing for his long journey to rejoin the expedition at Fort Enterprise. On February 9, 1821, after a hearty breakfast and some fond farewells to "a long range of women," he and a few men set out northward with their dogs and heavily laden sledges.

CHAPTER 24

Akaitcho's Warning

~

In January 1821, with Pierre St. Germain guiding, Tattannoeuck and Hoeootoerock snowshoed north from Moose Deer Island in Great Slave Lake to Fort Enterprise, arriving mid-month. George Back reached the fort two months later, on March 17, and received a hearty welcome, having brought more supplies than Franklin had anticipated. "I then heard," Back writes, "that it had been reported we were killed by the Slave Indians on our going to Fort Providence." The irrepressible midshipman lived on.

Of the four naval officers, he wrote by far the most about the voyageurs and the Inuit. He noted that Tattannoeuck "possessed a penetrating and quick discernment in the characters of strangers, and soon perceived their foibles—and being endowed with good natural abilities he made great progress in writing. He said that his Tribe lived a little to the northward of Churchill and came to the Fort with sledges in the spring. In the winter they live in circular snow houses (constructed with great ingenuity) on the seacoast—they kill seals when the ice begins to thaw—and in summer retire to the inland rivers and lakes where they obtain abundance of musk oxen—reindeer—and salmon—sufficient for their winter."

He noted also that Tattannoeuck was a proud man, "puffed up with the vanity of being made a 'great chief' and lorded it proudly over the easy disposition of his countryman [Hoeootoerock]—he would affect a superiority over our men sometimes and require that deference and respect which was shown only to the officers." In April, the two Inuit "erected a winter habitation similar to those used by their Tribe . . . which when finished was certainly one of the most delightful works of Art that can possibly be imagined. It was made of blocks of snow, so adjusted or scooped in the inner edge, as to form a dome about 6 feet high; on one side facing the south was a window of ice—and almost beneath it a square opening for the entrance—a piece of snow fitted to the size—serving as a door."

The interior, Back writes, "was divided into two parts, the one farthest from the entrance being elevated considerably above the other, which was the bed place—whilst the lower one was appropriated for the purposes of a kitchen—there was also a triangular division at each end of the bed place—the one for provisions and the other for rubbish—&c. On the outside there was a semi porch before the entrance—which kept out the wind—and added a finish to the building—the whole when viewed from the inside had such an imposing appearance and was so beautifully translucent—that it might be said to rival some of the 'thousand and one nights.'"

Tattannoeuck "employed himself in writing and smoking—and [Hoeootoerock] who was a perfect model of good nature, preferred the latter and using the bow and arrow—he would also carry wood and water for culinary purposes and was a great favourite with all. They paid a visit to Akaitcho our Indian chief and were highly pleased with the attention that was shown them." Because provisions were scarce at the Dene encampment, Hoeootoerock soon returned to Fort Enterprise, though Tattannoeuck remained until the end of May.

Meanwhile, at Fort Enterprise, food shortages meant people went hungry. Tensions had grown steadily through the cold, hard winter. On May 21, 1821, Akaitcho sent word that he would be coming to visit and wished to be received with a salute and such other marks of respect as he usually received on arriving in the spring at Fort Providence. Grudgingly, regretting the waste of ammunition, Franklin complied. Akaitcho arrived behind his standard-bearer, marching with a slow and stately step. All his men had painted their faces. They meant business.

Greeted by Franklin and Wentzel, the Dene chief entered and sat down on a chest, his men seating themselves on the floor around him. They passed the pipe around a couple of times, and Franklin had presents placed before the chief, among them cloth, blankets, capots, and shirts—in his view, "a present considerable for our circumstances." Akaitcho then started talking in what Franklin called a "very discouraging" manner. George Back wrote that he "continued the whole day—his ill humour increasing as his oration advanced."

If a coastal passage were discovered, Akaitcho asked, would Franklin or his officers be returning to his lands in a ship? With this answered in the affirmative, he asked whether some suitable present might then be forwarded to him and his nation, given that the Great Chief across the water "must see from the drawings and descriptions of us and our country that we are a miserable people."

Akaitcho again recalled that at Fort Providence, Nicholas Weeks had refused to pay Franklin's notes. If he could reject requests for such trifling amounts while the expedition was nearby, what would become of the promised large reward when Franklin and his men were far away and heading home? Franklin quoted Akaitcho as saying, "It really appears to me as if both the companies consider your party as a third company, hostile to their interests, and that neither of them will pay the notes you give to the Indians."

Working up a head of steam, Akaitcho said Franklin had failed to respect him as a chief and had sent him rum notable for its weakness. Now Franklin was putting forward a small collective present completely lacking in chief's clothing of the kind he received every spring at Fort Providence. This was unacceptable. He refused to receive the goods laid before him.

Shocked, Franklin responded that vague reports concerning Nicholas Weeks could not be trusted. He had heard many stories criticizing Akaitcho and dismissed them all. Stretching the truth, he claimed that the rum he had sent was mild but was what the great men of England drank. He and his officers had brought less than the fur traders because they had come a great distance in a short period. Because Akaitcho had not received his spring outfit, his debts to the NWC had been cancelled and a much greater present had already been ordered. Franklin went on the offensive. He was disappointed at not receiving any dried meat for the looming journey. Compared with that deficiency, the chief's complaints were trivial and looked to be made only to cloak his failure to fulfill the terms of their agreement.

Akaitcho shifted ground. He warned Franklin, not for the first time, that if he and his men went east along the coast in canoes, they would "inevitably perish." In this the British naval officer heard not a plea to reconsider but "an exact transcript" of opinions previously expressed by the interpreter Pierre St. Germain. He did not wonder if perhaps the two men had talked and come to the same conclusion. Instead he imagined that the interpreter had told Akaitcho that the white men had hidden some goods or rum, so inspiring him to come seeking more.

George Back noted that Akaitcho's words "tended towards dissuading us from proceeding along the coast. We examined the Interpreter [St. Germain] who had lived some time at the tents . . . to discover if possible if he had been tampering with [Akaitcho]—but nothing satisfactory was proved." Certainly, the Dene leader had changed his mind—"but from what motives we could not judge." Ultimately, Back attributed this change to Nicholas Weeks, the NWC man at Fort Providence, whose "continual aggravations" were, to quote him fully, "highly injurious to the credit and interest of the Expedition—and a marked disgrace to the Company he serves—or rather injures."

We don't know what Robert Hood thought of this long exchange with Akaitcho because his last journal entry is dated the previous month, April 16, 1821, when he observed that other duties had "compelled me to write it, from notes, within the last fortnight." Unlike Back, who never did revise his dash-ridden notes into grammatical English, Hood took care with his prose. Some of his later observations on the aurora borealis and the shifting magnetic pole did make their way into Franklin's journal. Much of the latter derived from the journal of John Richardson, who paraphrased Akaitcho as declaring "that if we attempted to make a voyage along the sea coast we would inevitably perish; and he advised us strongly against persisting in the attempt."

As afternoon turned to evening, Akaitcho accepted his usual dinner portion. He became friendlier, expecting that Franklin would now increase the collective present. When the naval officer said this was impossible because he had already presented all the remaining rum and every article he could spare, Akaitcho was shaken but undaunted. He said he would wait for the arrival of Humpy, his older brother. After he retired, however, the young hunters returned for the rum—according to Franklin, "a great step towards reconciliation."

Franklin now blamed Akaitcho's "defection" on St. Germain, "the most intelligent of our two interpreters, and the one who had the most influence with the Indians." He cited "unguarded conversations he had held with them." St. Germain half-admitted this and worked hard the next day to bring Akaitcho around. The chief remained in his tent while the young men showed their usual good humour, although they declined to hunt.

On May 25, 1821, Franklin issued the voyageurs clothing and other necessary equipment. He reserved some gifts for distribution among the Inuit—two or three blankets, some cloth, ironwork, and trinkets. He gave laced robes to the Inuit interpreters, who received them joyfully. That afternoon, led by Akaitcho's older brothers, Humpy and White Capot, and an unrelated leader, Long Legs, numerous Yellowknives arrived at Winter Lake, swelling the camp to 121 people, including 31 women and 60 children. The rest of the nation were on the Coppermine River.

That evening brought "another formidable conference." Akaitcho repeated his former complaints and Franklin offered the same answers. The talks went on until midnight. Akaitcho refused to say when he would be ready to make for the Coppermine and, according to Back, "continued in such a gloomy disposition that it was impossible to conjecture what he intended to do."

The next day, the Dene conferred in their tents all morning then came to the house. They seated themselves and passed the ceremonial pipe, filling the place with smoke. Franklin laid out the same gifts as before. Akaitcho flatly refused to distribute so few goods among his men, noting the absence of blankets, kettles, and daggers. He accused Wentzel of defrauding the Dene by distributing their intended gifts among the voyageurs.

Stung, Wentzel reminded Akaitcho that he had been told when he agreed to accompany the expedition that he should not expect any goods until he returned. This Akaitcho denied, Franklin writes, "with an effrontery that surprised us all." Humpy now intervened, saying that he had been present and Wentzel spoke the truth. White Capot took the same line, saying he had made a promise and would accompany the white people to the sea, confident that on his return, he would receive the stipulated reward.

Seeing how the wind blew, Akaitcho changed the subject and spoke of the treatment he had received from the fur traders "with an asperity of language that bore more the appearance of menace than complaint." Franklin dismissed this as irrelevant to the present discussion. He insisted that Akaitcho had a duty to provide comfort and safety to the Canadiens as well as the Indians. The voyageurs faced a long journey and would probably "be exposed to much suffering from cold on a coast destitute of wood." They therefore needed more clothing than the Dene, who would return to Fort Providence in August and receive their promised rewards.

Most of the Dene nodded assent. But according to Franklin, Akaitcho said, "I perceive the traders have deceived you. You should have brought more goods. But I do not blame you." Franklin answered that from England he had brought only ammunition, tobacco, and spirits. Not knowing what else the Dene needed, he had relied on the traders. He had worked hard to acquire more supplies, even sending George Back to Fort Chipewyan. Franklin added that he too was disappointed, but the shortage should be blamed on "the neglect of those to whom they had been entrusted."

Here was a way forward: both parties could blame the warring fur-trade companies. Never mind that in this territory widespread shortages were more the rule than the exception, or that the expedition had been an unrealistic proposition from the beginning—ill conceived, poorly equipped, badly planned. Akaitcho grew more amenable. Franklin reiterated that the expedition depended on the Dene to speedily furnish provisions. If he succeeded in his endeavour, a ship would soon bring an abundance of goods to the mouth of the Coppermine. The Dene conferred. Akaitcho asked for two or three kettles and some blankets for his young men. Franklin had no kettles, but his officers promised to provide one blanket each from their own beds.

After dinner, Akaitcho renewed his solicitations, but half-heartedly. In Franklin's view, he was clearly seeking to gain everything he possibly could. The naval officer steadily refused every request. This exchange, he wrote later, culminated in Akaitcho rising angrily to declare, "There are too few goods for me to distribute. Those that mean to follow the white people to the sea may take them."

The guides and most of the hunters stepped forward to receive a share of goods. Akaitcho withdrew from the meeting, but the hunters accepted ammunition from Wentzel so they could go hunting next morning. Everyone stayed late, playing voyageur-led games until two in the morning, when finally the sun went down.

After remaining absent the next day, Akaitcho resurfaced on May 28, looking cheerful. George Back interpreted this to mean that "finding his authority on the decline, and his character tarnished—from his recent feeble and capricious conduct—he suddenly reformed and with an abashed and servile countenance sought every means to please." Franklin wrote that "the knowledge that the sentiments of the young men differed from his own" had brought about the change. Indeed, he said he would set out for the river as soon as possible. The snow was still too deep to take sledges north and the moss too wet to make fires, but departure would not be far off. He now accepted the robe he had formerly refused.

Before leaving this subject in his official narrative—which inevitably reflects his own perspective and that of his Royal Navy editors—Franklin writes that he feels duty bound to alert future travellers to "the art with which these Indians pursue their objects, their avaricious nature, and the little reliance that can be placed upon them when their interests jar with their promises." He does not explain why putting their own interests before those of a foreign expedition should be considered greedy but assumes that Akaitcho should adopt a Royal Navy perspective, dismiss the needs of his own people, and put those of the expedition above all else. Franklin does think to add that "as has been already mentioned, their dispositions are not cruel, and their hearts are readily moved by the cry of distress." For this last he would have reason soon enough to be grateful.

Meanwhile, the weather having grown warm enough to work on canoes without cracking their bark, Pierre St. Germain had led the voyageurs in beginning repairs. Two canoes were in quite good shape and the third could be salvaged. When Franklin decided to send a first party off under Dr. Richardson, Akaitcho said he would appoint two hunters to accompany them. At the same time, he requested that "the Medicine Chief," as he called Richardson, might travel with his band.

That was not going to happen, but Richardson made up packets of medicine for several of the chiefs and, not for the first time, Akaitcho expressed his gratitude for the doctor's ministrations. Richardson set out on June 4 with George Back, fifteen voyageurs, and six Dene, including women—twenty-three persons in all, not counting children.

Akaitcho and his hunters remained at Fort Enterprise until 3 p.m., and through Wentzel, Franklin relayed that he wanted provisions left here at the fort for use if the expedition had to return this way. Akaitcho agreed and suggested hiding the goods in the house in case Dogrib visited. He grinned and told Franklin that he could see the supplies really were exhausted and that he would trouble the navy man no more but strive to acquire provisions: "I think if the animals are tolerably numerous, we may get plenty before you can embark on the river."

While the men were busy packing, a Dogrib woman slipped away and disappeared. Her Yellowknife husband had taken her from her relations by force and had then behaved abusively. The fellow was at Fort Enterprise when his mother told him the news. "You are rightly served," Akaitcho told him. "Now you will have to carry all your things yourself, instead of having a wife to drag them."

By the evening of June 7, Pierre St. Germain had finished repairing the two better canoes. By the night of the tenth, he had rebuilt the third. A letter came from Richardson at Point Lake, advising that the snow there was deeper and the ice thicker. The expedition was cleared to depart.

CHAPTER 25

Crisis *at* Bloody Falls

~

On June 14, 1821, accompanied by Dene hunters, the expedition set out from Fort Enterprise for the headwaters of the Coppermine River, four men dragging each canoe while others carried eighty pounds on their backs. Swarms of mosquitoes emerged from the swamps and were "very tormenting," Franklin wrote, yet the party rejoiced to set out at last "towards the final object of the expedition." The men made their way north, paddling and portaging over some of the roughest country in North America. According to George Back, "the poor dogs suffered the most— and left tracks of blood at each step." One of the dogs had already lain down on the shore ice, unable to drag his sledge farther, causing Franklin to lighten his load by abandoning the most damaged canoe. Back noted the water was so high and the current so fast that while running the rapids, "the men's hair, which is always long, flowed in straight lines behind them."

All except the navy men were "heavily laden with burdens of 60 or 80 pounds each," Back wrote. "Nor were we exempt—every officer carrying at least 20 pounds." Men and dogs hauled sledges over rough and melting ice until early July. Then they took to the rivers, though shallows and rapids necessitated frequent portages. While beating north, the hunters had only sporadic luck. By July 12, the expedition retained enough food for fourteen days at what Franklin called "the ordinary allowance of three pounds to each man per day."

In fact, this allowance was hardly "ordinary," especially for the hard-working voyageurs. In his journal, Richardson refers to "eight pounds of solid animal food, their customary daily allowance." Franklin himself writes of three fish of typical size being "the daily allowance to each man at the fort, and is considered . . . as equivalent to two geese, or eight pounds of solid moose-meat." The fur-trade standard was eight pounds per man per day. Not surprisingly, the voyageurs complained of hunger and exhaustion.

By the time the expedition reached Point Lake, their supplies had been reduced to two hundred pounds of dried meat. Richardson told Franklin that the hunters had expended all their ammunition but contributed no new provisions. Questioned about this, Akaitcho infuriated Franklin by revealing that he had given most of the ammunition to hunters accompanying women who had set out on a return journey to Fort Providence. The Dene leader redeemed himself somewhat in Franklin's eyes when a bear attacked a group of hunters deep in conversation, catching them by surprise.

Richardson called it a grizzly, while Back quoted Akaitcho as warning the men against wandering alone "for just now as we were conversing together a large white bear sprung upon us—which certainly would have dispatched someone (as all my young men missed their aim) had I not killed it." In Franklin's summary, Akaitcho "took deliberate aim and shot the animal dead." He added that the Dene do not eat bear flesh, but "knowing that we had no such prejudice, they brought us some of the choice pieces, which upon trial we found to be excellent meat."

The expedition had entered Inuit territory and Akaitcho grew cautious. The men were now within a dozen miles of Bloody Falls, scene of the infamous massacre witnessed by Samuel Hearne some fifty years before, when Dene marauders fell upon a party of sleeping Inuit. This had not been an isolated incident. Tattannoeuck told George Back that six years before, in this vicinity, "some of their Tribe were murdered by the Indians

On June 25, 1821, George Back depicted the expedition passing through Point Lake on the ice. Engraved by Edward Finden.

from the interior." Akaitcho himself may have been involved, though on a different occasion he told Franklin eight years had passed "since they went on a war party and actually destroyed some Esquimaux."

As the expedition continued north, there ensued what historian Richard Davis describes as "an elaborate ballet" involving people of four cultures: British, French Canadian, Yellowknife (Dene), and Inuit. At their camp by the river not far south of Bloody Falls, Akaitcho proposed to send out a scouting party. Franklin said no: among the Inuit, Dene scouts might cause alarm.

Akaitcho wanted to remain with the voyageurs because he feared Inuit aggression—and not without reason. Five years from now, at the mouth of the Mackenzie River, John Franklin's second overland expedition would come under attack, and only Tattannoeuck's extraordinary bravery would save the lives of the party. Alone and unarmed, the diminutive Inuk would stand in a throng of hostile hunters, proclaiming that the white men had come for their benefit. He stood arguing while more than forty men crowded around him, Franklin would write, "and all of them with knives, and he quite unarmed. A greater instance of courage has not been I think recorded."

But that was yet to come. Now, Franklin wanted Akaitcho and his hunters to wait here by the river while he pressed ahead with his officers and the voyageurs. Akaitcho refused. Together, he reasoned, Franklin and his own party might be powerful enough to repulse any attack, but his remaining Dene warriors, with most hunters already departed, were not now numerous enough to do so alone. "Therefore," he said, "we are determined to go on with you or to return to our lands." After much back and forth, Akaitcho agreed to stay where he was if Wentzel remained with him. He promised not to pass a range of hills unless he received notice.

On July 13, as the expedition came within hearing distance of Bloody Falls, Franklin dispatched Tattannoeuck and Hoeootoerock, instructing them not to mention their Dene travelling companions. The two Inuit carried pocket pistols and approached the falls with caution. As evening fell, they arrived near a campsite consisting of four tents. They hid until the next morning. Then Tattonnoeuck emerged, climbed to the top of a large rock, and addressed the strangers in their own language. "Nothing could equal their surprise," George Back wrote, "at beholding a strange form and voice, risen (as it were) from the rocks thus speaking to them."

The encamped Inuit became fearful, jumped into their canoes, and paddled to a nearby island. Then, overcoming their terror, "and perhaps not a little encouraged by understanding the language in which [Tattannoeuck] spoke—they ventured near him—but he could not persuade them to receive him into their skin barks." He showed the presents he had brought, said he was unarmed, and announced the white people had come with many gifts. "They listened attentively to all he said," Back writes, "but dreading some treachery was near, always remained a little distance from him. They did not however offer the least appearance of hostility."

Meanwhile, late on July 13, when the two Inuit did not return, Akaitcho—"ever ready to augur misfortune," according to Franklin—said he believed they had been killed and that "the Esquimaux were lying in wait for us." Franklin and a few men went forward and around 6 p.m. were excited to meet Hoeootoerock rushing back to tell them of having discovered the four Inuit tents at Bloody Falls. Tattannoeuck, having made contact, had remained on site but needed food. Soon after learning this, Franklin was "mortified by the appearance of the Indians with Mr. Wentzel, who in vain had tried to restrain them from following." Akaitcho waved off his criticism, saying only that he needed to know that Franklin meant to establish peace between the Dene and the Inuit. Apparently, the lack of trust flowed both ways.

Next morning, again, Franklin had trouble convincing the Dene to remain where they were. George Back wrote of an hour's "tedious and irritating conversation with the Leader, whose obstinacy or fear induced him to oppose all our propositions." He wished to go forward to make peace with the Inuit "with whom the Red Knives [aka Yellowknives] were at war." Akaitcho did not consent to stay behind until Franklin threatened to withhold the promised reward.

The navy men and voyageurs went forward cautiously, hoping to confer with the four families. But after agreeing to wait out of sight, Akaitcho and his men had moved forward. "What was our astonishment and indignation on approaching the spot to hear [Jean Baptiste Adam, the interpreter] say that the Esquimaux had seen the land party coming over the gigantic hill above us—and being frightened at their warlike appearance had thrown down their tents and fled in utmost consternation. At so critical a period of the voyage—at the very moment that we required the aid and advice of the natives—sure nothing could have been more unfortunate—but it was useless brooding over a misfortune which could not now be avoided—we therefore hastened to apply the only remedy in our power, which was that of sending [the two Inuit interpreters] after them—for this purpose we encamped—carried the canoes across the portage, and landed [the two men] on the opposite side of the River." Away they went, Tattannoeuck and Hoeootoerock, in search of the Inuit who had fled.

Franklin hoped that the Inuit families would return because surely they would be able to resolve "our state of absolute ignorance respecting the sea-coast." Having dispatched his Inuit interpreters to catch those who fled, he set up camp beside Bloody Falls, where some human skulls "bore the marks of violence" and many bones lay strewn about. George Back, who did a painting of the location, sought to rename it. In his journal about the Coppermine expedition, eventually published as *Arctic Artist*, he described his own arrival at Bloody Falls: "We were now at Massacre Rapid—celebrated in Hearne's voyage [*Journey to the Northern Ocean*] for the shocking scene that occurred there—the most interesting part of which I imagine to be unfounded—as one of our guides had accompanied him—said that [Hearne] was two days march from them at the time of [the Dene] attacking the Esquimaux. The havoc that was there made was but too clearly verified—from the fractured skulls—and whitened bones of those poor sufferers—which yet remained visible."

In fact, George Back's own imaginings were ill-founded. A close reading of his journal reveals that, initially, only one of the Dene claimed to have travelled with Hearne fifty years before. This man was Akaitcho's older brother, Humpy. As noted in chapter 14, another older brother, White Capot, later advanced a similar claim. According to Franklin's published narrative, a Dene named Rabbit's Head also declared that he had travelled with Hearne, bringing the total to three. And John Richardson writes of yet another "old Indian, who by the by, is considered as a hermaphrodite by his countrymen, and who remembers Mr Hearne's passing." How old were these Dene warriors fifty years before, when in 1771 Samuel Hearne reached the Coppermine? Those with whom he travelled deliberately left behind all women and children before advancing within striking distance. So the youngest participants would have been at least twelve or thirteen. By now, when Franklin and his men arrived, White Capot and Humpy and Rabbit's Head would have had to be at least in their sixties— and this in a world so filled with hardship and danger that the strongest men rarely survived beyond forty-five or fifty. Perhaps asserting a claim to having travelled with Hearne increased a guide's status with the credulous Englishmen.

In his official narrative, Franklin negated Back's suggested name change for Bloody Falls. "As the spot exactly answers the description given by Mr. Hearne," he wrote, "of the place where the Chipewyans who accompanied him perpetrated the dreadful massacre on the Esquimaux . . . We have, therefore, preserved the appellation of Bloody Falls, which he bestowed upon it."

On July 16, Franklin sent Jean Baptiste Adam and a voyageur to tell Akaitcho that the Inuit had fled. The two returned in a hurry with a gar-bled report that a party of Inuit were chasing some voyageurs who had gone to search for dried wood to make floats for nets. As Franklin set out to rescue those men, they arrived in camp, unconcerned, the focus of an unfounded rumour. They had stumbled upon a second party of Inuit, including six men with their families and dogs, all heading for Bloody Falls. The women hid, but the men began to dance in a circle, signifying a desire for a peaceful meeting. The voyageurs responded in kind, but then the Inuit withdrew.

Meanwhile, Tattannoeuck had chanced upon an old Inuk, Terreganoeuck, who had been unable to flee with the others. After some back and forth, he proved friendly enough. But he could do nothing to bring back the families who had fled, and who apparently numbered not four but eight. Franklin conveyed that he was travelling with some Dene who wanted to make peace with the Inuit, and when the old man said he desired the same, the navy man sent Adam to inform Akaitcho. The Dene chief arrived at camp that evening. He told an irritated Franklin that he too had communicated with Terreganoeuck. Still, things were progressing nicely.

The next afternoon, July 17, brought a reversal. A party of nine Inuit appeared on the east bank of the river about a mile below the expedition camp. They carried canoes and baggage but turned and fled as soon as they saw the expedition's tents. Even so, Akaitcho had seen enough. Who could say how many more Inuit would soon arrive? According to Back, three of Akaitcho's men, including White Capot, had already taken flight "from pure terror." The appearance of so many Inuit bands "terrified the Indians so much," Franklin wrote, "that they determined on leaving us the next day, lest they should be surrounded and their retreat cut off."

Franklin tried to retain two or three hunters by offering a greater reward, but they would have none of it. He had trouble even extracting a promise that they would wait at the Copper Mountains for Wentzel and four voyageurs he intended to discharge at the coast. Pierre St. Germain and Jean Baptiste Adam asked to be discharged along with them.

St. Germain argued that with the Indians gone, their interpretive services were no longer required. He claimed that he had agreed to remain only as long as the Dene and persisted in this until two different officers read his contract aloud. These two interpreters were among the best hunters on the expedition, and Franklin, fearing that they might try to slip away, alerted the other men to keep an eye out. Because St. Germain and Adam also feared the Inuit in their own territory, they would not try to flee once Akaitcho and his hunters were some distance away.

The next morning, July 18, Akaitcho and his men refused to reconsider. But perhaps Franklin would change his mind and abandon this mad plan that could only end in disaster? Franklin grew impatient. He reminded Akaitcho through Wentzel and St. Germain of the need to leave provisions at Fort Enterprise. The Yellowknife leader promised to do so. Franklin furnished the Dene with a bit of ammunition, and they departed, anxious to put as much distance as possible between themselves and what they imagined to be a growing army of vengeful Inuit.

CHAPTER 26

Franklin Reaches
the Coast

~

They lacked British grit and gumption. That was all John Franklin could think. These voyageurs, these Métis and *Canadiens*, were reputed to be tough and courageous. But now they were openly expressing terror. They were fearful beyond belief—scared to death of finishing the task for which he had hired them. It hardly bore contemplating.

Two years had passed since he left London. Two years and two months, almost to the day. What? Was he going to quit now? The young lieutenant stood on a bluff at the mouth of the Coppermine River gazing northward at islands rolling away into the mist. In his person the Royal Navy had reached the Arctic coast of North America. July 19, 1821—surely, the summer travel season had scarcely begun. A few miles upriver, at Bloody Falls, Franklin had taken sombre leave of Akaitcho, who had warned him against continuing his expedition this late in the year.

Having lived all his life in this part of the world, Akaitcho had told Franklin that if he and his twenty men now paddled east along the Arctic coast in birchbark canoes, they would not live to tell the tale. That brash interpreter Pierre St. Germain had persisted in repeating the same doom-and-gloom prophecy. These Indigenous leaders lacked courage. Worse, they had no Christian faith. The English lieutenant, so devoutly religious as to believe in miracles, had shrugged off their criticism and advice. Why, the voyageurs were as bad as Akaitcho and his warriors. They had been grousing since they joined the expedition. Their dogs were overloaded and would never last. Their packs were too heavy. But Franklin knew that sixty or eighty pounds, in addition to their personal items, did not constitute an unusual burden for these men. Wading through icy, waist-deep water with more than one hundred pounds on your back might be difficult; he could see that. But wasn't that what these men had signed on to do? And hadn't his own officers shouldered twenty-pound packs?

Yet these voyageurs never ceased complaining. Mainly they grumbled about the shortage of food. They said they weren't getting enough to eat. But the lack of provisions was more their fault than his. Weren't they supposed to be hunters? He had squeezed everything he could out of the fur traders and had driven a hard bargain with the Dene leader and his men.

These voyageurs lacked character. They gorged themselves when they could and gave no thought to tomorrow. Of moral fibre they had none. They were flagrant in their dalliances with Indigenous women. Even George Back had remarked on episodes that went "beyond decency or moderation between the Canadians and the young Indian girls." Back himself, like Robert Hood, had given in to his baser instincts with the young woman they called Greenstockings. But that was an exceptional circumstance, a youthful folly. As men more than a decade older, Franklin and John Richardson had set the British example and behaved impeccably.

Because he spoke fluent French and was naturally outgoing, midshipman Back had spent more time conversing with the voyageurs than was good for him. He would even listen and record the lyrics to their paddling songs—a wasteful pastime. At one point, Back had spoken of how "the perpetual fatigue of transporting canoes [and baggage] across the portages had harassed the men considerably, and having no other sustenance than bad dried meat—it is only surprising how they maintained sufficient strength to perform their daily labour."

Back had recovered from this excess of sympathy somewhat at Dissension Lake, where he wrote that "a mutinous spirit displayed itself amongst the men [and] they refused to carry the goods any farther, alleging a scarcity of provisions as a reason for their conduct." Even Back had approved of Franklin's response to this "apprehended insurrection."

Pierre St. Germain was the problem. The most rebellious of the hired men, he presented a threat to discipline, authority, and, indeed, the expedition itself. At Dissension Lake, St. Germain had led the voyageurs in threatening to cease working for lack of food. He said the men were starving and could go no farther. Franklin had been driven to warning that if he heard any more threats, he would make an example of the first person to come forward by blowing out his brains. Franklin would paraphrase St. Germain's response in a letter to a reverend friend, writing that the interpreter answered, "It is immaterial to me where I lose my life, whether it is in England, or accompanying you to the sea, for the whole party will perish."

As the only man on the expedition who could speak three languages—English, French, and Athabascan—St. Germain wielded disproportionate influence over Akaitcho and his hunters, and also shaped the thinking of the voyageurs. He used his influence to sow fear and discontent, asserting repeatedly and against all reason that if the men continued eastward along the coast, they would never return alive. This Franklin viewed as nothing but fearmongering.

On arriving at the coast, Franklin had written that the voyageurs "complained much of the cold, but they were amused with their first view of the sea, and particularly with the sight of the seals that were swimming about near the entrance of the river." But they plunged into "despondency before the evening had elapsed. They were terrified at the idea of a voyage through an icy sea in bark canoes. They speculated on the length of the journey, the roughness of the waves, the uncertainty of provisions, the exposure to cold where we could expect no fuel, and the prospect of having to traverse the barren grounds to get to some establishment."

On July 19, 1821, John Franklin and his men set up camp here at the mouth of the Coppermine River. A severe thunderstorm kept the expedition from proceeding next day, and at midnight on July 20, George Back drew this sketch, later engraved by Edward Finden.

Franklin "felt for their privations and fatigue," he had continued, "and was disposed to seize every opportunity of alleviating them." But the many instances of pilferage and "petty dishonesty with regard to meat showed how little confidence could be put in a Canadian voyager when food or spirits were in question." At Fort Enterprise, after he had learned of their siphoning off spirits while bringing forward provisions, one of them had come forward "with an artful apology for their conduct." The man stated that the voyageurs knew Franklin would treat them with a dram to mark the new year and so "helped themselves to a small quantity on that day, trusting to my goodness for forgiveness." Being unwilling to act harshly, Franklin had admonished them to be more circumspect in future. His leniency had availed nothing.

The voyageurs could have taken a lesson from Robert Hood. Franklin worried about that young man. He was the son of a preacher and not the strongest of men. Two months previous, during a night of games at Fort Enterprise, Franklin had been pleased to see Hood get involved. The young midshipman, immersed in his drawings, had "confined himself too much to the house in winter, and his health was impaired by his sedentary habits." Far from robust, at times he insisted on extending himself.

Just two days earlier, when Franklin had sent him with a party of men to talk with the old Inuk at Bloody Falls, Hood had descended into a chasm to retrieve some meat that had been deposited atop a column of rock. George Back reported that "the frightful appearance of the place was such that no one could conceive how or in what manner the natives had so carefully placed their provision." The meat had gone putrid and gave off such a "horrid effluvia" that the voyageurs refused to venture beyond the brink. "*Mais, c'est terrible,*" cried one. "*Jamais je descendrai la, moi!* [Never will I go down there.]"

Realizing that if he wanted to investigate the cache he must do it himself, Hood had tied one end of a rope around his waist and, with several men holding the other end, climbed down into the chasm. Back reported that if "the stench almost suffocated him on going down, [the meat's] putridness—and the large worms that made their appearance on [turning it over] had no less effect on his feelings. He was heartily glad to be hoisted up from so loathsome a sight and once more breathe the pure air of the atmosphere."

Robert Hood was made of the right stuff. But Pierre St. Germain? As recently as yesterday he had come forward yet again, bringing with him his fellow interpreter, Jean Baptiste Adam, and another of the voyageurs to request an early discharge. He argued that with the Dene gone, the expedition did not need him. He wanted to follow Akaitcho and proceed south with Willard Wentzel. Franklin had said goodbye to that useful North West Company trader earlier that day and released four voyageurs to travel with him. But St. Germain was not among them. Nor was Adam. Instead,

Franklin set the other men to watching over them. He could not afford to lose his two best hunters.

Franklin had reduced the expedition numbers to himself and twenty men. These twenty included three naval officers, one stalwart English seaman, four interpreters (two of them Inuit), and twelve voyageurs, mostly French Canadian but with one Italian, Antonio Vincenza Fontano, and one Iroquois, Michel Teroahaute. Franklin had named this part of the ocean Coronation Gulf, in honour of the coronation of King George IV, set for this date (July 19, 1821). Since arriving here, the English officers had behaved wonderfully, ridiculing the apprehensions of the voyageurs. And the way "our faithful Hepburn viewed the element to which he had been so long accustomed contributed not a little to make them ashamed of their fears."

What did Franklin care about the fears and misgivings of Akaitcho and St. Germain? Their concerns were groundless. They lacked tenacity and Protestant faith and any sense of discipline. As a naval officer, Franklin had his orders. He would follow them to the letter, as expected. What if Edward Parry arrived in his ship just to the east of this location and Franklin was not there to greet him? Why, he would be disgraced! And rightly so. Eastward along the coast, surely, they would encounter Inuit hunters eager to assist. John Franklin turned and headed for the tents. Tomorrow, the expedition would set out. If worse came to worst, the Good Lord would provide.

CHAPTER 27

East *of the* Coppermine

~

A day-long thunderstorm made departure impossible. Then came foggy weather and strong winds. But on July 21, 1821, after waiting until noon for the weather to clear, twenty-one men set out eastward from the mouth of the Coppermine River. They travelled along the Arctic coast in two birchbark canoes designed for lake and river travel. The men paddled all day inside a crowded array of islands. They put ashore when they spotted a deer, and the hunters managed to kill it—a fat male that amounted, Franklin wrote, to "a great acquisition in the present state of affairs."

Over the next few days, camping each night, the men beat eastward through cold, fog, fierce winds, and "heavy brash ice," or ice that was loose and crumbling. Five days out, after a rainy night, the voyagers awoke to see that a great deal of more solid ice had drifted into their path. While trying to force a passage, Richardson writes, "the first canoe got enclosed and remained in a very perilous situation for some time" as the wind drove pieces of ice into "its feeble sides." The men escaped onto an island without serious mishap and some went hunting, though without success.

By July 28, the men had consumed almost half their provisions. Worse, they were seeing no animals except, at a distance, elusive seals. Then they had "the mortification to discover that the pemmican upon which our principal reliance is based has become mouldy." The next day, Sunday, Franklin conducted divine service. The men set out just after noon and made some progress through the ice, though "with much labour and no small hazard to our frail vessels."

The paddlers again "got involved in a field of ice" on July 30 but broke free and paddled to the bottom of a deep sound and the mouth of a river. The party landed, and hunters chased deer without luck. That evening, they did kill one young deer, which provided at least some sustenance. The next day, Richardson wrote that supplies were now so low "that it has become a matter of first importance" to acquire more food. The men were "very anxious to discover some parties of Esquimaux."

At Bloody Falls, the old Inuk, Terreganoeuck, had said that at this season Inuit hunters frequented the rivers, and Franklin urged the men up one of those waterways. The expedition camped below a waterfall, and the party's Inuit interpreters killed a brown bear—a lean male. Franklin writes, "Our fastidious voyagers supposing, from its leanness, that the animal had been sickly, declined eating it; the officers, however, being less scrupulous, boiled the paws, and found them excellent."

Gale-force winds and heavy rains slowed progress as the men hugged the coast around the bottom of Bathurst Inlet. By August 9, Richardson writes, with provisions "reduced to two bags of pemmican and a small bundle of dried meat, the men began to apprehend the approach of absolute want." For some days, he added, the officers had been forced "to listen to their gloomy forebodings of the deer quitting the coast entirely" before long.

But now the hunters spotted and killed a large bear whose stomach contained the remains of a seal and several lemmings, all of which they ate. The next day, they killed a female bear and a cub, "neither of them very fat." The expedition emerged along the east side of the Bathurst Inlet, impeded by a heavy swell, but the hunters got three small deer. On August 12, the headwinds proved so strong that the men were driven ashore to camp. That night, unable to find driftwood to fuel a fire, the men "went supperless to bed."

The next day, running before a fresh breeze, the expedition made eighteen miles only to discover that they had reached a dead end. They had entered a deep bay, Melville Sound, which extends eastward from Bathurst Inlet and presented no outlet "but the one by which we had entered." No surprise, they grew increasingly discouraged. They spent August 14 paddling back west along the northern coast of the sound. The next day, the interpreters threatened to hunt no more and the steersman, Joseph Peltier, warned that the canoes were almost finished.

In writing of this, Richardson insists that "this conduct of our crew is not mentioned as influencing Mr. Franklin's determination," for that would never do. Rather, "it had long been evident to the officers that the time spent in exploring [the various bays and sounds along the coast] had precluded every hope of getting round to Repulse Bay." To have any chance "of a safe journey [back] across the barren grounds, our voyage along the coast must speedily terminate."

Franklin thought otherwise. With the expedition still beating east, Richardson complained that "the fears of our voyageurs have now entirely mastered their prudence and they are not restrained by the presence of their officers from giving loose to a free and sufficiently rude expression of their feelings." So he wrote on August 15 after the men set up camp.

~

Having been paddling for more than three weeks, the voyageurs feared they would never again see home but would die out here on the icy coast. Hadn't Akaitcho predicted precisely that? The stormy weather, the freezing cold nights, and the short rations, Richardson wrote, caused the men "to deem any attempt to proceed farther as little short of madness."

Lately, in what Franklin's second-in-command viewed as a shocking breach of Royal Navy code, they had "assumed the privilege of thinking for their Commanding officer." To force Franklin to end the voyage, interpreters Pierre St. Germain and Jean Baptiste Adam—the expedition's best hunters—"expressed their intention of killing no more deer." Given their recent lack of success, Richardson added, "we have reason to believe that they have actually begun to put their scheme in execution."

Earlier that afternoon, while trying to escape from among small islands along the coast of Bathurst Inlet, the men had found themselves in "considerable danger from a heavy rolling sea, the canoes receiving many severe blows and shipping a considerable quantity of water." Soon after putting ashore at 5 p.m., the steersman Joseph Peltier informed Franklin that the first canoe had twelve broken timbers and the second "was so shattered that they were in daily dread of the body dropping from the gunwales."

Trouble was, Franklin and his fellow officers "were all desirous of finding the shore trending to the eastward" before they turned back. This would establish that—in theory, at least—a passage could be found along the coast, and they were not now trapped in one great gulf. "To calm the minds of the voyageurs," Richardson wrote, Franklin told them he intended to proceed only until the coastline again trended east. He also limited further advance to four days.

The men welcomed this news, which the officers hoped would inspire the hunters into concerted action, especially since the food supply had now been reduced to a bag and a half of pemmican, "or not quite two days consumption." Richardson had been concerned about the lack of food even before setting out, writing at the mouth of the Coppermine that "our stock of provisions does not exceed 14 days consumption."

Although more worldly than Franklin, Richardson could not resist adding that "it is of no use to talk to a Canadian voyageur of going upon short allowance. They prefer running the risk of going entirely without hereafter, that they may have a present belly full, and if it is not given to them they will steal it and in their opinion it is no disgrace to be caught pilfering provisions."

Franklin was bent on seeing the coast trending eastward again. On August 15, he told the men that they would turn back in no more than four days. The next day, starting at 5 a.m., the men paddled west for ten miles and landed on a point beneath a cliff to eat breakfast. Back on the water, they entered a deep bay running north and rounded what, after his uncle Matthew, the navigator, Franklin called Cape Flinders.

Heavy seas kept the men ashore, and hunters bagged only a few geese. On Saturday August 18, Richardson, Franklin, and Back hiked ten miles north northeast along the coast. Ahead, the most distant land appeared to turn eastward, and Franklin called their location Point Turnagain. Richardson wrote, "This then is the limit of our voyage along the coast, which has occupied us nearly a month, but in which we have traced the open sea only five degrees and a half to the eastward of the mouth of the Coppermine River."

They had travelled little more than one-fifth of the distance from their departure point to Repulse Bay, though because they had hugged the indented coast, they had paddled more than 550 miles, "very little less than the estimated direct distance between the above-mentioned places." Tattannoeuck killed a deer in the afternoon, but the men who went looking failed to find it.

The next day brought gales and stormy weather. And on August 20, the men awoke to find snow on the ground. They located Solomon Belanger and Michel Teroahaute, who had got lost the previous day while looking for the dead deer. The next day, Richardson wrote that "our last bag of pemmican is now half done."

Six days before, Franklin had vowed to turn back in four days. He lingered still, partly because of turbulent seas, partly because he feared reprimand from the Admiralty, and partly because he was still hoping for a heaven-sent miracle. Maybe a party of Inuit would turn up or, better, Edward Parry would arrive at Point Turnagain in his ship. In fact, Parry was far away to the north. Having found his way forward blocked by ice, he had already begun sailing for England.

Finally, on August 22, Franklin left off waiting for a miracle and turned back toward Fort Enterprise. In his narrative, he drew attention to "the distance we had to travel before we could gain a place of shelter for the winter." He added, "I trust it will be judged that we prosecuted the enterprise as far as was prudent and abandoned it only under a well-founded conviction that a further advance would endanger the lives of the whole party, and prevent knowledge of what had been done from reaching England." After all, the coast appeared to run east–west, suggesting a connection with Hudson Bay, and the ice did not appear to be such that would prevent a Royal Navy ship from passing this way.

At last, having turned back, all the men of the expedition—officers, interpreters, voyageurs—shared a single purpose. Their very lives depended on acting as one. The men paddled with energy, taking short-cuts across the mouths of two small bays and covering twenty miles before noon. Afternoon winds forced a halt. The men went hunting but found nothing. So little pemmican remained that meals were reduced to two a day and again the men ate no supper.

The next day, having embarked at 2 a.m., the men made a dangerous twenty-five-mile paddle across the mouth of another bay. The lack of food "absorbed every other terror," Richardson wrote, "otherwise the most powerful eloquence would not have induced them to attempt such a traverse." Travelling then in tandem along the rocky shore, the men battled the recoil of smashing waves so high that at times they could not see those in the other canoe. Finally they landed on an open beach, though not before "splitting the head of the second canoe."

They were island hopping near the mouth of Bathurst Inlet. On August 23, they camped where they had breakfasted twelve days before. Again the men went hunting to no avail. For supper they ate a tiny bit of the remaining pemmican. The next day, the voyageurs landed on an unnamed island. They managed to shoot three female deer, Richardson reported, "which although very lean were highly acceptable." The day after that, on Algak Island (now Algaq), the men "found great plenty of deer" and managed to kill two.

On Sunday, August 26, the men re-embarked and, aided by a fair wind, reached the mouth of the Hood River. They paddled up it to a rapids, where they camped. "Our Canadians may be said to have in general showed considerable courage in bearing the dangers of the sea," Richardson writes, "magnified to them by their novelty, but they could not restrain their expressions of joy on quitting it." That the most difficult and dangerous part of the journey might lay ahead "did not depress their spirits at all."

Near the rapids on the Hood, the expedition planted the British ensign on a hill to attract the attention of any passing Inuit. They left a gift of iron work at the foot of the flag. The men proceeded six or seven miles up the river and camped at a falls twelve or fourteen feet high. Here a tributary river entered the Hood, which was two hundred yards wide. The men "enjoyed a delightful repast" of berries. One of the steersmen, the Métis Matthew Peloquin, nicknamed Credit, killed a small deer.

The next day, the crews worked hard carrying the canoes over the shoals and dragging them up the rapids, yet covered only seven miles. Evening found the men camped at the foot of a narrow, mile-long chasm whose walls were more than two hundred feet high. The river roared over a rocky wedge, creating what Richardson described as "two magnificent and picturesque falls close to each other." Franklin named these the Wilberforce Falls, for William Wilberforce, the evangelical abolitionist. Since renamed Kattimannap Qurlua, the upper fall is sixty feet high and the lower at least one hundred. Richardson estimated that "the whole descent of the river at this place probably exceeds 250 feet."

From the summit of a hill, the men surveyed the river. It ran so fast and shallow that Pierre St. Germain, the best rough-country traveller of them all, recommended breaking down the two large canoes, both badly damaged, and rebuilding them into two smaller ones. Through the next day, which brought a plague of sandflies and mosquitoes, he led several men in doing this work. Other men went hunting, and Credit and Hoeootoerock killed two musk oxen. On the evening of August 30, St. Germain finished the two canoes. The officers arranged and distributed loads by lot, and the next morning the heavily laden voyageurs set out, advancing at a rate of one mile per hour, including rests.

In his journal, Richardson here begins a new chapter entitled "Starvation on the Barrens." He describes how in the wee hours of Saturday, September 1, a wind blew down the officers' tent. Rain soaked their rough beds. Then came a fall of snow. At 6 a.m. the next day, the voyageurs set out along the rocky riverbank. High winds caught the two canoes, making them hard to carry, and even blew down the men holding them aloft. Loose stones made walking painful, "particularly so to men with heavy burdens on their backs, whose feet are protected only by soft mooseskin shoes."

In a heavy snowfall, St. Germain and Tattannoeuck killed a muskox and a deer. Next morning, the sun came out and cleared the snow. The men walked thirteen miles but found the river leading them due west rather than southwest toward Fort Enterprise. They crossed the river, climbed out of a valley, and resumed marching across level, treeless country interspersed with small lakes and marshes. On September 4, the travellers finished the last of the pemmican, which with "a little arrowroot formed a very scanty supper."

The next day the weather turned ugly. Heavy, continuous rain culminated in a severe gale that blew drifting snow into the tents. The men suffered from cold and hunger. They had to resume marching on September 7, Richardson writes, although "in a very unfit condition for starting, the ground covered a foot deep with snow and our garments stiffened by the frost, the tents having proved a very insufficient shelter from the rain." With the moss covered by snow, the men had no way to make a fire.

They were about to set out when "Mr. Franklin from exhaustion and sudden exposure to the cold wind was seized with a fainting fit." Richardson got a bit of portable soup into him—just enough to start him moving. The voyageurs carrying the canoes had been "repeatedly blown down by the violence of the wind," and now one of the two craft was so broken as to be utterly useless. This was "a serious misfortune": it meant they could not lash two canoes together as they had done while crossing the Hood River. Richardson doubted that, in a similar circumstance, a single canoe would suffice.

Sketch by George Back called "Richardson's Barren Ground Brown Bear." Franklin wrote that "our fastidious voyagers supposing, from its leanness, that the animal had been sickly, declined eating it; the officers, however, being less scrupulous, boiled the paws, and found them excellent."

The men built a fire from the bark and timbers of the broken canoe and cooked up what remained of the portable soup and arrowroot. The voyageurs, having fasted for three days, considered this "a poor substitute," Richardson wrote, "for eight pounds of solid animal food, their customary daily allowance" in the fur trade.

CHAPTER 28

Obstruction
Rapids

~

On September 8, 1821, the travellers arrived at a small, fast-moving river in a rocky channel. Here the remaining canoe proved useless. It needed gumming, "an operation we could not perform," John Richardson wrote. After trudging along the river for some distance, the men managed to dance across it on a row of large rocks. Several lost their footing and slipped into the water but were rescued by others. Most were wet to the middle, their clothes stiff with cold, and "we walked with much pain for the remainder of the afternoon."

The men camped at 4 p.m. and shared a few partridges and "some Tripe de Roche." In a separate entry, Richardson describes this as "various lichens . . . that cover the surfaces of most of the larger stones." He notes that "not having the means of extracting the bitter principle from them, they proved noxious to several of the party, producing severe bowel complaints." Robert Hood in particular began to suffer.

The next day, starting at 6 a.m., the men found themselves struggling through deep snow. They had to take turns breaking trail. Hoeootoerock, who frequently went hunting alone, turned up in the afternoon with about four pounds of meat, the remains of a muskox that had been eaten by wolves. Directly ahead lay a fast-moving stream 150 yards wide. The surviving canoe was leaky, but St. Germain and Adam "managed with much dexterity" to ferry the party across one at a time.

The snow grew deeper and walking more difficult. The heavily burdened voyageurs fell often between large angular stones. "If anyone had broken a limb here," Richardson wrote, "his fate would have been melancholy indeed. We could neither have remained with him nor carried him with us." At about noon on September 10, the sun broke out, and "to our great joy, we saw a band of musk oxen grazing in a valley before us."

The hunters approached the animals cautiously, taking two hours to get within shooting distance. The anxious officers watched from a hill and, when the men opened fire, thrilled to see one of the largest animals fall to the ground. Although the other beasts escaped over the hills, some of them wounded, "this success infused spirit into our starving party." The men quickly carved up and devoured the dead animal. "This was the sixth day since we had a good meal," Richardson wrote, as the *tripe de roche* served at best "to allay the pangs of hunger for a short time."

Heavy snow kept the men in camp through the next day. On the twelfth, the voyageurs "entreated us to set out" despite the wind and the deep, drifting snow. The men struggled onward until six in the evening. Richardson noted that "the whole party complained more of faintness and fatigue today than they had ever done before. Their strength seems to have been impaired by the recent supply of animal food."

Next morning, after marching in a thick haze, the men arrived at the edge of a large lake, which they recognized as Hearne's Contwoyto Lake, or Rum Lake, being the place, Richardson wrote, "where Hearne distributed his rum amongst the Indians." The expedition spent the rest of the day traipsing along its edge, labouring up and down steep hills while looking for a crossing place. Having finished the muskox meat, the men ate *tripe de roche* for supper—those who could keep it down.

On the morning of September 14, as the navy men sat warming their hands around a small fire of willows, Pierre St. Germain went round and, ceremoniously, gave each of the officers a small piece of meat he had saved from his allowance. Richardson wrote that the four of them felt immensely grateful, "and such an act of self-denial and kindness, being totally unexpected in a Canadian, filled our eyes with tears."

The voyageur Matthew "Credit" Peloquin, who had not returned from hunting the previous day, turned up to announce that he had killed two deer that morning. Credit and his joyful fellows shared the nearest one for breakfast. After retrieving the other deer, the party carried on to the fast-moving Burnside River, which was about two hundred yards wide as it thundered through a rocky channel. At the head of a rapid, where the stream flowed more smoothly, St. Germain put the canoe in the water and climbed into it with Franklin and Solomon Belanger.

Franklin was a dead weight, and with that too-heavy load, the small craft proved hard to control, especially for Belanger—powerful but not as agile and dexterous as St. Germain. A stiff breeze whirled it into the rapids and over it went, dumping all three men into the water. "By this disastrous accident," Richardson wrote, Franklin lost his briefcase containing his journal, which covered the period since leaving Fort Enterprise, along with his astronomical and meteorological observations. The three men fought their way onto a rock where the rushing river was only waist deep. Richardson wrote that St. Germain, "with great dexterity, emptied the water out of the canoe, replaced Mr. Franklin in it, and finally embarked himself . . . [leaving Belanger] in a very perilous situation on the rock." The canoe had been so damaged that it sank before the two men got far. Fortunately, they managed to scramble onto a small, rocky island. St. Germain again emptied the canoe. With Franklin riding in it, he attained the other bank of the river.

Meanwhile, Belanger stood shivering and "suffering extremely, immersed to his middle in a strong current" of freezing cold water. His upper body, covered in wet clothes and subject to a strong breeze, was faring no better than his lower half. He pleaded for help, and St. Germain piled back into the canoe, paddled out, and tried to haul him aboard. He proved unable and, exhausted, brought the canoe ashore. Now Adam tried and failed to retrieve Belanger, who had a deep channel on either side of him. Finally, with the freezing voyageur nearly finished, the men attached a rope to the canoe and floated it downstream to him. He held on and they dragged him ashore, "perfectly senseless through the rapid."

The voyageurs were no strangers to such mishap. They stripped Solomon Belanger and rolled him up in blankets, and then two of them also undressed and got under the covers to warm him with their body heat. Hours passed before Belanger recovered and regained sensation. The men spent the afternoon hauling each other across the Burnside River one at a time, and doing the same with the baggage, the canoe filling with water every time. By next morning, Belanger was well enough to walk, and Franklin dubbed this location Belanger's Rapids.

In his official report, he described a typical day. After choosing a campsite, the men would "thaw our frozen shoes, if a sufficient fire could be made." The officers wrote notes of the day's events, and Franklin led them in evening prayers. Then came supper, such as it was. The men crawled into their blankets and "kept up a cheerful conversation" until they were thawed by the heat of their bodies. "On many nights we had not even the luxury of going to bed in dry clothes, for when the fire was insufficient to dry our shoes, we durst not venture to pull them off, lest they should freeze so hard as to be unfit to put on in the morning."

By September 17, the men were fending off "the pangs of hunger by eating pieces of singed hides" and *tripe de roche*. "These would have satisfied us in ordinary times," Richardson insisted, dubiously, "but we were now exhausted by slender fare and travel and our appetites had become enormous." Two days later, after heavy snow all night, the men felt faint from hunger. They hoped to reach Point Lake on the twentieth, but "after a miserable march of eight or nine miles it seemed to fly from us. Men dispirited and exhausted. Supped on Tripe de roche."

The next day, Franklin took a clear observation and determined that the men were six or seven miles off course. They corrected and walked for a mile and a half before stopping and waiting for stragglers to catch up: "Nothing to eat. A gloom spread over every countenance." On the twenty-third, three of the strongest walkers—George Back, Pierre St. Germain, and Jean Baptiste Adam—went ahead to hunt. The main party then found the remains of a deer that had been devoured by wolves in the spring and made a meal of it. The surviving canoe had been damaged four days before in a fall, and earlier that day the voyageur carrying it fell and rendered it irreparable. "The men had become desperate," Richardson wrote, "and were perfectly regardless of the commands of their officers."

The main party had trouble tracing the tracks of Back and the hunters. They "became furious under the idea that they were deserted by the hunters, threw down their bundles, and prepared to set out after them with their utmost speed." The officers "prevented them from putting this mad scheme into execution" but sent Belanger ahead with orders to tell the three fast walkers to wait. They did so six miles farther, at the edge of Lake Providence.

On the morning of September 25, hunters killed five small deer—five! The voyageurs called for a day of rest and all agreed. The party consumed more than a third of the deer meat before evening. Next day, after a short hike, the men arrived at a powerful river that, from its size—and their observations—the officers knew to be the Coppermine. The men were doubtful. They despaired "of ever seeing Fort Enterprise again." The officers insisted that the distance to Fort Enterprise was no more than forty miles and the only problem was that they had to cross this formidable river roaring into Point Lake.

The voyageurs cursed their folly in having destroyed and burned the broken canoe. Repaired, it would have served them well. They spent the rest of the day wandering along the river, looking for a place to ford and concocting unworkable schemes. The men decided to build a raft and so, on September 27, began searching for wood along the coast of Point Lake. Four men went ahead to hunt—Back, St. Germain, Adam, and Beauparlant—and Franklin ordered the rest to stay together, especially the two Inuit, who had a habit of straying in search of animals, dead or alive.

Richardson noted that despondency had made the men "careless and disobedient." The lack of food was breaking down discipline. The strongest men had become shadows of themselves. Two of the voyageurs stole some food the officers had set aside for themselves. One British apologist-biographer, Martyn Beardsley, later explained that this infuriated the navy men because they were less accustomed to cold and physical hardship and so were suffering more. He forgets that the voyageurs were doing far more work.

One of the unruly voyageurs found and fetched the carcass of a deer that had fallen into a crevice. The men built a fire and ate most of the meat for breakfast. Though it was putrid, Richardson notes, "it was not the less acceptable on that account." Having faced the fact that they would find no wood without undertaking a gruelling march of twenty-five miles, the men resolved to make a raft and cross the Coppermine at a relatively narrow rapids they would later call Obstruction Rapids.

They camped in a valley among some large willows and consumed most of the rotting deer, along with blueberries and cranberries. On September 29, they finished building a raft of the largest willows they could find. They discovered that it could not support more than one man at a time, but still hoped that, as before, they could ferry the party across. Solomon Belanger, the strongest of the voyageurs—fully recovered from his dunking two weeks before—tried and failed to cross using the only available paddle. The men made a long pole by tying tent poles together, but this proved too short to reach the river bottom. The wind was blowing the wrong way, the water registered thirty-eight degrees Fahrenheit, and those who waded into the river to help Belanger emerged shivering from the cold.

As a last resort, Dr. John Richardson proposed to swim across the river with a line and drag the raft over. He stripped off his clothes. Then, shivering, he approached the freezing cold water across wet, uneven rocks. At any former period, Richardson wrote later, he would not have hesitated to plunge into still colder water. At this time, however, he had been "reduced almost to skin and bone and like the rest of the party suffered from degrees of cold [he would have] disregarded whilst in health and vigour."

He did not mention, though Franklin and George Back did, that as he approached the water, he slipped on the uneven rocks and rolled his foot onto a half-buried dagger that cut his ankle to the bone. He insisted on forging ahead. "I had advanced but a little distance from the bank," he wrote, "with a line round my middle, when I lost the power of moving my arms through the cold." He turned over onto his back, kicked his legs, and believed he was nearing the far shore "when my legs also became powerless and I sunk to the bottom." The men hauled him to the surface. While he struggled to keep his head above water, they dragged him back to shore, then bundled him into a blanket and placed him, scarcely able to speak, beside a fire.

Franklin wrote that Richardson "through the blessing of God was enabled in the course of a few hours to converse." By evening, the men felt they could move him into the tent, although then they discovered that he could feel nothing along his left side, a result of lying by the fire. He would not recover sensation on that side for five months. Franklin thought to add, "I cannot describe what everyone felt at beholding the skeleton which the Doctor's debilitated frame exhibited." When he stripped, the Canadiens cried out to see how thin he had become: "*Ah! Que nous sommes maigres!*"

CHAPTER 29

St. Germain
Finds *a* Way

∾

As October began, the navy men were in rough shape. George Back, recently returned from a long scouting sortie, was stiff and sore and struggled to walk unassisted. John Richardson was exhausted from his heroic attempt to cross the Coppermine, and his badly swollen ankle had left him limping heavily. Robert Hood had been "reduced to a perfect shadow," John Franklin wrote, "from the severe bowel-complaints which the *tripe de roche* never failed to give him." Franklin himself was dreadfully debilitated, George Back "was so feeble as to require the support of a stick in walking, and Dr. Richardson had lameness superadded to weakness."

While out hunting, Matthew "Credit" Peloquin had come upon a cap that had belonged to one of Akaitcho's men, a find that finally convinced the voyageurs they were indeed on the banks of the Coppermine. But now they had to cross. They had started gathering large willow branches to build a more buoyant raft, but the constant stormy weather had prevented them from acting. St. Germain had been scouting with Back for a better crossing place and, finding none, had just rejoined the main party. On examining the vessel they were building, he scoffed and shook his head.

He proposed to make a cockleshell out of pieces of painted canvas or sailcloth in which the men wrapped their bedding. He would need pitch to cover the seams of this craft, and so he took a couple of men and went back to their campsite of September 24 and 25, where he could collect sap from small pine trees. Two days later, with the increasingly despondent men trapped by the weather, Franklin realized that the singularly resourceful St. Germain was the expedition's last best hope of crossing the river. After breakfasting on *tripe de roche*, Franklin set out wading through deep snow to see what progress the man had made. The other camp was only three-quarters of a mile away, but the Royal Navy man spent three hours floundering through the deep snow before "returning quite exhausted and much shaken by the numerous falls I had got."

Next day, fortunately, St. Germain arrived with his newly built cockleshell. The weather had cleared and the whole party gathered anxiously on the beach. St. Germain tied a rope around his waist, then set out paddling and, Franklin wrote, "amidst our prayers for his success, succeeded in reaching the opposite shore." He attached the line to the cockleshell, and the men drew it back and forth, ferrying each other across one at a time. The cockleshell took a beating and toward the end would fill with water before reaching the far shore. Clothing and bedding got soaked. But having attained the far side of the Coppermine, the voyageurs were jubilant. "Each of them shook the officers cordially by the hand," Franklin wrote, "and declared they now considered the worst of their difficulties over, as they did not doubt of reaching Fort Enterprise in a few days, even in their feeble condition."

The one regret, widely shared, was that Hoeootoerock ("the faithful Junius") had failed to cross with everybody else. He had gone hunting and had been missing for several days. Tattannoeuck had spent a day and a half searching for him without success. But now, on October 4, 1821, Franklin "immediately dispatched" four men—Back, St. Germain, Solomon Belanger, and Beauparlant—to seek help from Akaitcho and his hunters. So he writes. The four were to speed ahead to Fort Enterprise, roughly forty miles away, where they expected to find food and a note from Willard Wentzel directing them to Akaitcho's winter camp. If along the way St. Germain were to kill any game, he should set aside a portion for those following.

In fact, Franklin could not have stopped Pierre St. Germain from forging ahead under any circumstances, not now that he knew where he was and could find his way to Fort Enterprise. Previously, he had been prevented from going on ahead because he did not know how to use a compass and take geographical observations. Three times he had urged George Back to join him in hurrying ahead to fetch help, but Franklin had never yet been willing to release his best hunter.

The four-man advance party set out at two o'clock in the afternoon, when the officers and half the men had finished crossing. They had to wade through knee-deep snow and so camped during a heavy snowfall after three hours. Back reports that they made a meal of *tripe de roche* and some leather from an old moccasin.

The next morning, the men floundered on through thigh-deep snow. They forged ahead, stopping frequently to catch their breath, encouraged by "the cheering hopes of reaching the house [Fort Enterprise] and affording relief to our friends." To their dismay, they ran out of *tripe de roche*. The men managed to kill four partridges, which made supper. That second day, they camped at five o'clock in a small clump of willows, Back writes, "very weak and sore in the joints and between the shoulders."

On October 6, they continued over a range of hills, quickening their pace when they saw a clump of large pines and a few willows. They were making good time when Solomon Belanger broke through the ice and "sunk as deep as the hips." The day was so cold that he was in danger of freezing, so the men gathered some brush and made a fire to warm him.

After resting for two hours, they resumed walking until five. Then they halted in some small brush "and made a sorry meal of an old pair of burnt leather trousers," washing it down with swamp tea. Back was using a stick as a cane and the pain in his shoulders became so acute that he "could not allow them to remain in the usual position for two minutes together."

That night was cold enough that, though the men slept in pairs, they could not keep warm. The following noon, they chanced upon a location on Martin Lake they had visited last year. Thanks to his artist's eye, Back recognized the location. The others remained dubious until he pointed out several landmarks and recalled incidents relating to them. The men cried as one, "*Mon Dieu! Nous sommes sauvés!*" My God! We are saved!

The ice on the lake was thick enough to support the travellers, and the four picked up the pace as they crossed through snow, hoping to reach the landmark Slave Rock—part of the ancient Slave Craton—by nightfall. Then poor Belanger, "who seemed linked to misfortune," broke through the ice near the head of a rapids and almost went under in deep water. The other men fastened their belts together and pulled him out but worried that he would freeze before they found any wood. They reached a few pines and kindled a fire, but hours passed before Belanger recovered. The men had nothing to eat but shared a kettle of tea.

The night brought stormy weather. Late the next morning, the men tried to go forward, but "we were all too feeble," Back writes, "to oppose the wind and drift, which blew us over" and, despite their best efforts, drove them backward. They sat out the storm in a small clump of pines and ate "a gun cover and a pair of shoes [moccasins] for our meal." George Back could scarcely stand upright.

The following morning, when the wind let up, he wrote, the men rose with difficulty and set out—"though had it not been for reaching the house (where I expected Indians—a cache of provisions—or at least a letter from Mr. Wentzel), I am certain, from the excessive faintness which almost overpowered me, that I must have remained where I was." The four passed Slave Rock, which meant they were nearing Fort Enterprise. They saw no signs of life except for the tracks of three herds of deer which had passed that way a few hours before.

Finally, they stumbled into the house. Back wrote that dismay washed over them: "what was our surprise—what our sensations?—at beholding every thing in the most desolate and neglected state—the doors and windows of that room in which we expected to find provision—had been thrown down—and carelessly left so—and the wild animals of the wood had resorted there as a place of shelter or retreat." The wolves had left a few bones from a deer they had consumed. Wentzel "had taken the trunks and papers but had left no note to guide us to the Indians."

Later, Back would learn that Wentzel had pencilled a note on a plank, indicating where to go. But none of the men spotted it. What Back took to be the absence of a note, he writes, "was the greatest disappointment." Without Akaitcho and his hunters, the men were in serious trouble, their situation made still worse because they knew that their friends on the trail expected them to send help.

Momentarily, the starving men forgot themselves and began to eat scraps of putrid and frozen meat, not pausing to cook but finding them "delicious raw as they were." After a while they built a fire and heated up a deer's neck and bones. With St. Germain, Back discussed what to do next. They could rest for a day and then search out the Dene. If they missed them, they could carry on to Fort Providence, the nearest fur-trade post, some 130 miles to the south. From there, they could send help to their fellows.

Unfortunately, the rivers and lakes in that direction had yet to freeze over. And the men had run out of food. St. Germain proposed "to follow the deer into the woods, and to make provision if possible, and then go down." George Back assented to this "as being the speediest manner of executing my purpose."

Night brought snow and cold, and St. Germain did not like the look of the frosty morning. Back considered him moody and difficult and recalled that he had once said "those might cross the river that would, but for his part, he had a good gun and would follow the woods." Not surprisingly, St. Germain had moments when he tired of being the main provider, and sometimes the only one. He headed out, traipsing through the snow, at around 11 a.m. and returned in the evening, having found tracks but no animals.

Back and Beauparlant made mittens and repaired snowshoes while Solomon Belanger searched out old bones from beneath the snow. Cooked and salted, these made what now passed for an excellent meal. The temperature fell further and the lakes and rivers froze over. The men breakfasted on a few old deerskins and set out southward toward the Dene hunting grounds.

This time, instead of Belanger, St. Germain went through the ice on a river, forcing the men again to halt and build a fire to prevent him from freezing. The cold was taking a toll. George Back froze his toes and, although he wore two pairs of mittens, could not keep his hands warm. The next day, St. Germain spotted ten deer but could not get within shooting range. For supper, the men ate scraps of old deerskin, drank tea made from leaves and, Back writes, "felt ourselves getting much worse." Again on October 13, St. Germain went hunting but found no animals. Blowing snow kept the other three men from moving: "Nothing to eat."

St. Germain grew increasingly worried. The previous summer, before leaving the expedition, Akaitcho had told him that he and his men would probably winter as usual within a triangle formed by three lakes—Winter, Snare, and Reindeer—that lay between ten and forty-five miles south and southwest of Fort Enterprise. But St. Germain was finding no signs. George Back began to panic. Maybe things would be better back at the fort? He sent Belanger—"much against his inclination"—to carry a note to Franklin, assuming he had reached Fort Enterprise.

He asked whether he should return to the fort, reasoning that a greater concentration of hunters might lead to more success in killing deer. He told Belanger to return to a spot four miles down the lake, where he intended to fish. But St. Germain and Beauparlant were now so weak they refused to move their campsite. After cutting firewood, Beauparlant "became dreadfully swelled," Back wrote, "so much so that he could scarcely see." Journal editor C. Stuart Houston, who was also a medical doctor, identified this condition as "nutritional oedema," or acute malnutrition resulting from a lack of protein in the blood. One of the symptoms is irritability, and Back admitted to losing his temper over trivial matters and to being "peevish."

On the evening of October 15, the three men—Back, Beauparlant, and St. Germain—resumed their southward journey. They had travelled three-quarters of a mile when St. Germain shot a partridge and they stopped to eat. By now, the hunter was ignoring the Englishman and doing as he thought best. The three men were subsisting mostly on *tripe de roche*. George Back, now twenty-four, had grown so emaciated that when he looked in a glass, he hardly recognized himself. Had it not been for the fact that others were depending on him, he would have lain down just to avoid "the miserable pain of attempting to move."

The men anxiously awaited the return of Belanger but finally set out for the narrows of Roundrock Lake, two miles away, where St. Germain said the Dene always enjoyed good fishing. The three had trudged halfway when Beauparlant complained of exhaustion. During a halt, he said he would never travel beyond the next camp. Back offered encouraging words, and Beauparlant asked where they would next put up. St. Germain pointed to a stand of pines not far away. Beauparlant told the other two to go on ahead and he would follow shortly.

While moving forward, St. Germain spotted ravens perched on a branch. He surmised that a dead animal must be nearby. Before long, he found the head and shoulders of a male deer frozen into the snow. Back writes that, a hundred yards farther on, he found six more deer heads, "being all perfect with the exception of the tongues and eyes." *Oh, merciful God! We are saved!* The two men shook hands, "not knowing what to say for joy."

Night was falling and a fog coming on when St. Germain started making camp. Back was too exhausted to help. He believed that if the Almighty had not intervened, he would have died within the next twenty-four hours. Their good fortune energized him sufficiently that he staggered around and collected six deer heads. Now the two awaited the arrival of Beauparlant. Several times they fired their guns as a signal and Beauparlant did the same in response. When the night grew dark and he did not turn up, they told themselves that he had camped nearby.

Through the cold, clear night, both Back and St. Germain suffered cramps from having gorged themselves—"excruciating pains." The next morning, October 17, they cleaned the ice and sand from the deer heads. They grew anxious about Beauparlant and, after collecting some firewood, St. Germain went to fetch him while Back boiled a deer head. Around 4 p.m., the hunter returned carrying Beauparlant's bundle, or at least contents that he knew belonged to Back.

St. Germain did not at first speak. Initially, Back imagined that Beauparlant "was coming behind—but not seeing him and the other not speaking, I said, well, was he asleep? Ah, Monsieur, il est mort—Dead? —I could not believe him—where?—how? In what manner?—Surely it cannot be. It is so Sir said the Interpreter." St Germain added that "after hallooing and calling his name to no purpose—I went towards our last encampment—and found him stretched upon his back on a sand bank— his limbs all extended and frozen to death—he is swelled enormously and hard as the ice that is near him." St. Germain could not move him but threw a blanket over the body and fixed it in place with the dead man's snowshoes.

Back was shocked and briefly gave vent to his grief. Now they were two. Belanger had yet to return and he and St. Germain could not help but wonder whether calamity had overtaken all their companions. They were more than seventeen days' march from the nearest outpost. Aware that he was "unaccustomed to carry burdens," Back feared what lay ahead but hid his feelings as best he could so as not to depress St. Germain. The two could only go forward. They gathered scraps from the remaining deer heads, lightened their bundles, and continued south toward Fort Providence.

On the morning of the eighteenth, at Roundrock Lake, they were cutting and sawing ice to get at another deer head when St. Germain pointed at a slowly moving figure in the distance and cried out, "*Monsieur! Belanger!*" Back ran ahead and inquired after his fellow navy men: "Are they alive? Does the Capt. live? Is anyone at the fort? The Doctor Mr. Hood Hepburn—said I—are my friends dead?" Belanger answered speaking of the whole party. Five men were at the house with Franklin. The rest had remained by the river just beyond Obstruction Rapids, unable to proceed. Belanger was too weak to elaborate. He had fallen into a river and nearly drowned in a rapid. Back wrote: "Oh my friend said I with tears in my eyes—render thanks to the Almighty for your preservation—we have found some deer—but come and eat!"

From farther away, St. Germain caught up and, on seeing Belanger, "was so affected that he cried—and we took the poor feeble man to our encampment." They built a fire, fed Belanger meat, and slowly learned the story of their companions, "at which the Interpreter could not avoid crying." In turn, Belanger wept to learn of the death of Beauparlant. He said the five men at Fort Enterprise were cold, swollen, and weak. Now he rummaged in his clothes and handed over a long letter from Franklin, which, Back wrote, "indeed was truly afflicting." Back had been able to contain himself while deciphering Belanger's colloquial French, but when he "read the story in another language, mingled with the pious resignation of a good man, I could not sustain it any longer." George Back wept.

Belanger was initially too weak to go anywhere and Back himself "was by far the weakest of the three—the soles of my feet were cracked all over—and the other parts were as hard as horn from constant walking." The three men survived on the remains of deer they found frozen into the ice. Finally, on October 30, they set out again for Fort Providence.

This leg of their journey has given rise to speculation. In a postscript to Back's Arctic journal, editor C. Stuart Houston notes that later, at Fort Chipewyan, Back would make a widely quoted remark to Willard Wentzel: "To tell the truth, Wentzel, things have taken place which *must* not be known." While reluctant to raise questions possibly "degrading to the memory of gallant men," Houston wonders if Back might have been alluding to events in which he himself had participated.

He analyzes Back's rough notes, noting that while encamped at Roundrock Lake, the young officer claims to have discovered an extraordinary number of caribou heads and other body parts frozen into the ice. Beauparlant died on the night of October 16. Earlier that day, the men had found seven caribou heads in the ice. They found four more the next day, plus caribou shoulders. Over six days starting October 20, Back claims to have found more frozen heads: five, three, a remarkable sixteen, a load, and then one and two. Twice more the men found caribou shoulders.

They remained at Roundrock Lake for sixteen days, too weak and despondent to resume their search for help. But then, on October 26, the day St. Germain and Belanger went back and buried Beauparlant, the men began to recover. The next morning, they started preparing to leave, and over the next two days, Back claims that they found half a caribou and two shoulders. How likely was all this? wonders Houston. Was the impressive turnaround of October 26 just a coincidence or were Back, St. Germain, and Solomon Belanger so starving and desperate that they ate from the corpse of the faithful Beauparlant and then lied about it? On October 30, they set out once more for Fort Providence. More than that we will never know.

CHAPTER 30

Shock *at* Fort Enterprise

~

B ack at Obstruction Falls, having crossed the Coppermine River and
seen Pierre St. Germain, George Back and two voyageurs leave to
seek help, the remaining men camped where they had landed. According
to Franklin, Dr. Richardson did not feel "so much inconvenience from his
wounded leg as he had expected." The next day, after a short march, several
men complained of weakness, particularly Matthew "Credit" Peloquin
and Registe Vaillant, both of whom suffered like Hood from an inability
to digest *tripe de roche*. The day after that, October 6, they both lay down,
Franklin wrote, "unable to move or in despair."

The doctor went back to urge them onward. He found Vaillant unable
to walk without falling. Of Credit, though Richardson walked another mile
and a half, he could find no sign. Separately, then, Richardson and Hood,
who was now suffering badly, suggested to Franklin that the men separate.
Most could not continue much longer carrying what they did. The two officers proposed that the expedition halt at the first woods. There the two of
them would remain and everyone else could leave their heavy goods, along
with some considerable ammunition to encourage the rescuers to return.

With the men travelling light, Franklin could lead the way more
quickly to Fort Enterprise. He "strongly combated our intentions,"

Richardson wrote, but finally approved. After trying and failing once more to rescue Credit and Vaillant, he felt compelled "to leave these poor sufferers exposed to the rigour of a bitter cold wind during the night," which apparently finished them both. That evening, the men had nothing to eat.

On Sunday, October 7, Richardson and Hood settled into a campsite near "a pretty extensive thicket of small willows." John Hepburn volunteered to stay with them. Franklin wrote that "Hood though very weak had marched better the last two days," and the other two men could have reached the fort, so their staying behind was "a generous sacrifice for the welfare of others." Having pitched the tent and lightened their loads, and with Franklin having given "thanks to almighty God," the main body of men pushed on toward Fort Enterprise, following in the footsteps of the advance party.

Hoeootoerock was still missing and Franklin had been forced to abandon Credit and Vaillant. Now, in a day's heavy slogging, he travelled four and a half miles. The snow was deep enough that wading through it was hard work. J.B. Belanger and Michel Teroahaute, the Iroquois voyager, fell behind the others. When they caught up they said they were exhausted and would never make it to Fort Enterprise. They wished to return to the tent and rejoin the three men there. Franklin held off giving permission, hoping they would change their minds.

The men tried and failed to raise the canvas tent. It was now too heavy to carry, so they cut it into blanket-size pieces. They searched for *tripe de roche* but found none. They drank tea and "ate a few morsels of burnt leather for supper." The night turned so bitterly cold that, although the men lay close to each other, they shivered through the night, unable to sleep. Gale-force winds made things worse. Come morning, Belanger and Teroahaute asked again to return to the tent. Franklin said they could go and gave them a letter addressed to Richardson. He tried to reassure the other men by insisting that they were only four days from the fort.

The party set out again but had not taken more than a few steps when Ignace Perrault and Antonio Vincenza Fontano "were seized with a fit of dizziness and betrayed other symptoms of extreme debility." The two drank tea and ate a few bits of burnt leather and said they wished to go forward. But now the other men, shaken by what they had seen, became dejected and said they could go no farther. Franklin told them that going forward was the only way to save their own lives.

With Belanger and Teroahaute at the campsite, preparing to join Richardson and Hood, the men resumed marching. They had not gone two hundred yards before Perrault became dizzy. He called for a halt and set out again but, bursting into tears, declared that he was totally exhausted. Franklin sent him back to join Teroahaute and Belanger.

Meanwhile, Tattannoeuck, having grown impatient, had forged ahead and disappeared. The other men carried on across a slippery lake, the wind knocking them down. This traverse exhausted Fontano, who recovered and went forward for a while. But then he was again "seized with faintness and dizziness" and fell repeatedly, so that finally he admitted he could go no farther. He wished to stay where he was.

Having travelled about two miles from their last camp, the men proposed that Fontano should return there along the beaten track. If the others had left, he could at least gather some fuel and *tripe de roche* and come after them the next day. In his narrative, Franklin writes of his anguish over separating from another companion under such circumstances, but clearly he had no alternative. The remaining men said a sad farewell and watched Fontano walk away slowly.

Now, after this series of "melancholy reductions," and with Tattannoeuck having gone ahead, the marching party was reduced to five— Joseph Peltier, Jean Baptiste Adam, Joseph Benoit, François Samandrie, and John Franklin himself. They struggled onward through the cold and frequently blowing snow, encouraged by seeing familiar landmarks. They spotted deer but Adam, their only hunter, was too weak to give chase. They passed Dogrib Rock and, camping among sizable pines, enjoyed a large fire for the first time since leaving the coast. "There was no *tripe de roche*,"

Franklin writes, "and we drank tea and ate some of our shoes for supper." He spoke of leather moccasins, but the word "shoes" would resonate.

Next day, October 11, the men tramped on, torn between hope and fear. At around noon, excited now, they stumbled into Fort Enterprise— "and to our infinite disappointment and grief found it a perfectly desolate habitation." No provisions, no letter from Wentzel indicating where Akaitcho might have gone. "After entering this miserable abode," Franklin writes, "and discovering how we had been neglected, the whole party shed tears—not so much for our own fate as for that of our friends in the rear, whose lives depended entirely on our sending immediate relief from this place."

Not for a minute does Franklin reflect that, if he had heeded Akaitcho's repeated warnings, he and his men would never have been reduced to weeping in this empty log house. He found a note left by George Back, who had set out from here two days before, making for a location where St. Germain thought Akaitcho might be found. If he failed to find the Yellowknives, he would carry on to Fort Providence and send supplies from there.

Obviously, any such help would arrive too late. Franklin proposed to join the search for Akaitcho, but only after resting for two or three days. The men found several deerskins and gathered bones from the heap of ashes. Together with *tripe de roche*, they would be able to subsist for a while. As temperatures hovered around twenty degrees below zero Fahrenheit, they did what they could to block the wind from entering through the open windows and the holes in the walls. They were sitting around the fire, singeing a deerskin for supper, when they rejoiced at the arrival of Tattannoeuck, who had found his way, Franklin wrote, without a compass through an area he had never visited—"a remarkable proof of sagacity."

~

When Franklin woke the next morning, his body and limbs were so swollen that he could not walk more than a few yards. Jean Baptiste Adam was unable even to stand without help. The other men, less debilitated, went to collect bones and *tripe de roche*. On October 14, Solomon Belanger arrived, exhausted, with another note from George Back. Belanger was almost speechless and covered in ice, having fallen into a rapid and narrowly escaped drowning. The men rubbed him, changed his clothes, and gave him some warm soup. They were no longer impatient or downcast, Franklin notes, "and had entirely given up the practice of swearing, to which the Canadian voyageurs are so lamentably addicted."

Back and St. Germain had seen no sign of Akaitcho, which suggested that the hunters and their families were already wending to Fort Providence. The best plan was to head in that direction with a view to overtaking them. Franklin wrote a note to Back suggesting that they meet at Reindeer Lake. But Belanger did not recover sufficiently to leave before October 18 and could not describe precisely where he had left his companions. He was bent on travelling thirty miles to where Akaitcho had camped the previous summer. At the very least, he would pick up a trail. He rejected the idea that the distance was too great, saying the track was beaten, and Franklin let him depart with a singed hide to cover himself at night.

The next day, Adam revealed that Belanger had remained vague about where George Back was camped because he worried that if all the men went there, they would consume everything St. Germain might kill. Belanger had also tried to get Adam to leave with him, but now the voyageur showed Franklin that he had such swelling in some parts of his body that he could not possibly march. Franklin abandoned the idea of having everyone set out for Fort Providence. He decided to set out with Benoit and Tattannoeuck, leaving Peltier and Samandrie to stay with Adam.

Some of Franklin's clothes were in tatters. The two men to remain, worried that he might suffer unnecessarily, traded garments with him. On the morning of October 20, having patched up three pairs of snowshoes and singed some skins, the three travellers set out. Franklin carried journals, charts, and other documents. He left a letter for Richardson and Hood and admonished the men staying in the house to eat two meals a day.

The three advanced slowly, working through deep snow to the river, where the snow was less deep on the ice. Still, the men covered only four miles in six hours. Tattannoeuck tried fishing but had no luck, and supper consisted of deerskin and tea. To the famished, emaciated men, the night felt bitterly cold. The next morning was mild and temperate, but after travelling a few yards, Franklin fell between two rocks and broke one of his snowshoes. This prevented him from keeping pace. Exhausted, he resolved to return to the house so Benoit and Tattannoeuck could proceed alone. He wrote another note to George Back and asked him to send meat from Reindeer Lake if St. Germain should kill any animals.

Back at Fort Enterprise, Franklin found Samandrie depressed and too weak to help Peltier fetch wood and *tripe de roche*. They had decided to take only one meal per day. Franklin got Samandrie moving and took over the cooking. The next day, a violent snowstorm confined the men to the house. Adam and Samandrie stayed in bed and, though Peltier and Franklin tried to cheer them, spent most of the day weeping.

On October 26 Samandrie rose and helped Franklin collect *tripe de roche*. Adam could no longer eat this lichen, only bones and a bit of soup. The men felt themselves weakening day by day. They often had to help each other out of their chairs. Yet they clung to the hope that one of their men would reach the Dene and send help. The three had burned all the expendable wood from the main house, and Peltier began pulling down partitions in the outbuildings. These were only twenty yards away, yet carrying wood that short distance exhausted him. His arms were so sore the next day that he could hardly lift the hatchet. Samandrie and Franklin helped fetch the wood but could bring enough that day only to replenish the fire four times. The bone soup made their mouths sore and they began boiling the skin instead of frying it.

Now the men found even light work difficult. They had trouble gathering *tripe de roche* because it was frozen to the rocks. Franklin turned up a few pieces of bark, which helped in kindling the fire. They spotted deer on the river, half a mile away, but nobody felt strong enough to pursue them, and none "could have fired a gun without resting it."

That evening, with everyone seated around the fire, Joseph Peltier exclaimed joyfully, "*Ah! Le monde!*" He had heard something and, for an instant, believed that help had arrived. But no. Instead, Dr. Richardson and Hepburn stumbled into the room and dropped their bundles. Peltier looked downcast but quickly recovered. Franklin saw that Robert Hood was not with the new arrivals, and Richardson revealed that he was dead, as was Teroahaute. Belanger had never reached the tent, nor had Perrault and Fontano. This news alone produced "a melancholy despondency" in those who heard it, and Richardson held off on sharing details. But finally he had to tell his story.

CHAPTER 31

Cannibalism, Murder, Starvation

~

Back on October 7, after the main party had set out for Fort Enterprise, Richardson, Hood, and Hepburn sat by the fire drinking tea. They went to bed and, with a storm blowing and snow drifting, stayed there through the next day. The two officers, still carrying a few religious books, read prayers to each other, which inspired them with "a sense of the omnipresence of a beneficent God." On the morning of the ninth, Richardson went searching for *tripe de roche* but found none. Back at camp, he found that Michel Teroahaute had arrived with a note from Franklin. It said that Teroahaute and Jean-Baptiste Belanger had become exhausted and so had returned to wait with them. Franklin also suggested that they move their tent forward a mile or two to a better site in a clump of pine trees.

Teroahaute said he and Belanger had spent the night a couple of miles away. That morning, Belanger had set out before him. Probably he had gone astray and would soon arrive. Teroahaute produced a hare and a partridge he had just killed. The three navy men received this "with a deep sense of gratitude to the Almighty for his goodness." Teroahaute complained of the cold, and Hood offered to share his buffalo robe at night. Richardson gave him one of the two shirts he wore. Hepburn exclaimed, "How I shall love this man if I find that he does not tell lies like the others."

The next morning, leaving Hood at the tent, Richardson, Teroahaute, and Hepburn carried the ammunition and most other goods to the pines. Teroahaute now said that on a hill above that site he had left a gun and forty-eight balls that Perrault had given him when he went with Franklin. He set out to fetch that, asking first for the hatchet, while Richardson and Hepburn rejoined Hood at the tent. On the morning of October 11, with Hood suffering "dimness of sight, giddiness, and other symptoms of extreme debility," the two other navy men fetched the remaining supplies. Teroahaute was nowhere to be found and Hepburn went back for the tent, arriving at the pines after dusk, exhausted.

Teroahaute arrived and said he had been chasing deer. He had shot none but had found a dead wolf and brought meat from it. "We implicitly believed this story then," Richardson wrote, "but afterwards became convinced from circumstances, the detail of which may be spared, that it must have been a portion of the body of [J.B.] Belanger or Perrault." Looking back, Richardson remarked that while hunters carry knives to use after killing a deer, Teroahaute had taken the hatchet to cut up "something that he knew to be frozen."

On October 12, Teroahaute went out early, declining Richardson's offer to accompany him. He returned late and slept not in the tent but beside the fire. A heavy gale kept the men by the fire for the next day and a half. Teroahaute went out to hunt on the fourteenth at around 2 p.m., returning shortly thereafter. His contradictory and evasive answers "excited some suspicions, but they did not turn towards the truth."

The next day, Teroahaute spoke of regretting that he had not gone forward with Franklin. If he knew the way, he said, he would now set out for Fort Enterprise. The men tried and failed to soothe him. He refused to help cut wood and eventually went out to hunt, though he returned in the evening with nothing. The sixteenth brought more of the same. Teroahaute refused to hunt or cut wood and threatened to leave. Richardson and Hood agreed that if he would hunt for four days, they would give Hepburn a compass and a letter for Franklin and send the two of them off to the fort.

Richardson walked three miles with Teroahaute and pointed to hills in the distance where he could expect to find Vaillant's blanket. The next afternoon, Teroahaute returned with the blanket and a bag containing two pistols that had been left with it. The men ate *tripe de roche*, although Hood could choke down only a couple of spoonfuls. "He was now so weak," Richardson wrote, "as to be scarcely able to sit up at the fireside."

Hood felt the wind blowing through him. At night he slept with Richardson, but their body heat could not even thaw the frost on the blanket produced by their breath. The men avoided talking of their increasing hopelessness, unable "to bear the contemplation of the horrors that surrounded us." Yet they remained calm and resigned and "were punctual and fervent in our addresses to the Supreme Being."

The muscular Teroahaute refused to hunt or even to help carry a log of wood that was too heavy for Richardson and Hepburn. Hood pointed out the cruelty of his proposed departure, but this only made him angry. Among other things, he said, "It is no use hunting, there are no animals, you had better kill and eat me."

On Sunday, October 20, with Teroahaute planning to depart next day, Richardson again urged him to go hunting so he could leave some provisions. He proved unwilling and stayed by the fire, ostensibly cleaning his gun. After reading the morning devotion, Richardson went to collect *tripe de roche*, leaving Hood by the fire in animated discussion with Teroahaute. Hepburn was cutting down a tree a short distance away. Richardson heard a gunshot, and ten minutes later Hepburn called to him "in a voice of great alarm." On hurrying back to the tent, Richardson found "poor Hood lying lifeless at the fireside, a ball having apparently entered his forehead."

At first Richardson was horror-struck with the idea that, in a fit of depression, Hood had killed himself, hurrying "into the presence of his Almighty judge." But the way Teroahaute behaved made him wonder, and "excited suspicions which were confirmed when, upon examining the body, I discovered that the shot had entered the back part of the head and passed out at the forehead, and that the muzzle of the gun had been applied so close as to set fire to the night-cap behind."

Richardson quickly determined that the gun was so long that Hood could not have pulled the trigger. When Richardson asked Teroahaute how this had happened, he said Hood had sent him into the tent for the short gun and in that moment the long gun had gone off, accidentally or otherwise. Hepburn later told Richardson that Hood and Teroahaute had been conversing "in an elevated angry tone." On hearing the shot, Hepburn had stood up and had seen Teroahaute rising from just behind where Hood was sitting.

Richardson did not dare voice his suspicions, yet Teroahaute repeated insistently that he was incapable of any such act. He remained on guard and avoided the two navy men. He wouldn't allow them to talk privately. Whenever Hepburn spoke to Richardson, Teroahaute asked if he were accusing him of murder. He was not a fluent English speaker, but he spoke well enough that the two naval men could not confer.

A copy of Reverend Edward Bickersteth's *A Scripture Help* lay open beside Hood's body, having fallen from his hand. Subtitled *Designed to Assist in Reading the Bible Profitably*, the book belonged to Franklin. "It is probable that he was reading it," Richardson wrote, "at the instant of his death." The two navy men moved Hood's body "into a clump of willows behind the tent and, returning to the fire, read the funeral service in addition to the evening prayers."

That night, the surviving men slept in the tent, all three of them on guard. Come morning, having decided to make for the Fort, they began to pack and prepare. They singed the hair off poor Hood's buffalo robe and boiled and ate that piece of clothing. Teroahaute spotted and killed several partridges, which he shared. On the morning of the twenty-third, having been delayed by stormy weather, the three men set out, carrying what remained of Hood's singed robe.

Teroahaute and Hepburn carried guns, and Richardson had a small pistol that Hepburn had loaded for him. Teroahaute acted strangely, muttering to himself about not going to the fort. He kept trying to persuade Richardson to head south into woods, where he could maintain himself all winter by killing deer. Richardson suggested that he go south on his own. At this he became angry. He muttered about freeing himself next day and accused Hepburn of telling stories against him.

For the first time, Teroahaute assumed a tone of superiority in addressing Richardson, suggesting he had him in his power. And he expressed hatred toward white people, among them some voyageurs who had allegedly killed and eaten his uncle and two of his relations. Richardson concluded that Teroahaute would try to kill him and Hepburn at first opportunity and had not yet done so because he did not know the way to the fort.

Teroahaute noticed that they were following in Franklin's footsteps and realized that by heading toward the setting sun, he could find his own way. The two navy men knew they could not survive an open attack, that even together they were not as strong as Teroahaute. Nor could they find any way to escape. Besides his gun, Teroahaute carried two pistols, a bayonet, and a knife.

In the afternoon, Teroahaute spotted some *tripe de roche* on a rock. He told the two navy men to go on ahead while he collected it, and that he would catch up. Safely alone and out of earshot for the first time, Richardson and Hepburn quickly agreed that they would not be safe until Teroahaute was dead. Hepburn said he would do the killing and the doctor said no. He was convinced of the necessity of the "dreadful act . . . and would take the whole responsibility" upon himself. When Teroahaute came forward, Richardson wrote, "I put an end to his life by shooting him through the head with a pistol."

He did so not just to save his own life, he wrote, but because he was entrusted with the protection of Hepburn, "a man who, by his humane attentions and devotedness, had so endeared himself to me, that I felt more anxiety for his safety than for my own." Teroahaute had collected no *tripe de roche*. He had halted to load his gun and prepare his attack.

Up until his return to the tent, Teroahaute had been an exemplary voyageur. "His conduct had been good and respectful of the officers," Richardson wrote, puzzling over why the man had suddenly changed. At Obstruction Rapids, the three naval officers on site—Franklin, Hood, and Richardson—remained so impressed that they "proposed to give him a reward upon our arrival at a post." Richardson, like Franklin, had no deep understanding of human psychology and regarded Christianity as the indispensable moral element—the *sine qua non*. Teroahaute's principles, he wrote, "unsupported by a belief in the divine truths of Christianity, were unable to withstand the pressure of severe distress." Many of his fellow Iroquois adhered to Christianity, but the man himself was "totally uninstructed and ignorant of the duties inculcated by Christianity."

Heavy snow kept Richardson and Hepburn from forging ahead. But on October 26, they resumed their march, sinking frequently into the deep snow under their load of blankets. After walking about three and a half miles, they saw a large herd of deer. Hepburn exhausted himself in fruitlessly pursuing them, so the men had to camp at an unfavourable spot.

The next day, they found a considerable amount of *tripe de roche*— supper!—and then came upon Little Marten Lake, which they recognized with joy. Hepburn followed a wolverine track until he found the spine of a deer, which proved "so acrid as to excoriate the lips." On October 28, Richardson felt so cold that he could not take his hands out of his mittens. The two pushed on past Dogrib Rock and over some large stones, Richardson falling to the ground "upwards of twenty times." If Hepburn had not made camp and kindled a fire, he "must have perished on the spot."

Next day, anxious to reach Fort Enterprise, the men pushed on through deep snow. Unable to think straight, they thought one lake was another and got lost. They climbed a hill to look for wood and caught a glimpse of the so-called Big Stone, a landmark on a hill opposite Fort Enterprise. They resumed slogging and, at dusk, spotted the house.

Moments later, in the growing dark, they threw open the door and stumbled inside.

~

Richardson was shocked by "the filth and wretchedness" to which Franklin and his companions had been reduced. He had grown accustomed to Hepburn's emaciated face, "but the ghastly countenances, dilated eye-balls, and sepulchral voices of Captain Franklin and those with him were more than we could at first bear." On the final leg of the journey, Hepburn had shot a partridge and now shared it around in six portions. For Franklin and his three housemates, this was the first morsel of flesh they had tasted in thirty-one days.

Richardson had brought his prayer book, his New Testament, and some other religious texts, and that first night, he and Franklin read passages aloud before retiring. The next day, the doctor went out early with Hepburn. They spotted some deer but failed to kill any. The cold forced Richardson to retreat, but Hepburn hunted into the evening without success. Franklin and the doctor dragged skins into the house, though several were putrid and inedible even for men starving to death. Richardson treated Adam, lancing his swollen welts so that water poured out, but still the hunter remained in his bed.

Only after the usual supper of skin and soup did Richardson share the story of how Robert Hood had died, and then the aftermath. Franklin was overwhelmed with sorrow at the death of Hood and reflected not only on the "excellent qualities of his heart" but on his scientific observations, maps, and drawings, which would have enabled him to become "a distinguished ornament to his profession."

On October 31, Adam rose from his bed and walked around. But Peltier and Samandrie had grown weaker—too weak to help with chores—and both complained of sore throats. Richardson and Hepburn were strong enough to chop wood, and Franklin searched for bones and did the cooking. In the evening, Peltier and Samandrie took to mending their clothes with pieces of a blanket, an activity that raised their spirits.

Hepburn went hunting next day, but his strength was failing. Peltier could not eat any *tripe de roche* on account of his sore throat. By afternoon he had trouble sitting up. He slid from his stool onto his bed, and after a couple of hours the men heard a rattling in his throat. He was unable to speak and that night he died. The death of Peltier weighed heavily on Samandrie, who now lay shivering, complaining of cold and stiffness. Others stoked the fire and covered him with blankets, but that night he followed Peltier. The remaining men moved the two bodies into another room but did not have the strength to bury them or even to carry them to the river.

Franklin paused his narrative to recall Peltier's "cheerfulness, his unceasing activity, and [the] affectionate care and attentions" with which he had nursed Jean Baptiste Adam. Samandrie had done his share until he was incapacitated. The two deaths shocked the survivors and took a noticeable toll on Adam, who had begun recovering. Franklin himself was so weak that he lay abed and only Richardson and Hepburn could collect wood. The two spent a day tearing down the storehouse and exhausted themselves in gathering enough wood to last twelve hours.

By November 3, Richardson and Hepburn were weakening. They had trouble fetching enough wood to keep the fire burning. Franklin kept company with Adam, who could not bear to be left alone. The four survivors ate soup for supper, so finishing their stock of bones. Next day, Richardson again lanced Adam's leg, relieving the swelling. Every morning and evening, he and Franklin took turns reading prayers and parts of the New Testament—an activity that renewed their "hope in the mercy of the Omnipotent, who alone could save and deliver us."

Franklin talked of his Christian faith, which had always been strong. A year before, in October 1820, he had written from this place to a brother-in-law, a man of the cloth, that he was finding "hope, comfort and support from religious books and especially the Bible during this season of leisure ... I am amazed at the state of ignorance under which I laboured with respect to its blessed contents."

The religious books, including the one Robert Hood was reading before he died, had been a gift from that famous evangelical Calvinist Lady Lucy Barry: "From the books she put in my hands," Franklin wrote later, to his fiancée, "I was certainly induced to read the Scriptures more attentively (in fact daily) and then I received through the blessing of God stronger grounds of hope in His divine mercy and goodness." As we have seen, Franklin was already a fervent Christian and a prayer after miracles when he embarked on his first overland expedition. His extreme experience at Fort Enterprise, which culminated in near starvation, and his immersion in evangelical literature cemented in him an unshakable faith and a narrowness of vision and understanding that he would never grow beyond.

Now, in the cold and the dark, the men continued to suffer. Hepburn's legs became swollen. Neither he nor Richardson could rise without help. Adam surprised his companions by standing and walking with energy, but according to Franklin, "his looks were now wild and ghastly, and his conversation was often incoherent." Adam's mood fluctuated wildly. The men no longer felt such acute hunger pains, but they developed sores because they slept on the hard floor wrapped in one blanket each. At night, they often dreamed of feasting.

During the day, while lying by the fire, the men tried to keep their conversation light. Usually, they avoided speaking of their sufferings or hopes for rescue. Still, they became peevish and short-tempered, and Franklin wrote, "Each of us thought the other weaker in intellect than himself, and more in need of advice and assistance." Men could irritate each other with a friendly suggestion to move closer to the fire or by trying to help carry wood. Adam had periods of being unable to speak. And Hepburn, noting the general deterioration, exclaimed, "Dear me, if we are spared to return to England, I wonder if we shall recover our understandings."

PART FIVE

Interweaving Expeditions

~

CHAPTER 32

Rescue *from* Enterprise

~

In 1995, Canadian historian Richard C. Davis published a transcript of John Franklin's original journal from this expedition—as distinct from his published account—complete with letters and a brilliant hundred-page introduction. Davis and other Canadian historians have argued that Franklin's hubris was more cultural than personal. C. Stuart Houston, who edited the journals of Robert Hood, John Richardson, and George Back, writes that Franklin was an old-school Britisher, rigid and stubborn, who drove his men too hard. And Davis suggests that the thirty-five-year-old lieutenant suffered from "a well-intentioned narrowness of vision that was systemic to his dominant culture, and that crippled Franklin when he found his culture dependent on others."

The ethnocentric arrogance of imperial Britain, Davis writes, "made it virtually impossible for Franklin to respect the traditionally-evolved wisdom of Yellowknife Indians and Canadian voyageurs, even though their assistance was crucial to the success of the expedition." What today we regard as insensitive, arrogant, and overbearing "was viewed as the epitome of civilized enlightenment by all those who basked in its nineteenth-century glow." Davis argues that despite the slipshod preparation and the damage wrought by fur-trade rivalry, the expedition "could have reached a far happier conclusion had Franklin been less a man of his times."

I would add that John Franklin augmented the ethnocentric arrogance of his time and place with a Christian evangelical's belief in God-sent miracles, a belief that led him to make some terrible decisions—lingering at Point Turnagain, for example. By late October 1821, Franklin's leadership had reduced the expedition to depending for survival on an advance party of three struggling men—Pierre St. Germain, George Back, and Solomon Belanger. These three reached Reindeer Lake at noon on November 2. Franklin had sent a note via Belanger saying he would meet them there, but they saw no signs of their companions. They began to think they were the only survivors of the expedition, and that everyone else had perished from cold and hunger. The next day, St. Germain led the way toward Akaitcho's favourite wintering area. Around 1 p.m., Belanger stopped and cried, "Footsteps! Indian tracks!"

Back had again been reduced to using a walking stick. The other two men were nearing their physical limits, but this news brought new hope. St. Germain examined the tracks, which were heading south toward Fort Providence, and determined that three persons had passed this way the previous day. With winter bringing colder weather, Akaitcho's whole party would be moving in that direction.

St. Germain set out alone to chase down the Dene leader and inform him of the need for help back at Fort Enterprise. Before seeing the tracks, George Back had been able to drive himself forward as the only way to save his life. Now, after making camp with Belanger, he collapsed and could hardly stand. The two were preparing to crawl into their tent when a Dene youth arrived bringing meat. St. Germain had found the tents of Akaitcho just before sunset and had sent the boy with a confusing note from Franklin.

St. Germain had received the note from Tattannoeuck and Joseph Benoit, who had located the Dene camp earlier that day. Akaitcho was out hunting but was expected tomorrow at a lake the boy knew. Back and

Belanger savoured a supper of dried meat and tongues. The next morning, Sunday, November 4, they broke camp and followed the boy. They met Benoit on the trail coming to fetch them. He told the two that Franklin and three men lived on at Fort Enterprise, though in desperate shape. Benoit had left before the deaths of Joseph Peltier and François Samandrie, and before the arrival of Richardson and Hepburn.

At about three-thirty, George Back and his fellow travellers reached the lake, where thirty people were encamped. Akaitcho had returned from hunting. He sat down and smoked the ceremonial pipe with the five men of the expedition: Back, St. Germain, Belanger, Benoit, and Tattannoeuck. As the only man who could speak Athabascan, French, and English, St. Germain did the talking. He communicated the urgency of the situation at Fort Enterprise, and Akaitcho responded without hesitation. "His conduct was generous and handsome," Back wrote later.

Through St. Germain, Akaitcho told Back that misfortune had dogged his own party since the expedition had set out along the coast. Three of their best hunters had drowned, and in keeping with Dene tradition, the people had mourned them by throwing away their clothes and guns. That was why they had left no provisions at Fort Enterprise: they had had none to leave. Then, at Fort Providence, almost incredibly, Nicholas Weeks of the North West Company had again refused to honour the notes Franklin had signed.

Early the next day, Monday, November 5, Akaitcho sent three men racing to Fort Enterprise, their sleds loaded with skins, shoes, and blankets. They covered the forty miles in little more than two days. On the morning of November 7, with Franklin and Adam still in bed, Richardson and Hepburn were in the storehouse cutting wood when they heard a gunshot and then a great shout. Looking along the river, they saw three Dene marching toward them.

Richardson raced into the house to tell Franklin, who "immediately returned thanks to the Almighty for his goodness." Later he would write that when the rescue party arrived, he was within a few hours of dying. He and Richardson immediately gave thanks, Franklin writes, not to the arriving Dene, but "to the throne of mercy." The good Lord had come through yet once more.

The three Dene—The Rat, Crooked Foot, and Boudelkell—laid out dried deer's meat, some fat, and a few tongues. Jean Baptiste Adam was so diminished that he could scarcely comprehend what was happening. The starving men stuffed food into their faces and then, Richardson writes, except for Adam, who was unable to feed himself, "all suffered dreadfully from distention of the abdomen and had no rest during the night." In his view, this was the fault of the Dene hunters, who "incautiously permitted us to eat as much as we could." Franklin shared this view, noting that the three men "imprudently presented [food] in too great abundance, and in consequence we suffered dreadfully from indigestion."

The youngest of the three new arrivals, Boudelkell, rested for one hour and then set out to bring word that they had found four men alive. Of the two Dene who remained Richardson wrote, "The ease with which these two kind creatures separated the logs of the storehouse, carried them in, and made a fire, was a matter of the utmost astonishment to us, and we could scarcely by any effort of reasoning, efface from our minds the idea that they possessed a supernatural degree of strength." And Franklin wrote that "their frames appeared to us gigantic and their strength supernatural."

While the men recovered—Jean Baptiste Adam "with amazing rapidity"—the Dene cleared the room of filth. They refused to stay in a house containing two dead men, and Richardson and Hepburn managed to drag the bodies a short distance away and pile them with snow. The hunters prevailed on those in the house to wash themselves and shave, their beards having grown to an offensive length. They kept the fires burning far better than before, so the white men felt that the weather was becoming milder rather than colder. Crooked Foot caught four fine trout. Because now they could eat, Adam and Hepburn recovered quickly. Soon the latter was able to fetch wood while the Dene went hunting or fishing.

On November 12, the men ate the last of the dried meat. The Dene had expected their fellows to arrive with more supplies and began to worry that Boudelkell had suffered an accident. They waited all the next day and then, in the evening, they gave each man a handful of pounded meat. Anticipating opposition, they "went off suddenly" without explanation. Under interrogation, Adam explained that they had set out to march night and day until they reached Akaitcho, and then to send aid back to the house.

This plan bore fruit on the fifteenth, when three men, two women, and Benoit arrived with more provisions. The next morning, everyone departed from Fort Enterprise with mixed feelings—"a species of joy tempered with regret and elevated by a deep sense of gratitude to the Supreme Being that pervaded all our minds." The Dene treated the convalescents "with the utmost tenderness, gave us their snowshoes and walked without themselves, keeping by our sides that they might lift us when we fell." The party camped when Richardson, his legs swollen, could go no farther. "The Indians cooked for us and fed us," he wrote, "as if we had been children, evincing a degree of humanity that would have done honour to the most civilized nation."

After struggling through deep snow for several days, the party came to the lodges of several older Dene and stayed the night. Finally, on November 26, having marched for ten days, they reached Akaitcho. He and his band received them with sympathy, compassion, and a quarter hour's silence, meant to express their condolences for the dead. Akaitcho showed the men "all kinds of personal attention," Franklin wrote, "even to cooking for us with his own hands, an office which he never performs for himself."

On December 1, in company with the Dene, the Fort Enterprise survivors started slowly south for Fort Providence. George Back, having already reached that destination, sent word that the Hudson's Bay Company and the North West Company had united on June 1, 1821, and now formed one. Yet he had still not been able to send the goods intended to reward Akaitcho and his people. Richardson described this as "a grievous disappointment to us."

The men also learned that Willard Wentzel, in returning from the northern coast, had suffered his own hardships, at one point surviving for eleven days on *tripe de roche*. It turned out that at Fort Enterprise, he had written a note on a piece of wood and placed this where John Franklin usually slept, but nobody had noticed it.

The retreating travellers arrived at Fort Providence on December 11 and were "kindly welcomed" by the same Nicholas Weeks who had caused them so much grief. Franklin now absolved him because he had been acting on "a mistaken idea that he was serving the interest of his employers." Here, Franklin received a few items Back had sent from Moose Deer Island "as a temporary present to Akaitcho and his band," who arrived at the fort on December 14.

On learning that he would receive only a fraction of what was owing, Akaitcho expressed disappointment on behalf of his band but did not blame anyone. And judging from the record, he refrained from saying "I told you so"—even though he had repeatedly warned Franklin not to proceed along the coast. Now, according to Franklin, Akaitcho said, "The world goes badly. All are poor. You are poor. The traders appear to be poor. I and my party are poor likewise, and since the goods have not come in we cannot have them." He continued in this vein, indicating that he felt no regret at having supplied the travellers, "for a Copper Indian can never permit a white man to suffer from want on his lands, without flying to his aid." He trusted that he and his band would, "as you say, receive what is due to us next autumn." In a joking tone, he added, "This is the first time that the white people have been indebted to the Copper Indians."

Akaitcho distributed what he was given. He ran out of goods before rewarding all those who had helped, but nobody complained. The next day, before Franklin and Richardson set out southward, Akaitcho said a fond farewell. He asked that, back at home, they would speak well "of the character of his nation." Richardson added, "We felt a deep sense of humiliation at being compelled to quit men capable of such liberal sentiments and humane feelings in the beggarly manner in which we did."

From Fort Providence, the travellers crossed Great Slave Lake to Moose Deer Island, where chief trader Robert McVicar received them warmly. Here they joyfully rejoined George Back. In this vicinity, over the next few months, the men regained their health. Late in May 1822, they were preparing to set out for Fort Chipewyan when a canoe arrived from that place carrying the provisions they owed Akaitcho and his hunters. They were thrilled by this, especially since they had heard that several recent deaths had plunged the tribe into mourning. They were able even to send along some extra ammunition for every man who had been attached to the expedition.

CHAPTER 33

The Trouble *with* Polar Bears

~

What caused the disaster of 1845, when John Franklin disappeared into the white booming emptiness with two ships and 128 men, never to be seen again? We know what happened in general terms because researchers have been working at it since 1847. The expedition crossed Davis Strait, entered Lancaster Sound, probed Wellington Channel northward, and then spent the winter of 1845–46 on Beechey Island. Today, forty or fifty yards above the graves, visitors can see an array of rocks marking Franklin's main wintering camp. Most then hike along the coast to the remains of Northumberland House, built by British searchers in 1852–53 as a supply depot and shelter in case Franklin should return. But if you hike a few hundred yards along the coast in the opposite direction, you arrive at a second rough site, complete with fireplace. Some have identified this as a washing or storage area, but I would argue that mainly it served as a lookout post to guard against the sudden intrusion of polar bears, which are known to come racing over the isthmus or land bridge that connects Beechey to Devon Island.

In 1846, when the ice melted, the two ships started south into Peel Sound. They were beset off the northwest coast of King William Island on September 12, 1846, probably after getting caught in a storm. Nine months later, on June 11, 1847, John Franklin died. A bit over ten months after that, on April 22, 1848, 105 men departed from the two ships, which were still ice-locked. The Victory Point Record tells us that already, nine officers and fifteen seamen had died. With three buried on Beechey, that means twenty-one men died in the two years between spring 1846 and April 1848.

What happened? No such catastrophe engulfed the Royal Navy expedition of John and James Clark Ross, who spent four winters, from 1829 to 1833, trapped in the Arctic ice at the bottom of Prince Regent Inlet. Researchers have gone so far as to exhume the remains, on Beechey Island, of the first three sailors to die on the Franklin expedition. As noted in chapter 20, "What Do We Know for Sure?," leading experts have ruled out lead poisoning as the primary cause of the expedition's breakdown.

But here's a corollary question: What if those first three deaths were anomalies that contribute nothing whatever to solving the larger mystery? The Victory Point Record reveals that 37 per cent of the officers had died, but just 14 per cent of the regular seamen. Why such disproportion? Equally fascinating: What galvanized 105 men to abandon the ships (though some of them, clearly, later reboarded)? And why were so many men so sick that, according to Inuit accounts, they could not walk in a straight line? Why did the faces of some men look black? Why did some appear to be sheltering (and dying) onshore in what seems to have been a hospital tent, as if under quarantine?

But here's a surprise: While researching Franklin's first overland expedition, I chanced upon evidence that supports a new answer to questions raised by the 1845 catastrophe. Perhaps the twenty-one men who died early off the west coast of King William Island fell victim to an accident or else ingested something. The discrepancy between the mortality rates of officers and men is particularly puzzling.

Some writers have followed Scott Cookman (*Ice Blink*) in pointing to botulism as an alternative cause to lead poisoning. But this, as Russell Potter observes, "seems highly unlikely." He notes that the poorly sealed tin cans admitted oxygen and that the concentrated soups were high in salt and nitrates, all of which would have constrained botulism. Early letters sent home from Greenland find the sailors raving about the soups and making no mention of dramatic illness as produced by botulism. Years later, Inuit who found and opened some cans liked their contents very well indeed. Bottom line: the symptoms and pathology of botulism do not align with what we know of the Franklin expedition.

Yet that does not eliminate questions about differing diets and food preparation as pertaining to officers and men. This book is the first to investigate and advance the argument that there is a link between the final Franklin disaster and the calamitous Jens Munk expedition, outlined earlier. Over a period of eleven months, Munk lost a staggering sixty-one men out of the sixty-four who landed at Churchill, leaving only three survivors. Most accounts blame the debacle on scurvy. But while that disease was almost certainly a contributing factor, an article by Delbert Young, published five decades ago in *The Beaver* magazine (Winter 1973), suggests a different scenario. In an article titled "Was There an Unsuspected Killer aboard 'The Unicorn'?," Young argued that the root cause of the catastrophe was trichinosis, the disease arising on this occasion from eating poorly cooked or raw polar-bear meat. And here, the symptoms fit.

Soon after reaching Churchill, as noted above, Jens Munk shot and killed a "large white bear" that turned up to feed on a beluga whale. His men relished the bear meat. Munk had ordered the cook "just to boil it slightly, and then to keep it in vinegar for a night." He had the meat for his own table roasted and wrote that "it was of good taste and did not disagree with us."

During his long sailing career, Jens Munk had learned how to treat scurvy. Two English navigators on board the *Unicorn* also knew enough to boil the needles and gum of evergreens and drink the broth. All three were also familiar with the symptoms of scurvy, which is caused by severe vitamin C deficiency. According to the Mayo Clinic, scurvy "causes anemia, bleeding gums, bruising and poor wound healing." Not primarily indicated: diarrhea or dysentery.

Even the initial signs and symptoms of trichinosis, on the other hand, include diarrhea, abdominal pain, nausea, and vomiting. Abdominal symptoms can occur one or two days after infection. Other symptoms "usually start two to eight weeks after infection," as larvae enter the bloodstream and burrow into muscle. These symptoms include high fever, muscle pain and tenderness, weakness, headaches, and sensitivity to light. In severe cases, the larvae can "migrate to vital organs, causing potentially dangerous, even fatal, complications."

Jens Munk himself stated that "a rare and extraordinary" disease was killing his men. Writing in the 1890s, Danish writer and editor C.C.A. Gosch, a zoologist who rejected Charles Darwin and the theory of evolution, rejected Munk's opinion. He argued that the captain's paragraph about the extraordinary disease "only mentions as remarkable the contraction of the limbs"—a symptom that echoes "muscle pain and tenderness." But Young answers that, having spent twenty-eight years at sea, the Danish captain surely knew scurvy when he saw it.

Young also ranges widely and mounts a convincing circumstantial case. He reviews puzzling deaths that occurred on two different expeditions, and notes that the one thing they shared with the Munk misadventure was the eating of raw or undercooked polar bear meat. The first expedition, a voyage led by the Welsh Royal Navy officer Thomas Button in 1612–13, lost many men to a strange illness during a hard winter in Hudson Bay at the mouth of the Nelson River.

The second, led in 1897 by Swedish engineer Salomon Andrée, was an attempt to reach the North Pole with two other men by balloon. After flying only 295 miles, the three survived the forced landing of their balloon onto the Arctic ice but then died mysteriously. They were plagued, according to their diary notes, by digestive troubles, illness, and exhaustion. In 1952, Ernst Tryde, a Danish physician who examined the remains of a polar bear found near the crash site, published a book called *The Dead on White Island*, in which he argued that the men died as a result of eating polar bear flesh carrying *Trichinella* parasites, which induce trichinosis.

This parasitical disease, unidentified until the twentieth century, is conveyed by a parasite frequently found in polar bears—and, indeed, in bears of all kinds. Infected meat, undercooked, deposits embryo larvae in a person's stomach. These tiny parasites embed themselves in the intestines. They reproduce, enter the bloodstream and, within weeks, encyst themselves in muscle tissue throughout the body. They may remain dormant for years. But they cause the terrible symptoms Munk describes—diarrhea and stomach pains—and, left untreated, can culminate in death as early as four to six weeks after ingestion, or months later.

Descriptions published by the Mayo Clinic and David Waltner-Toews, one of Canada's leading epidemiologists, confirm this pathology. And in 2019, scientists from Lancaster University determined that certain immune responses can eliminate *Trichinella*, the causative agent of trichinosis. This might explain why the Inuit do not suffer from the disease, though they have always eaten polar-bear meat (minus the liver, which contains dangerous amounts of vitamin A).

Delbert Young asks whether, "at the very least, the first men to die may have met their deaths from eating the bear meat," improperly prepared. Munk never identifies those men who were at his table and so ate roasted as opposed to uncooked bear meat. In his 1890s analysis, Gosch makes clear that the surgeons would not have been among those eating with the captain.

He writes that in Munk's time, surgeons "were, almost without exception, men who had learnt to perform surgical operations, but were otherwise almost destitute of medical knowledge ... Surgeons were classed with ordinary handicraftsmen, like tailors and shoemakers." One of those accompanying Munk, "Mester" Casper Caspersen, appears "to have been a particularly ignorant specimen of his class." Munk accorded the other, David Volske, no "Mester," which indicates that he "was, therefore, no doubt, an even inferior person."

Probably, Munk's "table" would have included some of the ships' mates, all of whom died. But one wonders whether the two men who survived—two of those who went ashore with Munk on May 21—might also have been among those at his table who ate their bear meat roasted as opposed to raw. If those two were suffering from only scurvy, then they might have cleared the symptoms with the fresh root vegetables, and the same is true of Munk.

In an email exchange with me, epidemiologist Waltner-Toews explained that "a lot of diseases can kill a person if they are already weak or co-infected, so pin-pointing one cause in the Munk outbreak is a challenge." In his book *Food, Sex and Salmonella*, Waltner-Toews writes of a hunting party from France that in August 2005 killed a black bear in northern Quebec. They cut it up and ate it after varying degrees of preparation, from well-done to raw. Some smuggled meat home and entertained friends. End result: seventeen cases of trichinosis.

As to Delbert Young's suggestion that trichinosis was a root cause of the sweeping destruction of Munk's expedition, a situation complicated by cold and scurvy, Waltner-Toews writes that this "version of events is as reasonable as any, and more reasonable than most."

Extrapolating from all this, and flashing forward from the 1600s to the 1840s, I would suggest that trichinosis engulfed the final Franklin expedition. And terrified the surviving men, galvanizing them into abandoning the ships. And rendered many of them so sick that they could hardly walk straight. And made others of them so horribly ill that they were quarantined in a separate tent. All of which accords with Inuit testimony.

~

In recent years, while visiting Beechey Island, more than once my fellow voyagers and I have been driven off by polar bears. Rather than fire guns into the air, we retreat into Zodiacs at first sighting. On September 18, 2008, as keeper of the Adventure Canada logbook, I wrote, "This morning we got driven off Beechey Island by a polar bear, a massive creature capable of outrunning a racehorse. It came charging along the isthmus as some of us walked along the beach while others lingered at the graves. As soon as we retreated to the Zodiacs and fired up the engines, the bear changed its mind and went running off in the opposite direction."

Two years later, on August 21, 2010, I registered a similar incident on Beechey Island. And in August 2012, I wrote of an encounter at Dundas Harbour, located in the same channel as Beechey: "Today began with a polar bear. Quarter to eight in the morning. With breakfast ending and voyagers preparing to go for a hike, scouts spotted the big white fellow rambling along the ridge overlooking our intended landing site. Instant change of plans." Instead of landing, we loaded eleven Zodiacs and cruised along the coast, careful not to frighten the bear. "No problem. He ambled along the side of the ridge, looking our way occasionally, and then sat on his haunches as if waiting for us to arrive."

For people voyaging in the Northwest Passage, polar-bear sightings are to be expected. Adventure-travel companies understand that, at first sign of a polar bear, you vacate the area. And so I found myself wondering: Is that how Franklin's men would have reacted? Obviously, the answer is no. On Beechey Island, especially, they would have encountered and eaten any number of polar bears. They might have killed some that were free of disease. But trichinosis was and remains endemic among polar bears, which do not hibernate because they devour seals through the winter. And so, almost inevitably, Franklin's men killed a bear—and probably more than one—infected with *Trichinella*. And then they ate the bear meat without cooking it properly. That undercooked polar-bear meat, unevenly distributed among officers and crew, almost certainly led to the lopsided fatality statistics . . . and to all the rest.

By the mid-nineteenth century, some sailors might have heard that polar-bear meat could be dangerous. But can anyone doubt that the men of the Franklin expedition, subsisting on short rations, desperate for a change of diet, would have risked eating it anyway? Like Munk's men, they would not have seen terrible and baffling symptoms arise until later. Not only that, but Franklin was expected to hunt and store fresh meat whenever possible,

English artist Edwin Landseer painted *Man Proposes, God Disposes* in 1864. Inspired
by the catastrophe of John Franklin's final expedition, it shows polar bears tearing
at wreckage that includes a red ensign, a sail and human bones. Widely construed as
commenting on the hubris of British imperialism, the painting was first shown at the
Royal Academy in the 1864 summer exhibition. Lady Franklin declined to attend.

and to salt and conserve seabirds, for example, in the casks emptied of the
salt meat with which he sailed. Surely he would have salted away fresh bear
meat. When the expedition departed from Beechey Island, the men would
have brought along casks of bear meat infected with trichinosis.

When in 2017 I floated my as yet undeveloped polar bear theory in a
blog post, some readers resisted. By the time Franklin sailed, they argued,
Royal Navy officers knew that bear meat could wreak havoc in the human
body, even if they did not understand exactly how. This is probably true—
though Waltner-Toews notes that the first clinical diagnosis of trichinosis
did not come until shortly after Christmas 1859. Friedrich Albert von
Zenker, a Dresden pathologist, treated a young servant girl who, having
prepared meats for the holiday, complained of dizziness and aching mus-
cles. Initially, he thought she had typhoid fever. But then, after suffering in
extreme pain for fifteen days, the girl died. Zenker did a post-mortem. He

crushed a sliver of muscle, examined it under a microscope, and discovered countless tiny worms. The girl had died of trichinosis.

Meanwhile, in 2017, a truth-seeker drew my attention to a video broadcast in which a well-known American hunter describes how he and his companions got horribly sick after eating poorly cooked bear meat. On an episode of *MeatEater*, outdoorsman Steven Rinella admits to feeling mortified: "I have been preaching about the importance of cooking bear meat to my viewers and readers for a decade now," he says, "and it's really embarrassing." Rinella knew very well that bear meat could be dangerous. But he went ahead and ate it anyway. Can anyone doubt that the ravenous men of the Franklin expedition would have made the same decision?

Until now, I could respond only that Parks Canada would soon turn up some decisive evidence—written records or human remains or both—as divers investigated the *Erebus* and *Terror*. That was all I had. End of discussion. While researching the book you hold in your hands, however, I came across a smoking gun.

In chapter 25, "Crisis at Bloody Falls," you have already encountered this evidence. John Franklin writes of arriving within a dozen miles of Bloody Falls on July 12, 1821: "In the evening two musk-oxen being seen on the beach, were pursued and killed by our men. Whilst we were waiting to embark the meat, the Indians rejoined us, and reported they had been attacked by a bear, which sprang upon them whilst they were conversing together. His attack was so sudden that they had not time to level their guns properly, and they all missed except Akaitcho, who, less confused than the rest, took deliberate aim, and shot the animal dead. They do not eat the flesh of the bear, but knowing that we had no such prejudice, they brought us some of the choice pieces, which upon trial we found to be excellent meat." Franklin was here paraphrasing from Richardson's journal.

Having lost his own when he tumbled into the Burnside River, he could only draw on the two surviving accounts. The first was that of George Back, who wrote, "'You should not let one person go alone,' Akaitcho said, 'for just now as we were conversing together a large white bear sprang upon us—which certainly would have dispatched someone—(as all my young men missed their aim) had I not killed it. If an Indian cannot perceive danger in his own country—much less can a Canadian do so.' After this information we put up—and sent the men for the meat . . . I must not forget to state that we tasted for the first time—some of the bear which Akaitcho had shot—it was rather fishy but otherwise not bad."

In the second account, John Richardson wrote, "The Indians arrived in the evening with a report that a bear had sprung upon them whilst they were walking in earnest conversation with each other. This attack was so sudden that they had not time to level their guns properly and they all missed except Akaitcho who less confused than the others took a deliberate aim and killed it on the spot. The Indians do not eat the flesh of the Grizzly-bear themselves but knowing that we had no such prejudice they brought us some of the choicest pieces and upon trial we unanimously pronounced them to be superior to the best musk ox meat we had seen."

George Back suggests polar bear, Richardson grizzly. I am inclined to believe the former, who quoted Akaitcho and mentioned the colour of the bear. Possibly it was an extremely rare white grizzly, but no matter. The point is that Franklin and Richardson took a scoffing, superior tone toward the Dene "prejudice" about eating bear meat. Amused by this compunction, they proudly proclaimed that they had no such superstitious qualms. They happily devoured the bear meat and got lucky: no trichinosis.

Take this attitude and experience into the late 1840s. Do the hungry sailors on those two ice-locked ships, the *Erebus* and the *Terror*, have an opportunity to eat polar-bear meat? Can there be any doubt? Polar bears were ubiquitous in the Arctic, more then even than now. Do they hesitate to eat bear meat? Don't even ask. Do the officers end up with most of the best cuts? That would explain, certainly, why a much greater percentage of them—37 per cent to 14—met an early death. What does the expert David Waltner-Toews say? "Your description sounds about right," he wrote in a final exchange of emails. "And it really does sound like trichinosis."

The overlanders of 1821 got lucky: the bear Akaitcho killed was free of the parasite *Trichinella*. The sailors of the late 1840s were not so lucky. One or more of the bears they ate was infected. They paid the price with trichinosis, which led directly to the disaster that ensued—the greatest catastrophe in the history of polar exploration.

CHAPTER 34

The Man Who Could
Do No Wrong

~

The aftermath of the 1845 expedition is fascinating, with countless historians, biographers, and other scholars striving to find in the debacle
some kind of triumph—preferably geographical, but at least spiritual. I am
equally struck by how the catastrophe of the Royal Navy's first Arctic overland expedition gave rise to the veneration of John Franklin. He published
his account of the Arctic Land Expedition in 1823 and promptly became
famous as "the man who ate his boots." After the still greater disaster of
the 1840s, the truth of geography notwithstanding, Lady Franklin led
the world in celebrating her husband as the "Discoverer of the Northwest
Passage." This was a man who could do no wrong.

In the introduction to his 1823 narrative, after writing of the kindness,
good conduct, and cordial co-operation of "all the Gentlemen associated
with me in the Expedition," Franklin would remember the "unfortunate
death" of Robert Hood as "the only drawback which I feel from the otherwise unalloyed pleasure of reflecting on that cordial unanimity which at all
times prevailed among us in the days of sunshine, and in those of 'sickness
and sorrow.'"

No other drawbacks? No more unfortunate deaths? Well, not that
merit counting, apparently. One was an Inuk interpreter: Hoeootoerock.

Sir John Franklin at his most heroic. Inset: originally captioned "Opening the cairn containing the relics of Franklin," this is a romanticized depiction of finding the Victory Point Record in 1859.

And nine were non-British voyageurs: Matthew Pelonquin (Credit), Registe Vaillant, François Samandrie, Gabriel Beauparlant, Ignace Perrault, Jean-Baptiste Belanger, Antonio Vincenza Fontano, the murderous Michel Teroahaute, and Joseph Peltier. As it happens, I am distantly related to this last voyageur through my grandmother on my father's side. Celina Pelletier sprang from an early immigrant line rooted in seventeenth-century France and a man named Eloi Peltier (a.k.a. Pelletier, 1568–1620). So there you have it—full disclosure, my bias revealed.

About survivors, we do have some information. Akaitcho said goodbye at Fort Providence and thrived for the next three years. But in 1825, a large party of Dogrib ambushed and murdered most of his men, including those who had saved the Franklin expedition. Soon afterward, Akaitcho made peace with the Dogrib and so ended years of hostilities.

With his Inuk friend dead, Tattannoeuck made his way home and resumed working for the Hudson's Bay Company as a hunter and interpreter. Then he served with Franklin's second overland expedition. In July 1826, during a crisis at the mouth of the Mackenzie River—described in chapter 25—he showed extraordinary courage in saving the lives of

Franklin, Back, and a dozen other men. In 1833, after another stint with the HBC, he set out from Fort Churchill to join a George Back–led expedition at Fort Resolution. After travelling for weeks, he got lost a short distance from his destination and died in a snowstorm.

Of the other two interpreters, Jean Baptiste Adam requested his discharge at Fort Providence so he could join Akaitcho. Franklin complied, giving him a bill to draw on the HBC for his wages. Pierre St. Germain, that peerless jack-of-all-trades, drew criticism in the published journals of both Franklin and Back. Richardson showed him respect and even affection as the one who distributed morsels of meat from his own share to the starving officers and then solved the riddle of Obstruction Rapids, building a cockleshell without which the entire expedition would have perished. Toward the end, St. Germain was the one who communicated with Akaitcho in his own language, inspiring him to send immediate assistance to Fort Enterprise, so averting more deaths, including that of Franklin himself.

On January 7, 1822, soon after Franklin reached Moose Deer Island on his way home, St. Germain requested and received his discharge. He spent the next decade working in the fur trade as an interpreter and hunter in the Mackenzie River District. In September 1834, he retired to Red River Colony, where he bought fifty acres of land and farmed with his wife. He fathered at least two sons and three daughters. In 1841, St. Germain took advantage of HBC incentives and moved with his family to what is now Lewis County in the state of Washington. He died there in the 1870s.

Meanwhile, in the mid-1820s, John Franklin led that second overland Arctic expedition. He then received a knighthood and married a wealthy, well-connected woman (Jane Griffin) who eventually got him appointed lieutenant-governor of Van Diemen's Land (Tasmania). This adventure ended badly—a story I detail in *Lady Franklin's Revenge*—but even so, his wife managed to get him appointed leader of the 1845 expedition that, as we have seen, became the most famous catastrophe in Arctic exploration history.

Franklin's second-in-command, Dr. John Richardson, returned to
the Arctic twice more. He travelled with Franklin on his second overland
expedition and then in 1848 in search of the two lost ships. Knighted in
1838, he became England's leading naturalist, published authoritative texts
on plants and fishes, and served for years as senior physician to the Royal
Naval Hospital at Portsmouth.

With Franklin and Richardson, George Back too ventured down the
Mackenzie. In the 1830s, he became a captain, led two of his own Arctic
expeditions, and received a knighthood. Ill health forced him to retire, but
in 1867, thanks to his seniority, he became an admiral. His paintings of the
Arctic stand as a singular legacy.

That faithful seaman John Hepburn went with Franklin to Van
Diemen's Land, where in the 1830s he ran parts of a convict settlement. He
later sailed in search of his old commander on a voyage sponsored by Lady
Franklin, during which he told Joseph-René Bellot of how Back and Hood
had nearly fought a duel over Greenstockings. In 1856, Hepburn received a
government appointment to the Cape of Good Hope, where he lived until
his death in the early 1860s.

By then, British writers had begun churning out hagiographies of
Sir John Franklin. In 1853, Admiral Clements Markham insisted that
Franklin's "voyage along the shores of the Arctic Sea must always take rank
as one of the most daring and hazardous exploits that has ever been accom-
plished in the interest of geographical research." Other writers followed
Markham's lead. As late as 2002, Martyn Beardsley would write in *Deadly
Winter*, a biography published by the Naval Institute Press, that Franklin
survived because he had the physical and mental strength to do so. And his
Dene rescuers? Who? What?

One prominent early Franklin-skeptic was Canadian-born explorer
Vilhjalmur Stefansson, who in the 1930s suggested that the English naval
men were a dead weight on that first expedition: "Was it beneath their
dignity to co-operate in securing food? Was helping the workers, in their
minds, detrimental to discipline?" In 1988, Canadian popular historian

Pierre Berton argued in *The Arctic Grail* that Lady Franklin created a mythical hero out of "a likeable but quite ordinary naval officer," noting that Franklin's first expedition was a disaster, his second was uninspiring, and his third ended in the worst tragedy in the history of polar exploration.

In 1994, in a CBC interview, Margaret Atwood summed up the emerging Canadian consensus that Franklin "was a dope." Then she added, "After we've had Franklin the dope for a while, undoubtedly we're going to get a different Franklin. People will say, 'Wait a minute now, Franklin wasn't such a dope. Really, he was a mystic.'"

Or maybe—here's an idea—maybe he was not an explorer at all but rather a navigator? That is what, in 2009, Royal Navy historian Andrew Lambert argued in seeking to reframe the discussion with *Franklin: Tragic Hero of Polar Navigation*. His clever hair-splitting ignored countless inconvenient facts. For example, Franklin self-identified as an explorer and spent twice as much time exploring overland (more than five years) as he did sailing aboard expeditionary ships (two and a half years).

Against this background of contention, I present John Franklin as a well-meaning plodder who could not learn from Canada's Indigenous Peoples for two reasons. First, he was a Royal Navy man from head to toe. He had a career to pursue and so would follow orders no matter how stupid, dangerous, and potentially costly. Second, and perhaps even more tellingly, he was an evangelical Christian with a mission. How could he take advice from non-believers who had no conception of the way, the truth, and the life? John Franklin's God could intervene in the affairs of men whenever He chose, and so could be expected to work a miracle if His faithful servant prayed hard after running into trouble on the Arctic coast.

Could a more psychologically developed man have listened to Akaitcho and so fared better? The answer is yes. I think of Samuel Hearne, who from the age of eleven also spent his boyhood in the Royal Navy (1756–63). As he became a man, and after he left the navy, Hearne embraced the work of Voltaire, a deist who believed in God but rejected Christianity. Arriving in North America, he was able to develop his received belief system, apprentice himself to leading Indigenous figures, and so succeed in making a life in the fur trade and becoming the first explorer to reach the Arctic coast of North America.

Samuel Hearne could listen. When Matonabbee said, "We follow the animals," Hearne said, "Ready, aye, ready." John Franklin could not listen. When Akaitcho told him, "We do not eat bear meat," Franklin did not ask, "Why not?" Instead, he said, "Ha! What do you know?"

In *Searching for Franklin*, Akaitcho emerges as an outstanding Dene leader and Pierre St. Germain as a most magnificent voyageur. John Franklin stands revealed as something more than the quintessential Royal Navy man. He was also an evangelical Christian, a true believer, who could preach but could not listen. Louie Kamookak, my late friend, the latest of the great oral historians and interpreters, cries out for a more personal evocation.

On Top *of* *the* World

~

A nd so, Louie, I find myself speaking to you once more, telling you
stories that you originally told me. That is how I relive them, how
I keep them alive. Stories, stories, stories—but yours, after all, is an oral
culture. I think again of how your particular Franklin quest sprang from
the stories your great-grandmother, Hummahuk, told you when you were
six or seven. Stories of how she found strange objects made of wood and
a rope or chain going into the sea, and then came upon a curious mound
the size of an adult human body. At one end stood a stone with strange
markings. A slightly older you, Louie, recognized this as a burial site.
Hummahuk's stories launched you on your lifelong quest. And after you
read the Supunger and Peter Bayne stories, about the gravesites they found,
nothing could stop you. You were bent on finding Franklin's grave on King
William Island—*your* island.

You talked with any Elder who had a story to tell and spent more than
three decades doing informal interviews, circling back always to Franklin.
And, oh, how you searched the island! In winter 2004, you came upon
a promising site measuring four feet by twelve and covered by long, flat
rocks. You hoped to return the next summer but then you ran into health
problems. You lost your house and had to move some distance out of Gjoa

Haven: "People in town were saying it was the curse of Franklin—that I was getting too close."

You came back! Though you never did get back to that promising site. But in 2006, with some French and British researchers and Robert Grenier, an underwater archaeologist with Parks Canada, you submitted a search proposal for International Polar Year. That failed to secure a grant, but Parks Canada brought you to Ottawa the following year and consulted you frequently thereafter. In 2008, when federal government officials launched a new search for the Franklin ships, leaders brought you to Ottawa for the announcement.

Environment minister John Baird stated that the research you shared "has provided incredibly valuable insight." He added that "local Inuit involvement has been absent in previous searches, and it will undoubtedly be a key to a successful expedition this summer or next summer." You told reporters, "For the first time in 160 years, I feel that the witnesses of the Franklin tragedy events have a chance to really contribute to an important search party."

Six years later, when in 2014 the Parks Canada team located the *Erebus* off Adelaide Peninsula, government officials hailed your contribution. Without it, said Doug Stenton, director of heritage for Nunavut, the team might not have found the ship. "It's very satisfying to see that testimony of Inuit who shared their knowledge of what happened to the wreck has been validated quite clearly." You yourself hailed the finding as showing Inuit oral history to be "very strong in knowledge."

I know you would want me to mention that Canadian geographer Tom Zagon, an expert in ice movement and remote sensing, was also pointing to the correct general area. The real value of ice studies, Zagon said, emerges "when you bring it together with historical evidence." The latter, while very valuable, is "obviously not enough to find the ships on its own and ice information is not going to do that either." By combining ice studies, remote sensing, archaeology, and Inuit oral history, searchers finally found the *Erebus*.

Meanwhile, you kept hunting for Franklin's burial vault. In 2016, you embarked on your most elaborate search, the Hummahuk Expedition. You acquired the requisite archaeological permit from the Nunavut government and, after landing a grant, bought a camera, camping gear, and enough gas for three ATVs. Delayed by heavy rain, you set out on July 27, leading two young hunters. You travelled with a four-person dome tent, three air mattresses, sixty-nine litres of gas, a tool bag with spare parts, food for six or seven days, a fishing rod, and, of course, three guns.

You went west beyond the Todd Islets to Douglas Bay, where the rivers were deep and muddy. At Peabody Point, you investigated the ruins of a Greenland-style stone house built in 1923 by Danish explorer Knud Rasmussen and an Inuk named Arnarulungnuaq. Farther west, you located tent rings and a cairn erected in 1979 to commemorate the Franklin expedition. But no sign of a burial site, and in the end, the unusually wet, spongy terrain forced you to use so much gas that you had to turn back without reaching your destination.

Given our different obsessions, I realize now how lucky I was in 1999 to go searching with you on the west coast of Boothia Peninsula. You will remember how, after reaching the John Rae cairn, we three—you, me, and Cameron Treleaven—spent the better part of an hour exploring the boulder-strewn tip of Pointe de la Guiche before starting back to camp. We arrived at 9:45 p.m. with the sun still high in the sky. All told, we had slogged back and forth across marshy tundra for twelve hours and covered roughly twenty miles—a minuscule distance by John Rae's standards, but far enough to get the idea. This was rugged country. Still, more than once you had made me laugh. On our way back to camp, we chanced upon an overturned rowboat. You alluded to a well-known Franklin site and dubbed it "the boat place." We sat on the boat and Cameron took our picture.

Next morning, a bright August day, is vividly present to me. We awake to the challenge of transporting the plaque. This brings another special moment—one I think of as "The Chase." The John Rae cairn lies

In August 1999, returning to camp after locating the John Rae cairn, the author and Louie Kamookak stopped to rest on an overturned rowboat.

roughly five miles north of our campsite. While returning the previous evening, we stumbled, miserable and soaking wet, through bog and muskeg. Detouring around that stretch would mean a round trip of roughly twelve miles—not a great distance compared with our first day. Now, however, we have a plaque to transport—a plaque that, screwed to a waist-high stand you built of welded steel, weighs at least thirty-five or forty pounds.

I suggest that we use the motorboat to shorten the trek, but you and Cameron will not hear of it. In the end, I have to admit that you are right. If we cannot hope to emulate John Rae, that consummate overlander who on snowshoes hauled a sledge most of the way here from Repulse Bay, we can at least pay homage to the spirit of his achievement by lugging the memorial plaque overland. You create a sling out of a sweatshirt and propose we carry the awkward creation "traditional Inuit style."

While Cameron and I stuff last-minute items into our daypacks, you set off across the tundra at a pace I consider unsustainable. To tell the truth,

Having placed a memorial plaque beside the John Rae cairn in August 1999, three adventurers—Cameron Treleaven, Louie Kamookak, and the author—toast Rae, Mistegan, and Ouligbuck, who arrived at this location on May 6, 1854.

I am stunned by how fast you can run. How you almost glide over the spongy tundra despite the awkward weight you carry across your shoulders—the aluminum plaque, the heavy metal stand. You have covered half a mile by the time we two stragglers depart, and we expect that you will pause to rest. But after half an hour, you show no signs even of slowing.

Cameron and I maintain a rigorous pace, but you, gliding effortlessly over the land, increase your lead. Slowly the truth dawns. Like a champion cycling racer making a move to leave the pack, you are bidding to become the only one of us to carry the plaque to its destination. I raise my eyebrows at Cameron. No way we can let this happen.

I am what, fifty-two years old? I work out four or five times a week and consider myself physically fit. In fact, I am. But Cameron is used to running fifty miles a week, plays squash well enough to compete nationally, and makes a habit of scrambling up peaks in the Rockies. I feel that he, better than I, can do what has to be done. As I lengthen my stride, Cameron Treleaven, lugging a twenty-five-pound daypack, breaks into a steady trot.

After fifteen or twenty minutes of non-stop running, as you may recall, he finally catches you on a ridge, foiling your mischievous bid for solitary glory. The two of you sit down and rest and, when I catch up, you grin at me: "You thought I was going to put the memorial in the wrong place?"

"Not exactly," I reply.

But Cameron and I take turns carrying it the rest of the way. Ah, Louie . . . A few feet south of the ruined cairn, we jam the stand into the ground and pile rocks around it. Then, with a bottle of dry red wine, we toast John Rae and the two men who reached that location with him—Thomas Mistegan and William Ouligbuck. Having waited for this moment, you read the plaque out loud: "This plaque marks the spot where Arctic explorer John Rae (1813–1893) discovered the final link in the Northwest Passage." The homage summarizes the original three-man trek through gale-force winds, blowing snow, and bitter cold. At the bottom of this screed, you find our three names written in large italics. You let out a whoop and say, "That's the first time I've noticed. I waited until now to read the inscription."

We stand a while looking out over Rae Strait in the sunshine, savouring the notion that we have created a memorial that can endure the High Arctic climate for at least half a century. The sun is high in the sky and will remain so for hours. After a while, we shoulder our daypacks and start south. Mission accomplished.

Yet one highlight remains. Having hiked back along the coast to camp, dismantled the tent, and packed our gear into your boat, we set out for Gjoa Haven. You announce that, before recrossing Rae Strait, you want to investigate a spot where sometimes you find good hunting. So, yes, you have a passionate interest in all things Franklin. But also you are an Inuk living—and helping *preserve*—a traditional way of life. You are a hunter at home in this High Arctic world. In summer, you venture out in your twenty-foot boat. In winter, you use a dog team or a snowmobile. The water, the ice—they belong to your world, and to the way your Inuit ancestors lived for generations. With you at the helm, we roar south along the west coast of Boothia.

We enter another nondescript bay, haul the boat onto a sandy beach, and climb a ridge to scan the horizon. I see nothing. There is nothing to see. But you point and whisper, "Caribou!" A huge-antlered animal, all but invisible against the brown tundra, stands in profile more than one hundred metres away. He is far too distant, in my opinion, to even contemplate. But you fall to one knee, bring your gun to your shoulder, aim carefully, and fire. Nothing happens. I think you have missed completely. That's how far we are from the animal.

But no! Look! The caribou drops down dead in his tracks. I can hardly believe my eyes. We three go charging across the tundra. You are jubilant. When you reach and examine the caribou, you whoop and cry, "Straight through the heart!"

You say a few words in Inuktitut over the dead animal. Then Cameron and I watch, awestruck, as you skin the body, cut off chunks for us to carry, and hoist the bulky carcass up onto your shoulders. With that you stagger back to the boat. After heaving the carcass into the stern, you look up at the sky and throw open your arms: "Meat will last all winter."

We haul the boat into deep water and again set out for Gjoa Haven, returning from what has evolved into a successful caribou hunt. You are feeling good. We all three are on top of the world, almost literally. Gone now, at least for the moment, all thought of John Rae, of John Franklin, of lost ships or vaults. And as we pound across Rae Strait in the wind, I hear myself whooping and realize that I am in love. I have fallen in love with the Arctic.

A Note *on* Sources

~

J ohn Franklin was history to me. I had written about him in all five of
my Arctic narratives. In *Lady Franklin's Revenge*, I had word-painted Sir
John as the second largest figure in the book. Now I realize that researching that work provided me with a considerable foundation. I spent days in
the archives at the Scott Polar Research Institute in Cambridge researching Lady Franklin, many of whose letters and journals involve her husband.
Also in England, I explored Franklin's birthplace (Spilsby, Lincolnshire),
ransacked the National Maritime Museum at Greenwich, and visited sites
relevant to both husband and wife.

As well, I had spent ten weeks in Tasmania, where from 1837 to 1843
Franklin served as lieutenant-governor of what was then the penal colony
of Van Diemen's Land. While serving as a writer-in-residence, I visited
prison cells in Port Arthur and on Sarah Island, perused obscure documents in the Hobart archives, and turned up nasty portrayals of Franklin
written by Canadian and American political prisoners. But after 2005,
when I published my book about Lady Franklin, I believed I was done
with Sir John.

Then, in 2017, along came Louie Kamookak: "When are you going
to write your big book about Franklin?" We were kibbitzing, but Louie
planted a seed. Meanwhile, in 2014 and 2016, searchers had located the
Erebus and the *Terror* in the Canadian Arctic. Invited to comment in various forums—*Canadian Geographic*, *The Globe and Mail*, a documentary

film called *Franklin's Lost Ships*—I naturally found myself reflecting on the unresolved mysteries of the 1845 expedition. I had read about Jens Munk and wondered if trichinosis might have doomed the final Franklin expedition.

Further research would turn this speculation into what I think of as the framing tale in the present volume. But that formulation came later. Another story had already caught my eye—one that evolved into our main narrative. In my 2017 book, *Dead Reckoning*, I had devoted a chapter to the Yellowknife Dene rescue of those who survived Franklin's first overland expedition. Intrigued by this little-known story, usually downplayed, I had begun researching.

Five books provide eyewitness accounts (see Selected References). Inevitably, while telling the same story, these five sources sometimes contradict each other. When a disagreement is significant, I quote both parties and indicate what I believe. If I quote an individual, I am drawing on his own published journal. As usual, after a preliminary investigation enabled me to develop an outline, I wrote and researched as I went along. Only when I had produced a first draft of the main narrative did I see what was missing: a larger frame of reference. And only when I began fitting together the two narratives did I see that, in response to Louie Kamookak, I was writing my "big Franklin book."

Endnotes

~

Part One

By 2017, when the prologue opens, I had been voyaging with Adventure Canada (AC) for ten years, giving talks on Arctic exploration history. Accompanied by my wife, photographer Sheena Fraser McGoogan, I had talked my way through the Northwest Passage almost annually, visiting history-rich locations like Beechey Island, Gjoa Haven, Fort Ross, and Dundas Harbour. I would write a logbook and later publish articles in places like *The Globe and Mail*, *National Post*, *Canadian Geographic*, *Canada's History*, and the British magazine *Geographical*.

All through part one, which opens in 1999, I draw on my personal experience of the Arctic. In addition, I make use of research I did for three books in particular: *Fatal Passage*, *Lady Franklin's Revenge*, and *Race to the Polar Sea*. All three have extensive bibliographies. For a detailed analysis of donors who contributed to Lady Franklin's drive to fund the voyage of the *Fox*, I would refer you to allegrarosenberg.com.

Part Two

In part two, after introducing John Franklin, we begin the process of inter-weaving accounts of his first overland expedition. Where I could, because it makes for a better reading experience, I tracked the narrative through a single point of view for long stretches. In chapters 8 and 9, I drew mostly on the journal of midshipman Robert Hood, who kept the best record of the ocean voyage and the early slogging.

In chapter 10, I turned to the journal of George Back, widening the lens to include occasional commentary. My main source for Back's biography is Peter Steele's book *The Man Who Mapped the Arctic: The Intrepid Life of George Back, Franklin's Lieutenant*. I had John Richardson step forward in chapter 11. For background I drew on a 1976 biography by Robert E. Johnson: *Sir John Richardson: Arctic Explorer, Natural Historian, Naval Surgeon*.

Having introduced all four eyewitnesses, I felt more comfortable mixing and matching. The journey to Fort Chipewyan demanded that I cut back and forth between the journals of Back and Franklin—and with this approach I carried on. Research I had done for previous books came into focus as the expedition arrived in Dene territory. For detail about Akaitcho and Pierre St. Germain, I drew on articles by C. Stuart Houston (1927–2021) published in *Lobsticks and Stone Cairns: Human Landmarks in the Arctic* (ed. Richard C. Davis). For additional colour I turned to the first-ever history of Red River Settlement, *The Fur Hunters of the Far West* by Alexander Ross.

Several other books inform part two, among them my own *Lady Franklin's Revenge* and two biographies from different eras: *The Life of Sir John Franklin* (1896) by H.D. Traill and *Franklin: Tragic Hero of Polar Navigation* (2009) by Andrew Lambert. Also useful: *The Search for Franklin* (1970) by Leslie H. Neatby and *The Arctic Grail* (1988) by Pierre Berton.

Part Three

Personal presence is the hallmark of creative non-fiction, even that variation I think of as historical narrative. We launch part three with Our Narrator in the Arctic in 2010, when I got caught up in the quest for Franklin documents. About the 2010 adventure, I published three real-time articles in the *Montreal Gazette*, all of which were picked up by newspapers across the country.

I had met Tagak Curley in 2008, when we both travelled to London to play ourselves in John Walker's *Passage*—a feature-length docudrama based on *Fatal Passage*. We were delighted to meet again in 2016 on board the *Clipper Adventurer*, while voyaging with Adventure Canada. Curley drew my attention to Tulugaq, and I extracted that Inuk's story from two books written in the early 1880s: *Schwatka's Search: Sledging in the Arctic in Quest of the Franklin Records* by William Henry Gilder and *Overland to Starvation Cove: With the Inuit in Search of Franklin 1878–1880* by Heinrich W. Klutschak.

Regarding William Ouligbuck, I have a painful memory of Louie trying to correct my pronunciation: "Not Oulig*buck*, Ken. Ou*lig*buck. Ou*lig*buck." I researched Ou*lig*buck, Taqulittuq, and Ipiirvik for *Fatal Passage* and *Dead Reckoning*, and gleaned a great deal from David C. Woodman's classic work, *Unravelling the Franklin Expedition: Inuit Testimony*. About Supunger, mainly I learned from Tom Gross, with whom I exchanged emails about his continuing search for Franklin's vault.

Frozen in Time: The Fate of the Franklin Expedition by John Geiger and Owen Beattie, first published in 1987, is a foundational work. It raises questions that are still resonating. In 2014, when Parks Canada located *Erebus* in the Canadian Arctic, I went overboard in hailing the achievement in a *Canadian Geographic* article as "The Discovery of the Century." I should have reserved that encomium—and now do so—for the finding of Franklin's vault. As for the Munk expedition of the early 1600s, that did not catch my eye until 2015, when I turned up a 1970 translation by James Mcfarlane and John Lynch of *The Way to Hudson Bay: The Life and Times of Jens Munk* by Thorkild Hansen.

Part Four

That Robert Hood and George Back came close to fighting a duel over a young Dene woman is well known. In his introduction to Hood's journal, *To the Arctic by Canoe, 1819–1821*, C. Stuart Houston mentions that in 1851, while enduring a winter in the Arctic ice, sailor John Hepburn shared the tale with Joseph-René Bellot, who recorded it for posterity. In chapters 23 and 24, we follow George Back as he treks south to Fort Chipewyan. Then, at Fort Enterprise, we draw on both Franklin and Back, and Richardson becomes a major source during the Crisis at Bloody Falls.

With the attack of the bear, we encounter one of those instances where primary sources disagree. Then comes what Richard C. Davis, in his introduction to *Sir John Franklin's Journals and Correspondence: The First Arctic Land Expedition, 1819–1822* (1995), describes as "an elaborate ballet" involving people of four cultures. In clarifying the claims of Dene warriors to have accompanied Samuel Hearne to the Arctic coast in 1771, I drew on research I did for my book about that explorer and for a foreword I wrote to a 2007 edition of Hearne's *Journey to the Northern Ocean*.

Chapter 27, "Franklin Reaches the Coast," exemplifies a writing technique I call "implied stream-of-consciousness." The stream is implied rather than explicit because I am writing non-fiction. While apparently offering Franklin's thoughts, never do I declare that at a certain moment "he thought." Instead, drawing on everything I know about who, where, and when he is, I create a word-movie of his mind.

Heading east along the coast, we follow Richardson, cutting occasionally to Franklin and Back. When Richardson stays with Hood, we travel ahead with Franklin. Then, for chapter 31, "Cannibalism, Murder, and Starvation," we return to Richardson, who supplies the only original account of the cannibalism and murder. When he reaches Fort Enterprise, Franklin takes over, leading the way into fervent Christianity.

Part Five

As suggested by its title, "Interweaving Expeditions," this part resolves what we now perceive to be three related quests. First, Canadian scholars Richard C. Davis and C. Stuart Houston sweep us into the final days of the overland expedition by suggesting that Franklin's hubris was more cultural than personal. They argue that the ethnocentric arrogance of imperial Britain created a narrowness of vision that made it impossible for him to learn from the Indigenous Peoples. We hear from George Back as he searches for Akaitcho, who shines as he saves the lives of Franklin and his remaining men.

In chapter 33, "The Trouble with Polar Bears," we turn to our second quest—an attempt to determine the root cause of the 1845 disaster. After laying out the challenge and repudiating prevailing theories, we recall the Jens Munk catastrophe of the early 1600s. We investigate the theory offered by Delbert Young in a 1973 article ("Was There an Unsuspected Killer aboard the 'Unicorn'?," *The Beaver*)—that the disaster derived from trichinosis, caused by the eating of undercooked polar-bear meat. In addition to relaying information from the Mayo Clinic, I contacted leading Canadian epidemiologist David Waltner-Toews, who affirmed Young's analysis.

Our third main quest, to find the man behind the myth of the Arctic Hero, opens with Franklin suggesting that "the only drawback" he could recall from his first expedition was the "unfortunate death" of Robert Hood. British biographers like H.D. Traill, Richard Cyriax, and Martyn Beardsley perceived no blind spot here. Canadians Stefansson, Berton, Houston, and Davis challenged their perception, and I follow them in suggesting that John Franklin could preach but could not listen.

Acknowledgements

~

M argaret Atwood appeared out of nowhere and seized me by the shirt sleeve. I had been standing by the food table in a crowded room at the annual post-Christmas party she and Graeme Gibson used to hold for Toronto-based "waifs and strays." Yes, I have told this story before, but it bears repeating. The year was 2005, and I had just published my third Arctic book. "Come with me," Atwood said. "There's someone I want you to meet." She hauled me from that first jam-packed room into a second, where she introduced me to Matthew Swan, owner and CEO of Adventure Canada, a travel company that specializes in expeditionary voyages in the Northwest Passage. "You two should talk," she said, and vanished. So we did. A few weeks later, Matthew called and said maybe I would like to sail as a resource person on one of their voyages, give a few presentations.

So I owe both Atwood and Swan a massive thank you. From 2007 to COVID-19, Sheena Fraser McGoogan and I went voyaging with AC at least once a year, and sometimes twice. As a result, I met and learned from such outstanding Arctic experts as Latonia Hartery, Tagak Curley, John Houston, Susie Evyagotailak, Mark Mallory, Pierre Richard, Lynn Moorman, David Reid, Kenn Harper, Mike Beedell, and Susan Aglukark. That experience informs this work.

My sixteenth book, *Searching for Franklin*, is my first publication with Douglas & McIntyre, and I am thrilled to join the mighty list of authors who have published with that storied firm. They include Anna Porter, Fred

Stenson, Mark Zuehlke, Michael Byers, Will and Ian Ferguson, Wayne Grady, J.L. Granatstein, Charlotte Gill, Mark Abley, John MacLachlan Gray, Richard Wagamese, Daniel Poliquin, John Ralston Saul, Alan Twigg, Madeleine Thien, Christopher Moore, Bill Richardson, and Irshad Manji. But why stop? Among them we also find Robert McGhee, Rudyard Griffiths, Robert Hough, Zacharias Kunuk, Dany Laferrière, Ross King, Stephen Hume, Dorothy Eber, Adrienne Clarkson, Lorna Crozier, Silver Donald Cameron, Susan Delacourt, James P. Delgado, Stephen R. Bown, Wade Davis, Samuel Bawlf, Shelagh Grant, Douglas Hunter, and Farley Mowat.

Editor Derek Fairbridge made a huge difference to this book with his meticulous, detailed, and constructive substantive edit. Copy editor Stephanie Fysh also made a significant contribution, showing why she is recognized as one of the best in the business by ridding the text of an embarrassing number of small errors. I want to thank my editor-friend Jonathan Webb, now retired after working at McClelland & Stewart and Key Porter Books, for casting his professional eye over an early version of this book and inspiring a restructuring. The crucial work of the late C. Stuart Houston in editing journals by George Back, Robert Hood, and John Richardson deserves special mention, as does that of Richard C. Davis for editing and introducing John Franklin's journals and correspondence. Kudos to the publishers of those works: McGill-Queen's University Press and the Champlain Society. For taking care of business, I will always owe Beverley Slopen, my literary agent and savviest friend.

To write this book, I received a grant from the Canada Council, and for that I am sincerely grateful. Down through the years, several agencies have helped keep me afloat: the Ontario Arts Council, the Access Copyright Foundation, and the Public Lending Right Commission. I want to thank the editors at *Canadian Geographic*, *Canada's History*, *Maclean's*, *Celtic Life International*, *Geographical*, *Polar Record*, *Arctic*, *Literary Review of Canada*, *Up Here*, *Alberta Views*, and *The Globe and Mail*, *Toronto Star*, *National Post*, *Montreal Gazette*, *Times Colonist*, and *Calgary Herald* for publishing my sundry articles. I also owe a shoutout to my mentoring colleagues in the MFA program at University of King's College in Halifax for keeping me engaged and inspired. And I want to say hey to fellow members of the Facebook group *Remembering the Franklin Expedition*, who frequently dazzle me with their arcane knowledge.

I owe my greatest debt to my immediate family: Keriann and Travis, Carlin and Sylwia, Veronica and James. Above all, I give thanks for Sheena Fraser McGoogan, my artist-wife and life partner—first reader, fellow traveller, and long-suffering photographer—without whom this book would not exist. Long may we run.

Selected References

~

For the main narrative in *Searching for Franklin*, treating the overland expedition of 1819–22, I drew on the following works.

Back, George. *Arctic Artist: The Journal and Paintings of George Back, Midshipman with Franklin, 1819–1822*, ed. C. Stuart Houston. Kingston, ON, and Montreal: McGill-Queen's, 1994.

Franklin, John. *Narrative of a Journey to the Shores of the Polar Sea in the Years 1819-20-21-22*. London: John Murray, 1823.

Franklin, John. *Sir John Franklin's Journals and Correspondence: The First Arctic Land Expedition, 1819–1822*, ed. Richard C. Davis. Toronto: Champlain Society, 1995.

Hood, Robert. *To the Arctic by Canoe 1819–1821: The Journal and Paintings of Robert Hood, Midshipman with Franklin*, ed. C. Stuart Houston. Montreal and Kingston, ON: McGill-Queen's University Press, 1974.

Richardson, John. *Arctic Ordeal: The Journal of John Richardson, Surgeon-Naturalist with Franklin, 1820–1822*, ed. C. Stuart Houston. Kingston, ON, and Montreal: McGill-Queen's University Press, 1984.

~

Selected References

For what I call the framing narrative, I built on the foundation I laid with my five previous books about Arctic exploration.

Ancient Mariner: The Amazing Adventures of Samuel Hearne, the Sailor Who Walked to the Arctic Ocean. Toronto: HarperCollins Canada, 2003.

Dead Reckoning: The Untold Story of the Northwest Passage. Toronto: HarperCollins Canada, 2017.

Fatal Passage: The Untold Story of John Rae, the Arctic Adventurer Who Discovered the Fate of Franklin. Toronto: HarperCollins Canada, 2001.

Lady Franklin's Revenge: A True Story of Ambition, Obsession, and the Remaking of Arctic History. Toronto: HarperCollins Canada, 2005.

Race to the Polar Sea: The Heroic Adventures and Romantic Obsessions of Elisha Kent Kane. Toronto: HarperCollins Canada, 2008.

∾

In addition, I incorporated research I did while writing forewords to three books:

Hearne, Samuel. *A Journey to the Northern Ocean: The Adventures of Samuel Hearne*. Victoria, BC: TouchWood Editions, 2007.

Rae, John. *The Arctic Journals of John Rae*. Victoria, BC: TouchWood Editions, 2012.

Rae, John. *John Rae's Arctic Correspondence, 1844–1855*. Victoria, BC: TouchWood Editions, 2014.

∾

For background and context, these works are among those that most shaped my thinking:

Beardsley, Martyn. *Deadly Winter: The Life of Sir John Franklin.* Rochester, UK: Chatham Publishing, 2002.

Bellot, J.R. *Journal d'un voyage aux mers polaires à la recherche de Sir John Franklin,* ed. M. Paul Boiteau. Paris: Garnier, 1875.

Berton, Pierre. *The Arctic Grail: The Quest for the North West Passage and the North Pole, 1818–1909.* Toronto: McClelland & Stewart, 1988.

Bown, Stephen R. *The Last Viking: The Life of Roald Amundsen.* Vancouver: Douglas & McIntyre, 2012.

Bown, Stephen R. *White Eskimo: Knud Rasmussen's Fearless Journey into the Heart of the Arctic.* Vancouver: Douglas & McIntyre, 2015.

Burwash, L.T. "The Franklin Search." *Canadian Geographical Journal,* vol. 1, no. 7 (November 1930), pp. 587–603.

Byers, Michael. *Who Owns the Arctic? Understanding Sovereignty Disputes in the North.* Vancouver: Douglas & McIntyre, 2009.

Cookman, Scott. *Ice Blink: The Tragic Fate of Sir John Franklin's Lost Polar Expedition.* New York: Wiley, 2001.

Craciun, Adriana. *Writing Arctic Disaster: Authorship and Exploration.* Cambridge: Cambridge University Press, 2016.

Cyriax, R.J. *Sir John Franklin's Last Arctic Expedition: A Chapter in the History of the Royal Navy.* London: Methuen, 1939.

Davis, Richard C., ed. *Lobsticks and Stone Cairns: Human Landmarks in the Arctic.* Calgary, AB: University of Calgary Press, 1987.

Dodge, Ernest S. *The Polar Rosses: John and James Clark Ross and Their Explorations.* London: Faber & Faber, 1973.

Eber, Dorothy Harley. *Encounters on the Passage: Inuit Meet the Explorers.* Toronto: University of Toronto Press, 2008.

Fleming, Fergus. *Barrow's Boys: The Original Extreme Adventurers.* London: Granta Books, 1998.

Franklin, Jane. *The Life, Diaries and Correspondence of Jane Lady Franklin 1792–1875*. London: Erskine MacDonald, 1923.

Franklin, John. *Sir John Franklin's Journals and Correspondence: The Second Arctic Land Expedition, 1825–1827*, ed. Richard C. Davis. Toronto: The Champlain Society, 1998.

Geiger, John, and Owen Beattie. *Frozen in Time: The Fate of the Franklin Expedition*. Vancouver: Greystone, 1987/2004.

Geiger, John, and Alanna Mitchell. *Franklin's Lost Ship: The Historic Discovery of HMS Erebus*. Toronto: HarperCollins Canada, 2015.

Gilder, William. *Schwatka's Search: Sledging in the Arctic in Quest of the Franklin Records*. New York: Charles Scribner's, 1881

Grant, Shelagh D. *Polar Imperative: A History of Arctic Sovereignty in North America*. Vancouver: Douglas & McIntyre, 2010.

Hall, Charles Francis. *Life with the Esquimaux: A Narrative of Arctic Experience in Search of Survivors of Sir John Franklin's Expedition*. London: Sampson Low, Son, and Marston, 1865.

Hansen, Thorkild. *The Way to Hudson Bay: The Life and Times of Jens Munk*, trans. James McFarlane and John Lynch. New York: Harcourt, Brace, 1970.

Harper, Kenn. *Give Me My Father's Body: The Life of Minik the New York Eskimo*. South Royalton, VT: Steerforth Press, 2000.

Hempleman-Adams, David. *At the Mercy of the Winds: Two Remarkable Journeys to the North Pole: A Modern Hero and a Victorian Romance*. London: Bantam, 2001.

Henderson, Bruce. *True North: Peary, Cook, and the Race to the Pole*. New York: W.W. Norton, 2005.

Holland, Clive. *Arctic Exploration and Development, c. 500 BC to 1915: An Encyclopedia*. New York and London: Garland Publishing, 1994.

Kenyon, W.A., ed. *The Journal of Jens Munk 1619–1620*. Toronto: Royal Ontario Museum, 1980.

Klutschak, Heinrich. *Overland to Starvation Cove: With the Inuit in Search of Franklin, 1878–1880*. Toronto: University of Toronto Press, 1987.

Krupnik, Igor, ed. *Early Inuit Studies: Themes and Transitions, 1850s–1980s*. Washington, DC: Smithsonian Institution Scholarly Press, 2016.

Lambert, Andrew. *Franklin: Tragic Hero of Polar Navigation*. London: Faber & Faber, 2009.

Loomis, Chauncey C. *Weird and Tragic Shores: The Story of Charles Francis Hall, Explorer*. New York: Modern Library, 2000.

McClintock, Francis Leopold. *The Voyage of the Fox in the Arctic Seas: A Narrative of the Discovery of the Fate of Sir John Franklin and His Companions*. London: John Murray 1859.

McGoogan, Ken. "Defenders of Arctic Orthodoxy Turn Their Backs on Sir John Franklin." *Polar Record*, vol. 51, no. 2 (March 2015), pp. 220–221. (Published online October 2, 2014.)

Mills, William James. *Exploring Polar Frontiers: A Historical Encyclopedia*. 2 vols. Santa Barbara, CA: ABC-CLIO, 2003.

Nanton, Paul. *Arctic Breakthrough: Franklin's Expeditions 1819–1847*. Toronto: Clarke Irwin, 1980.

Neatby, Leslie H. *In Quest of the North West Passage*. Toronto: Longmans, Green, and Company, 1958.

Neatby, Leslie H. *The Search for Franklin*. Toronto: The Ryerson Press, 1970.

Newman, Peter C. *Company of Adventurers: The Story of the Hudson's Bay Company*. Toronto: Viking, 1985.

Owen, Roderic. *The Fate of Franklin*. London: Hutchinson, 1978.

Parry, Ann. *Parry of the Arctic: The Life Story of Admiral Sir Edward Parry*. London: Chatto & Windus, 1963.

Parry, William Edward. *Journal of a Voyage for the Discovery of a North-West Passage . . . in the Years 1819–20*. London: John Murray, 1821.

Potter, Russell. *Finding Franklin: The Untold Story of a 165-Year Search.* Montreal and Kingston, ON: McGill-Queen's University Press, 2016.

Potter, Russell, ed. (with Regina Koellner, Peter Carney, and Mary Williamson). *May We Be Spared to Meet on Earth: Letters of the Lost Franklin Arctic Expedition.* Montreal and Kingston, ON: McGill-Queen's University Press, 2022.

Rasky, Frank. *The Polar Voyagers.* Toronto: McGraw-Hill Ryerson, 1976.

Riffenburgh, Beau. *The Myth of the Explorer: The Press, Sensationalism, and Geographical Discovery.* Oxford: Oxford University Press, 1994.

Roobol, John. *Franklin's Fate: An Investigation into What Happened to the Lost 1845 Expedition of Sir John Franklin.* Canterbury, UK: Conrad Press, 2019.

Ross, John. *Journal of a Voyage for the Discovery of a North-West Passage.* London: John Murray, 1819.

Ross, M.J. *Polar Pioneers: John Ross and James Clark Ross.* Montreal and Kingston, ON: McGill-Queen's University Press, 1994.

Schwatka, Frederick. *The Search for Franklin: A Narrative of the American Expedition under Lieutenant Schwatka, 1878 to 1880.* London: T. Nelson, 1888.

Smith, D. Murray. *Arctic Expeditions from British and Foreign Shores.* Southampton, UK: Charles H. Calvert, 1877.

Steele, Peter. *The Man Who Mapped the Arctic: The Intrepid Life of George Back, Franklin's Lieutenant.* Vancouver: Raincoast Books, 2003.

Stefansson, Vilhjalmur. *Unsolved Mysteries of the Arctic.* New York: Macmillan, 1938.

Stein, Glenn M. *Discovering the North-West Passage: The Four-Year Arctic Odyssey of H.M.S.* Investigator *and the McClure Expedition.* Jefferson, NC: McFarland & Company, 2015.

Sundman, Per Olaf. *The Flight of the Eagle,* trans. Mary Sandbach. New York: Pantheon 1970.

Sutherland, Patricia, ed. *The Franklin Era in Canadian Arctic History 1845–1859.* Ottawa: National Museum of Man, 1985.

Traill, Henry Duff. *The Life of Sir John Franklin, R.N.* London: John Murray, 1896.

Watson, Paul. *Ice Ghosts: The Epic Hunt for the Lost Franklin Expedition.* Toronto: McClelland & Stewart, 2017.

Woodman, David C. *Strangers Among Us.* Montreal and Kingston, ON: McGill-Queen's University Press, 1995.

Woodman, David C. *Unravelling the Franklin Mystery: Inuit Testimony*, 2nd ed. Montreal: McGill-Queen's University Press, 2015.

Young, Delbert A. "Was There an Unsuspected Killer aboard the 'Unicorn'?" *The Beaver*, Winter 1973, pp. 9–15.

Image Credits

~

All images available through Wikimedia Commons except those on pages viii–x, 6, 15, 41, 108, 122, 124, 167, 195, 213, 230, 250, 306, 314, 315.

pp. viii–xi, maps by Stuart Daniel

p. 2, Gordon Leggett

p. 6, Sheena Fraser McGoogan

p. 16, courtesy Cameron Treleaven

p. 23, *Illustrated London News*, 24 May 1845

p. 31, James Hamilton, based on sketch by Elisha Kent Kane and engraved by John Sartain

p. 33, Thomas Addis Emmet

p. 39, William Armstrong; courtesy University of Calgary/Glenbow Collection

p. 41, George Simpson McTavish; courtesy Kenn Harper

p. 53, Thomas Bock

p. 57, painter unknown; courtesy Royal Museums Greenwich

p. 66, courtesy National Maritime Museum, Greenwich, London

p. 73, courtesy Dibner Library Portrait Collection

p.100, Walter J. Phillips; courtesy HBC Archives/Archives of Manitoba

p. 102, print by Louis Haghe, based on a sketch by George Robert Lewis; courtesy British Museum

p. 108, sketch by Thomas Phillips, engraved by Edward Finden, courtesy London's Wellcome Library

p. 122, George Back

p. 124, George Back, engraved by Edward Finden; courtesy University of Calgary/Glenbow Collection

p. 137, Robert Hood; courtesy Library and Archives Canada

p. 165, Daniel Georg Nyblin; courtesy National Library of Norway

p. 167, Sheena Fraser McGoogan

p. 170, Henry Klutschak; first appeared in *The Illustrated London News* in 1881

p. 172, Giles Bishop

p. 177, G.W. Pach

p. 182, frontispiece to Charles Francis Hall's *Arctic Researches and Life Amongst the Esquimaux* (Harper & Brothers, 1865)

p. 195, Jonathan Moore diving at wreck of *Erebus*, 2022; Parks Canada photo (89M11768EF) by Marc-Andre Bernier

p. 208, Robert Hood; courtesy Library and Archives Canada

p.213, Robert Hood; courtesy Library and Archives Canada

p. 230, George Back, engraved by Edward Finden; courtesy New York Public Library

p. 239, George Back, engraved by Edward Finden; courtesy Toronto Public Library, Special Collections

p. 250, George Back; courtesy Library and Archives Canada

p. 301, Edwin Landseer

p. 306, originally from D. Murray Smith, *Arctic Expeditions from British and Foreign Shores from the Earliest Times to the Expedition on 1875-76* (Edinburgh, Jack, Grange Publishing Works, 1877)

p. 314, courtesy Cameron Treleaven

p. 315, courtesy Cameron Treleaven

Index

~

Adam, Jean Baptiste, 140, 244–45, 272–73, 281–83, 290, 307

Advance, 31–34

Adventure Canada (AC), 3, 162–63, 320

logbook, 299–300

Akaitcho, **137**, 136–43, 147–49, 155–57, 220–27, 229–32, 306–7

accusation, 224

Akaitcho's men, 235, 289, 291–92, 306

at odds with John Franklin, 150–54, 158, 221–22, 229, 232

leadership, 154

search for, 271–72, 288

son, **137**, 141

to leave provisions (Fort Enterprise), 235, 259, 271, 289

warnings, 148, 222–23, 229, 236, 244, 292

Amundsen, Roald, 4, 17, 46, 162, 165, **165**

records, 166

Andrée, Salomon, 297

Arctic Council, 26, 28

Arctic Land Expedition, 133, 305

Arctic Research Foundation, 190

Atwood, Margaret, 309

Australia, 75

Back, George, 101–**2**–4, 212–16, 237, 263–67, 308

Cumberland House departure, 113–15

duel with Robert Hood, 209

expedition to Fort Chipewyan, 113–21, 205, 215

left behind, 83

on Christianity, 105–6

route to Coppermine River, 152

struggle to walk, 258, 260–61, 266, 288

Back, George (*cont.*)
  supplies from fur-trade
    companies, 217–18
  writing, 119, 123–24, 233
  See also under Greenstockings
Back River, 26, 64, 176, 178
  See also Great Fish River
Barrow, John, 21, 73, 78–80
Barry, Lucy, 105, 283
Bathurst Inlet, 243–44, 247
Bayne, Peter, 183–85
  testimony, 187–88
Beads, Jacob, 42, 45, 47
bears, 229, 243, **250**
  grizzly bears, 148
  See also polar bears; trichinosis
Beattie, Owen, 7, 193
Beauparlant, Gabriel (Paul), 116,
    215, 263–66
  corpse, 267
Beechey Island, 33–34, 36, 62, 192,
    299–300
  graves, 30, **31**, 34–35,
    193–94, 294
Belanger, Jean-Baptiste, 275–76
Belanger, Solomon, 253–54, 256,
    260–61, 263, 265–66, 272
  Belanger's Rapids, 254
Bellot, Joseph-René, 208–9
Bellot Strait, 62–63
Benoit, Joseph, 288–89
Bernier, Marc-André, 1–4

Berton, Pierre, 73, 309
Bloody Falls, 232–33, 243
  massacre, 229
  name, 234
Boat Place, 67, 313
Boothia Peninsula, 17–18, 45–46,
    63–64, 173
botulism, 194, 295–96
Boudelkell (Dene man), 290–91
British Admiralty, 19, 26–29, 55, 80
  Lords of the, 56
Brown, Robert, 78
Burnside River, 253–54

Canada's History (The Beaver), 13,
    166, 197, 324
cannibalism, 53–55, 68, 174–75, 191
canoes
  accidents, 134–35, 247
  birchbark canoes, 236, 242, 245,
    248–49
  canot du maître (Montreal
    canoe), 144–45
  Hudson's Bay Company, 127–29
  North West Company, 210
Cape Felix, 170, 176, 185–86, 192
Cape Victoria, 63–64
Christianity, 280
  Bible, the, 157
  John Franklin, 24–25, 105, 153,
    236–37, 282–83, 309–10

Churchill, 28, 40, 137, 155, 198–99, 202, 213, 219, 296, 307

Clarke, John, 117–19

Clouston, William, 84

Coleman, Patrick, 183–84

Contwoyto Lake (Rum Lake), 252

Coppermine River, 125, 236, **239**, 255–56

 expedition, 138–40, 150–52, 154, 206, 228, **230**

 See also expedition, 1819–22

Crozier, Francis, 65, 187, 194

Cumberland House, 94, 96, 99–100, 107, 112

Curley, Tagak, 168–69, 322

Davis, Richard C., 154, 287, 321, 323, 324, 326

Davis Strait, 62

Davison, John, 82–83, 87, 89

Dease, Peter Warren, 19, 41, 45, 125

Dickens, Charles, 54–55, 169

 The Lost Arctic Voyagers, 54

Disko Island, 23, 31–32, 62

Dissension Lake, 146, 209, 238

Eddystone, 87–89

Erebus, HMS, 22–23, **23**, 178–79, 192, 194, **195**

 artifacts, 195

 discovery (2014), 179–80, 189–90, 312

men, 35–36, 191–92

 present day, 1–4

 size, 26

 trapped, 65, 178

Erebus Bay, 67, 174, 187–88, 191

ethnocentrism (British), 287–88

expedition, 1845–46, 6, 23, **301**

 around King William Island, **xi**

 logbooks, 161–65

  See also Gjoa Haven

 mystery, 50, 191, 294–96

 survivors, 7, 172–73, 191–93, 306–8

  See also Franklin, John

expedition, 1819–22, 27, 72, 81, 82

 Fort Providence to Point Turnagain, **x**

 York Factory to Fort Providence, **viii–ix**

 See also under Coppermine River

expedition, 1619 (Jens Munk), 197–202, 296–99

 See also trichinosis

Fatal Passage, 168, 320, 322

fire accidents

 campfire, 142–43

 signal fire, 149

 tent fire, Union Jack, 139

Fitzjames, James, 21–22, 187

Flinders, Matthew, 74–78

Fontano, Antonio Vincenza,
269–70
Fort Chipewyan, 120–**22**–23, 125,
131, 205, 215
See also under Back, George
Fort Enterprise, 154–56, 205,
207–8, 210, 212, 218–20,
226–28, 235, 239–40, 246,
249, 253, 255, 259–60, 263,
266, 268–69, 271, 273,
275–76, 280, 283, 288–89,
291–92, 307, 323
Fort Providence, 134–36, 138, 140,
207, 262, 292
Fort Resolution, 135, 145–46
Fox, **57**, 58, 59–63, 67
Fox Islands, 63
Franklin, Jane, 20, 22–23, 25–29, **53**,
53–56, 60, 307
expedition, 57–58, 59
financial support, 60
petition, 57
Franklin, John, 20, 71–72, **73**,
74–78, 272, 305, **306**
appointment, 1819 expedition,
78–81
as Christian, 8, 24–25, 84, 89,
105, 153, 157–58, 236–37,
282–83, 288, 309–10, 323
expedition to Fort Chipewyan,
113–21

fainting fit, 249
journal transcript, 287
leadership, 154, 287–88
missing, 25–27, 36
vault, 13–14, 185
waterfall accident, 97
See also Akaitcho; Christianity
frostbite, 45, 47, 113–14, 215
Frozen in Time, 7, 193, 322
fur-trade co-operation, 91–92
united, 291–92
See also Hudson's Bay Company
(HBC); North West
Company (NWC)

Geddes, George, 84
Geiger, John, 7, 190
Gibson, William (Paddy), 13,
163, 193
cairn, 163–64, **167**
Gilder, William Henry, 169,
177–78, 192
Gjoa Haven, 4, 161–64, 316–17
visitors, 13
See also under expedition,
1845–46
Great Fish River, 26, 192
corpses, 48–49
See also Back River
Great Slave Lake, 126, 135, 138,
212, 293

Great Yarmouth, 82, 106

Greenland, 24, 31, 58, 61–62

Greenstockings, 208, **208**

  duel, 205, 237

  See also Back, George; Hood,
    Robert

Gross, Tom, 185–88

Hall, Charles Francis, 173–74, 176,
    181–82, **182**, 184

Harris, Ryan, 189–90, 195

Hearne, Samuel, 80, 93, 100, 125,
    138, 233–34, 309–10

Hepburn, John, 139, 205, 208–9,
    275–81, 290, 308

  failing strength, 282–83

  missing, 149

Hobson, William, 64–65

Hoeootoerock (Junius), 213, **213**,
    220, 231–33,

  missing, 259, 269

Hood, Robert, 82, 85–86, 93–94,
    96–97, 127–29, 240, 275–77

  death, 277–78, 281

  duel with George Back, 209

  indigestion, 258, 268

  See also under Greenstockings

Houston, C. Stuart, 91, 96, 101, 263,
    266–67, 287, 321, 324, 326

Hudson Strait, 86

Hudson's Bay Company (HBC), 29,
    48, 56, 91–92, 95, 125–26,
    210, 217

  rivalry, 91–92, 145

  See also canoes; fur-trade
    co-operation; North West
    Company (NWC)

Hummahuk (great-grandmother
    to Louie Kamookak),
    13–14, 311

Humpy (brother to Akaitcho),
    223–24, 233–34

Île-à-la-Crosse, 92, 129, 217–18

  journey, 116–17

Indigenous peoples

  Assiniboine, 114, 116, 123

  Cree, 96, 114, 117, 129, 134, 198

  Dene, 133–34, 155–56, 158, 209,
    214, 224–25, 229, 288–91

    Chipewyan, 117, 120, 129, 134

    Yellowknives ("Copper
      Indians"), 133, 140, 223, 232

    mythology, 153–54

    relations with Inuit, 229–34

  Dogrib, 156, 306

  In-nook-poo-zhe-jook (Inuit man),
    43, 174

  Inuit, 15, 48–49, 52, 55, 63, 134, 235

    languages, 134

Inuit (*cont.*)
 Mackenzie River Inuit, 117–18
 testimony, 52–53, 67, 173–76,
  176–80, 186, 190–91, 312
Inuit-style (traditional), 314,
  316–17
 snowhuts, 41–42
Investigator, HMS, 75
Ipiirvik (Ebierbing) (Inuit man),
  172–73, 176, 177, **177**,
  179, **182**
Isbester, 114

Jean, Louis Saint, 129
Johnston, James, 45

kabloonas (white men), 44, 48–49
Kamookak, Louie, 3–5, **6**, 11–**16**–
  18, 162–64, 166, 180,
  185–86, 311–**14**–**15**–17
 on Inuit oral history, 190
Kane, Elisha Kent, 30–**33**–36, 58
Keskarrah, 143, 207, 208, **208**
 Birdseye, wife of, 139, 143
King, Richard, 26–27
King William Island, 3–4, 13–15,
  44–46, 64–65, 67, 176, 183
Klutschak, Heinrich (Henry), 169,
  171, 178–79
Kogvik, Sammy, 190

Lambert, Andrew, 72, 191, 309
Lancaster Sound, 32–33, 36, 62
lead poisoning, 193–94, 295

McClintock, Francis Leopold,
  59–65, 67–68, 192
 letters, 68
McClure, Robert, 47, 61
McGoogan, Ken, **6**, 191, **314–15**
 writing, 5–6, 164
Mackenzie, Alexander, 94
Mackenzie River, 117–18
McVicar, Robert, 145, 212
Martin Lake, 261
Massacre of Seven Oaks, 98
measles, 96, 114
Middle Ice, 61–62
Mistegan, Thomas, 17–18, 40–41,
  46, **315**
Montagu, John, 20, 24
Moore, Jonathan, 189–90, **195**
Moose Deer Island, 135, 207,
  213, 293
mosquitoes, 96, 126–27, 129–31
Muddy Lake, 99
Muir, Tom, 84
Munk, Jens
 See expedition, 1619 (Jens
  Munk)
musk oxen, 252

Napoleonic Wars, 71, 76–77,
  101–3, 111
North West Company (NWC), 92,
  117–18, 125–26, 210, 217–18
  rivalry, 91–92, 145
  See also canoes; fur-trade
    co-operation; Hudson's
    Bay Company (HBC);
    Nor'westers
Northwest Passage, 17, 26, 30,
  45–46, 61, 197, 300
  north–south link, 45, 316
Norway House, 38, 98, **100**
Nor'westers, 92, 98–99
  See also Massacre of Seven Oaks;
    North West Company
    (NWC)
Nunavut, 133, 169
  government, 162–63, 166, 313

Obstruction Rapids, 256, 280, 307
Ocean Endeavour, **2**–4, 168
Oo-na-lee (Inuit man), 63–64
Oot-joo-lik, 177, 194
  "Ook-joo-lik," 175
  "Oot-loo-lik," 64, 175
  See also Wilmot and Crampton
    Bay
Open Polar Sea, 34, 36, 79
Orkney, 23, 38, 72, 83–84, 92, 100
Ouligbuck Jr., William, 40, **41**, 47,
  171–72, 177, **315**

Parks Canada, 1, 179, 189–90, 312
  divers, 195, 302
Parry, Edward, 22, 73–74, 81, 246
Peel Strait, 62
Pelly Bay (Kugaaruk), 42, 47–48
Peltier, Joseph, 273–74, 281–82
Peloquin, Matthew (Credit), 253,
  258, 268–69
Penny, William, 32, 34
Perrault, Ignace, 269–70, 276
Petersen, Carl, 63–64
Point de la Guiche, 46–47
Point Lake, 206–7, 229, **230**, 255
Point Turnagain, 246
polar bears, 11, 170–71, 294,
  298–300, **301**, 303, 324,
  299–300, **301**
  See also trichinosis
Porden, Eleanor, 105
Porpoise, 75
Portage La Loche (Methye
  Portage), 119–20, 131
Porter, Wally, 162–66, **167**
  family, 162–63, 165
Potter, Russell, 194, 295
Prince of Wales, 73, 82–89
Prince Regent Inlet, 62–63, 295
provisions, 40, 42, 114, 135, 139,
  146, 156, 211, 235, 243, 271,
  289, 293
  daily allowance, 229, 250
  pemmican, 42, 95, 123, 131, 247

Puhtoorak (Inuit man), 178–79

Rabbit's Head (Chipewyan Dene
man), 125, 233–34
Rae, John, 15, 28, 38–**39**–51, 54–56
cairn, **16**, 17–18, 313–16
report, 52–53
Rae Strait, 12, 15, 316–17
Red River Colony, 87, 92, 98, 307
Reid, David, 11–12
Reindeer Lake, 272, 288
relics, 34, 48–50, 54, 63–65,
173, **306**
Repulse Bay (Naujaat), 40, 45, 47,
52, 183, 244
Resolute, 58
Resolution Island, 86, 106
Richardson, John, 28, 80, 107–**8**–
12, 126–29, 131–32, 138–39,
245, 249, 268–69, 308
Coppermine accident, 256–57,
258
Michel Teroahaute death,
279–80
Robert Hood death, 277–78
weakening, 282–83, 291
Riffenburgh, Beau, 7
Ross, James Clark, 20–22, 27–29
Ross, John, 25–26, 28, 32–33, 74
Roundrock Lake, 264–65, 267
Royal Canadian Geographical
Society, 14, 190

Royal Navy, 22, 56, 158, 191,
226, 244
Rupert's Land, 72, 80, 216

St. Germain, Pierre, 135, 144–46,
206, 235, 236, 244–45,
248, 253, 258–60, 265–66,
288, 307
hunting, 262–64
influence, 151, 222–23, 238
Samandrie, François, 273, 281–82
Saskatchewan River, 99, 115, 128,
Schimonwski, Adrian, 190
Schwatka, Frederick, 169, **170**,
176–77
Scoresby, William, 79
Scottish Highlanders, 87, 92
scurvy, 75, 193, 198, 299
symptoms, 200–201, 296–97
Simpson Strait, 64, **170**
Simpson, George, 38, 145, 210–11,
216–18
Simpson, Thomas, 19
cairn, 45, 65
Smith, Edward, 126, 212, 214
starvation, 48, 106, 209, 262, 283
Steele, Peter, 72–73, 79, 102–3,
105–6
stones, 181–82
Stuart, John, 120
Supunger, 181–83, 185, 187
Swan, Matthew James (M.J.), 2–3

Taqulittuq (Tookoolito) (Inuit
 woman), **172**, 172–76,
 182, 182
Tattannoeuck (Augustus), 119, **213**,
 213, 219–20, 231–32, 234,
 259, 270–71, 306–7
Teroahaute, Michel, 269, 274,
 275–80
Terreganoeuck (Inuit man),
 234, 243
Terror, HMS, 22–23, **23**, 65
 discovery (2016), 177, 190, 192
 size, 26
 trapped, 65
Terror Bay, 67, 174, 177, 190, 192
Thanadelthur, 133–34
Treleaven, Cameron, **315**, 316
trichinosis, 296, 299–304, 319, 324
 symptoms, 297–98
 See also polar bears
Tulugaq (Inuit man), 169–71

Vaillant, Registe, 268–69
Van Diemen's Land (Tasmania),
 19–22, 153, 308
Victoria Strait, 46, 52, 61–62
Victory Point, 65
Victory Point Record, 65–**66**–67,
 176, 187, 192, 194, 295, **306**

Waltner-Toews, David, 298–99, 301,
 303, 324
Washington, 1814 invasion of, 111
Weeks, Nicholas, 154–55, 209–11,
 214, 222, 292
Wellington Channel, 37, 44
Wentzel, Willard Ferdinand, 135–
 36, 155, 207, 224, 262, 292
White Capot (brother to
 Akaitcho), 138, 224, 233
whooping cough, 96, 117
 See also measles
Williams, William, 91, 93, 99
Wilmot and Crampton Bay, 3,
 189, 194
 See also Oot-joo-lik
Wilmot Bay, 179
 See also Wilmot and Crampton
 Bay
Winter Lake, 148, 150, 223
Woodman, David, 174–75, 183,
 186, 194

York boats, 40, 93–94, **100**
York Factory, 84, 91–93,
 99–100, 107
Young, Delbert, 296, 298, 324

Zagon, Tom, 312